A THORN
— IN THEIR —
SIDE

The Hilda Murrell
Murder

Robert Green
with Kate Dewes

Published by Rata Books,
PO Box 8390,
Christchurch 8440,
New Zealand
www.hildamurrell.org

First published October 2011
Reprinted 2012

ISBN: 978-0-473-19685-1

Publishing consultants: Fraser Books, Masterton, New Zealand
Printed by Choice Development, Inc, Printing Group, Taiwan
Distribution: Nationwide Book Distributors, PO Box 65, Oxford,
North Canterbury, New Zealand

The cover depicts the Hilda Murrell rose, propagated and named by
leading rose grower David Austin. From a painting by Jeanette Mitchell.

CONTENTS

ABOUT THE AUTHOR

Robert Green served for twenty years in the Royal Navy from 1962-82. As a Fleet Air Arm observer/bombardier-navigator, he flew in Buccaneer nuclear strike aircraft and anti-submarine helicopters. On promotion to Commander in 1978, he worked in the Ministry of Defence before his final appointment as Staff Officer (Intelligence) to the Commander-in-Chief Fleet. Having taken voluntary redundancy in 1981, he was released after the 1982 Falklands War, and trained as a roof thatcher in Dorset.

In 1984, the murder of his beloved aunt and mentor Hilda Murrell led him to examine and then challenge the hazards of nuclear electricity generation. This, plus the break-up of the Soviet Union, followed by the 1991 Gulf War, caused him to speak out against nuclear weapons – the first ex-Commander with nuclear weapon experience to do so.

Commander Green chaired the British affiliate of the World Court Project (1991-2004), an international citizen campaign which led to the International Court of Justice judgement in 1996 that the threat or use of nuclear weapons would generally be illegal. Now co-director with his wife, Dr Kate Dewes ONZM, of the Disarmament & Security Centre in New Zealand, his previous book, *Security Without Nuclear Deterrence*, was published in 2010.

AUTHOR'S NOTE

Chronicling my pursuit of the truth about how and why my aunt Hilda Murrell met her violent death in 1984 has been arduous, but deeply cathartic. My primary and immediate motive is to expose explosive new evidence which proves at least one other man was involved in Hilda's murder. This would probably acquit Andrew George of abducting and murdering her. In addition, suspicious loss by the Forensic Science Service of key parts of Hilda's body relating to toxicology testing means the case must be re-opened. However, I have no illusions that – barring some extraordinary new whistleblowing – her killers will ever be found.

My experience of sitting through the five-week trial of Andrew George in 2005 was that the English adversarial judicial process proved woefully ineffective in discovering who murdered Hilda. I believe this book provides enough evidence, known to both prosecution and defence but not put to the jury or the Appeal Court judges in 2006, to re-open the coroner's inquest into Hilda's death. As Michael Mansfield QC explained in his *Memoirs of a Radical Lawyer* in 2009, an inquest is unique in English law, because it is inquisitorial. It is a genuine search for the truth, exploring all the possibilities – including those raised by the victim's next of kin. My hope is that out of that will come political pressure for a public Commission of Inquiry into the investigation by the West Mercia Police.

A powerful topicality and sense of *déjà vu* surrounds this cautionary tale about a distinguished elderly woman and law-abiding, true British patriot. Hilda loved her country so much she was not prepared to have it damaged by the nuclear machinations of the State, regardless of which political party holds power. As the current British government presses to replace nuclear power plants and weapons, Hilda's prophetic arguments against both have lost none of their force. Indeed, the nuclear catastrophe at Fukushima, Japan in March 2011 highlighted the hazards of relying upon such an unforgiving power source. Hilda stands vindicated regarding the uniquely intractable and long-lived characteristics of radioactive waste.

Hopefully this book also clears my name and puts the record straight about my involvement in the 1982 Falklands War – which did nothing to solve the still festering conflict over these resource-rich islands in the South Atlantic. In March 2010, the start of British oil exploration in Falklands waters angered the Argentine government, which gained widespread international support for pressure to be applied to the British government to negotiate on the future of the Falklands.

Sources

Every proffered fact can be backed up by source material, much of it not publicly available before and giving new information about the case. This includes Hilda's and my diaries; police videotapes and forensic reports; witness statements; the suppressed Northumbria Report; transcribed notes from the 2005 trial of Andrew George and his failed Appeal in 2006; notes and audiotapes from interviews and meetings with police and key witnesses; books; transcribed tapes of TV and radio programmes; newspaper reports and correspondence. Some names have been withheld for their protection. All photographs from the West Mercia Police have previously been released to the media. Passages in italics are from documents, including witness statements disclosed before and during the trial.

For permission to use his archive of material I must thank Andrew George.

Every attempt has been made to gain permission to use other material. In some cases there has been no response to requests; in others, it has not been possible to trace relevant people.

Acknowledgements

Researching and writing this book has been a long haul. I could never have done it without my wife Kate's tireless enthusiasm and determination, as well as her research, transcribing and record-keeping skills. On the many occasions when 'Murrelling' fatigue set in for me, she kept me going. Her dedication to Hilda and what she stood for has been inspiring and humbling. Also her three daughters have sustained me with wonderful affirmation, support and encouragement.

During the last fifteen years of intimidation, indications of surveillance, and occasional mysterious break-ins and reports of intruders, we were grateful for support from several New Zealand parliamentarians. These included two former Prime Ministers, David Lange and Helen Clark, as well as Kate Wilkinson. I would also like to thank Dr Warren Tucker, Director of the New Zealand Intelligence Service, who visited our home to be briefed, and reassured us his officers were not involved. He also undertook to ask the Police Commissioner to provide intermittent protection.

Special mention must go to Michael Mansfield QC for his Foreword. For years he followed the case and my pursuit of the truth and, on countless occasions, offered advice and encouragement.

Andrew Fox also deserves a special tribute for his help with early drafts.

Over so many years I have received help, support and encouragement from countless good people. Some I cannot name for reasons they will understand. In alphabetical order, I wish to acknowledge and thank the late Don Arnott's family, Norman Baker MP, Kathy and Rick Beech, Dr Rosalie Bertell, Gladys Bury, Ian and Thalia Campbell, Trina Child (Guthrie), Alex Cooke, the late Patsy Dale's family, Tam Dalyell, Chris Eldon Lee, Nick Fielding, Michael Fitzgerald, Brian George, Jane Gilmore and Pat Dymond, the late Philip

Griffith's family, Christopher Haydon, Lord Peter Hennessy, Robert Hunt, Lawrence Lifschultz, Paul Marsden, Christopher Mileham, Gary Murray, John Osmond, Laurens Otter, Anna Parker, Tatjana and the late Dr Murray Parsons, Jenny and the late Dr Edward Radford, Dr Paul Rogers, Marnie Sweet, the late Joan and Clive Tate's family, David Watson, Derek Woodvine, and Stuart and Angela Wright-Stow.

For editing, I am indebted to Ian and Diane Grant. For assistance with and permission to use illustrations, I thank David Burrows at the *Shropshire Star*. His fine newspaper has played a vital and honourable role in following the case.

Robert Green
Christchurch,
New Zealand.
September 2011

FOREWORD

This is a tale of mystery and intrigue which touches all our lives. Carefully researched and lovingly told, you cannot remain unmoved. The questions come thick and fast. There is always another stone to be overturned. Far more than a 'who dunnit', about which so much has already been written, it is also a 'why' and 'what dunnit'. Echoes of the death of Dr David Kelly.

The book's achievement is a testament to the courage and commitment of two people in their relentless search for truth: the author Robert Green and his aunt Hilda Murrell. It is a story which uncovers the life-threatening risks that have to be endured by a few for the many who 'dare not speak'. No healthy democracy can survive without such examples, and their endeavours have an extraordinary resonance in the rapid succession of events and revelations that have surfaced on a daily basis throughout 2011. As George Santayana famously observed, "Those who cannot remember the past are condemned to repeat it."

On 12 September 2011, not quite within spitting distance of where I write these words, there was an explosion and a fire at a French nuclear waste plant in Marcoule. One person was killed and four were injured. It occurred in a furnace used to melt so-called low-level nuclear waste. Although there is no reactor at this site, it has been at the heart of the French nuclear industry from 1956, and had been used for atom bomb research. France now has 59 nuclear power plants with 75 percent of its electricity being generated from this source. President Sarkozy has reaffirmed his belief in this technology, and this same site had been earmarked to host a European Pressurised Water Reactor (PWR). Hardly surprising, therefore, that this incident is being played down – despite the fact that there have been 20 complaints over the last ten years about the subsidiary of Électricité De France which operates the plant, and another earlier explosion and fire further north in the Rhône valley at Tricastin (Drôme) which houses four PWRs, two days after 32 safety hazards had been identified by the authorities.

These incidents are precisely what Hilda, a spritely 78-year-old rose grower with an internationally respected reputation, had recognised and forewarned of 27 years ago, before she was murdered. She had replaced the trowel with the pen, and was diligently digging away to uncover the risks posed by the first British PWR at Sizewell promoted by the Thatcher Government.

Hilda's concerns were twofold. The process of energy generation itself creates a highly hazardous material, plutonium, as well as the potential for radioactive fallout should there be a breach in safety. A secondary complication is the need for secure containment of radioactive waste. She became vociferous in her condemnation: "The nuclear thing is totally evil and must be abolished". She was well aware she was under surveillance, aware of interference with communications, and of the risk of infiltrators. Such measures have not abated, as was dramatically unveiled by an undercover cop, Mark Kennedy, in January 2011. For eight years he and other officers pretended they were environmental activists and befriended individuals in order to accumulate information for the National Public Order Intelligence Unit.

Hilda was killed in March 1984, just when she was gearing herself up to appear as an independent objector at the Sizewell Inquiry where she would have presented her research and arguments in person.

In March 2011, a nuclear catastrophe shook not only Japan but the rest of the world. Following both an earthquake and tsunami in an area susceptible to such natural forces, nuclear power plants at Fukushima were blighted as were the lives of thousands. Initially, there were the usual bland assurances that everything was under control. There were two explosions in the plants, and the resultant leaking of radioactive material has still not been contained. Two thousand square kilometres of land have been contaminated, and some scientists have assessed that radioactive caesium from the disaster is circulating in the currents of the Pacific Ocean and will return to the shores of Japan in twenty or thirty years. Small wonder, therefore, that an increasing number of countries have reconsidered using nuclear energy – among them Germany, Switzerland and Italy – and that the Japanese Prime Minister, Naoto Kan, resigned on 28 August 2011. Somehow the memory of Three Mile Island and Chernobyl had faded in the mists of time.

Shortly after Three Mile Island, Margaret Thatcher swept to power in the UK. Her reign was marked by several cataclysmic enterprises. One was the 1982 Falklands War, during which the *Belgrano* was torpedoed by a British nuclear submarine *HMS Conqueror*. Rob Green was then a Commander in the Royal Navy, helping run Intelligence support for British forces. In his work he had become familiar with the proposed replacement of Polaris with Trident nuclear-armed submarines. He, like his aunt, became increasingly uneasy about the deployment of nuclear power, in his case in relation to weaponry. As part of a massive controversy about the *Belgrano* sinking, Clive Ponting, head of a Ministry of Defence department, stood trial in 1985 for blowing the whistle on how Parliament had been misled. He was rightly acquitted by a jury despite strong directions from the judge to convict.

These were highly charged times, and Rob himself became embroiled in false accusations about possible leaks of signals intelligence to Hilda. Both he and his aunt were staunchly loyal citizens and nothing could have been further from the truth. Nevertheless, perceptions within the portals of power were running rife and provide a backcloth for the sub-plot of this book.

The bizarre and incredible circumstances surrounding the killing of Hilda Murrell have been trawled over a thousand times in books, articles, films, documentaries and plays. A man has been convicted – but this cannot be the whole story. Rob Green and his wife Kate Dewes, in the face of unmitigated harassment, have painstakingly pieced together from contemporary documents and eye-witness accounts a scenario that is irreconcilable with the police version that this was a random lone burglar, or with the convicted man's own varied accounts. It is, of course, for the reader now to make up her/his mind; but I doubt anyone will imagine the whole exercise from house, to car, to lane, to field, to copse in broad daylight, was accomplished by a slightly built sixteen-year-old who had merely been looking for cash.

Critics have tried to dismiss thoughts of conspiracy in high places behind these events as though such contentions are the product of a fevered brow. Their naivety has been sorely exposed by the continuing revelations during the British summer of 2011 thrown up by the phone hacking scandal. As usual, it is a very British coup. It works behind the scenes; nothing is too explicit, nothing is officially recorded. The Prime Minister, David Cameron, employed as his head of communications and press liaison Andy Coulson, who was editor at the *News of the World* during illegal phone hacking. He has now been arrested. It now turns out he retained substantial remuneration from the newspaper whilst in Government employment. The Commissioner of the Metropolitan Police, Sir Paul Stephenson, resigned over links with a former *News of the World* editor, Neil Wallis, who has also been arrested. Assistant Commissioner John Yates has also resigned in relation to these matters. The press room at Scotland Yard employed ten ex-*News of the World* staff. In addition, there are serious allegations that the police received large payments from the newspaper for information. There is little doubt that a series of prime ministers had an unhealthily close relationship with Rupert Murdoch.

On top of this comes the disclosure by Human Rights Watch in Tripoli, Libya, that both the CIA and MI6 had been collaborating closely with a regime whose human rights record was appalling, which indulged in torture and co-operated with unlawful acts of extraordinary rendition by the USA and its allies. Needless to say, all this has been denied by the British authorities – the sort of denials constantly confronting Rob Green throughout his investigation.

There can be no doubt that Rob and Kate will give every last breath to this trail of truth. On the way, they have galvanised thought and action not only about the case but also at a higher international level. They both played pivotal roles in the World Court Project, which I supported wholeheartedly. The object was to obtain an Advisory Opinion from the International Court of Justice in The Hague on the legality of the use or threat of use of nuclear weapons. The Opinion overwhelmingly confirmed either was illegal, and reminded states of their obligations under nuclear disarmament treaties.

There is now an initiative to make states and corporate bodies responsible for environmental destruction of the kind that might occur as the result of a nuclear power plant or weapon explosion. The idea is to create a new international crime alongside the other four presently drafted for the new International Criminal Court in The Hague, if the UN can be persuaded to adopt it. I present the case for the prosecution in London at the end of September 2011. It is to be called Ecocide, the nearest equivalent being Genocide. Hilda would have felt totally vindicated.

Michael Mansfield QC

MAIN CHARACTERS

Mr A – Police informant at Andrew George's trial.

Dr Peter Acland – The pathologist who performed the first autopsy on Hilda, for many years he was a media spokesman on forensic aspects for the West Mercia Police.

Michael Appleby – Forensic scientist and DNA expert who was a key prosecution witness at Andrew George's trial.

Don Arnott – Retired nuclear scientist living in Wales who Hilda went to for advice 1983-4.

Anthony Barker QC – Defence counsel at Andrew George's trial.

Detective Chief Superintendent David Cole – Based at West Mercia Police HQ in Hindlip Hall, Worcester, he led the investigation into Hilda's murder from 1984-1990.

Judith Cook – Journalist, author and playwright who wrote two books and a play about the case.

Tam Dalyell – Backbench Labour MP who led a campaign criticising the controversial sinking of the Argentine cruiser *General Belgrano* on 2 May 1982 by the British nuclear submarine *HMS Conqueror*.

Police Constable Robert Eades – Organised the search which found Hilda's body in Moat Copse on Saturday 24 March 1984.

Andrew Fox – Documentary film maker and producer of the pulled 1989 Central Lobby television programme on Hilda's case, who later helped write early drafts of this book.

Detective Chief Inspector Chris Furber – DCS Cole's right-hand man on the investigation based at Shrewsbury Police Station.

Adrian George – The younger brother of Andrew George.

Andrew George – Convicted of Hilda Murrell's murder in May 2005, in 1984 he was a 16-year-old petty thief living at Besford House, a home for delinquent boys in Shrewsbury.

Brian George – No relation to Andrew, Adrian or Stephen, he was a neighbour of Hilda.

Stephen George – Andrew's elder brother.

Trina Guthrie – Botanist daughter of a friend of Hilda who became her unofficial niece during the early 1980s, and documented a prison confession about MI5 involvement in Hilda's murder.

Richard Latham QC – Prosecution counsel for Andrew George's trial.

Mrs Betty Latter – Hilda's cleaning lady and neighbour.

George Lowe – A relation and former neighbour of Hilda.

David McKenzie – A compulsive confessor who was charged with Hilda's murder in 1990 but acquitted.

John Marsh – Hunkington farmer who reported Hilda's crashed car three times to the police.

Christopher Mileham – Telephone engineer who examined Hilda's Ravenscroft phone.

Gerard Morgan-Grenville – Director of European ecological action group Ecoropa who was in frequent contact with Hilda 1982-84.

Gary Murray – Former MI5 agent whose 1993 book *Enemies of the State* highlighted Hilda's case.

John Osmond – Harlech TV producer of a succession of programmes probing Hilda's case.

Laurens Otter – Anti-nuclear activist and Secretary of the Shropshire Peace Alliance.

Detective Constable Nick Partridge – The 'walking memory' of Hilda's case from 1985-2003 and member of the Cold Case Review team.

Constance Purser – A longstanding friend of Hilda who ran a farm museum in Shropshire.

Ian Scott – Owner of the Moat Copse who checked every tree there on Thursday 22 March 1984 and confirmed Hilda's body was not there.

John Stalker – Former Deputy Chief Constable of Manchester who made a programme on the murder for Central TV in 1994.

Detective Chief Inspector Jim Tozer – Leader of the Cold Case Review into Hilda's case.

Justice Richard Wakerley – Judge presiding over the trial of Andrew George in 2005.

Mark Webster – Forensic scientist who was a key prosecution witness at the trial.

Derek Woodvine – Shropshire Councillor and member of the West Mercia Police Authority who challenged the police about the state of Hilda's telephones.

Hilda Murrell

*'Oh no man knows through
what wild centuries roves
back the rose.'*

Dedicated
To life on Earth,
She grew roses
For our pleasure.
The measure
Of her trust to us
Must be
That roses live
For centuries
To come.

Kay Ekevall

CHAPTER 1

MUCH MORE THAN MY AUNT

A 4.00 am phone call usually means trouble – especially if it is from police. "What? He was only sixteen at the time?"

In Britain it was 5 pm on 7 June 2003, and Detective Chief Inspector Jim Tozer of West Mercia Police was calling from Shrewsbury. He rang us in New Zealand to tell us Andrew George, a 35-year-old local labourer, had been arrested and charged with abducting and murdering my aunt, friend and mentor, Hilda Murrell on 21 March 1984. Her mutilated body had been found three days later in a poplar copse six miles outside the ancient capital of Shropshire, where Hilda had lived all her 78 years. It was one of the biggest and most famous British murder cases of the twentieth century, with allegations of political conspiracy and cover-up around the nuclear industry and the 1982 Falklands War.

Tozer's reply to my incredulous question was chilling: "Yes, Rob – but we can make it fit the facts". George's DNA had been identified on clothing on Hilda's body, and his fingerprints had been found in her house. He was remaining silent, but would be held in custody for questioning over the next 72 hours.

My wife Kate and I got no more sleep that night as several British newspapers and the BBC sought my reaction as Hilda's next of kin. As leader of the Cold Case Review, Tozer had spent two weeks in Christchurch, New Zealand the year before, when he had heard why my relationship with the police had broken down in 1986. He had formally apologized on their behalf, and seemed prepared to follow up some new leads suggested by us. With a sinking sense of dread and disappointment, I realised he was now asking me to believe a truant teenager had abducted and murdered Hilda.

―――∞∞∞―――

In March the following year, Kate and I flew to Britain for a weekend of events in Shrewsbury to commemorate the 20th anniversary of Hilda's murder, starting with an expedition to three of her favourite haunts. Coincidentally, we were also able to be in court when Andrew George pleaded not guilty on 21 March 2004.

On the morning of Saturday 19 March 2004, about twenty of Hilda's friends and supporters met outside the Shropshire Wildlife Trust opposite the Norman sandstone abbey, immortalized as the *alma mater* of Ellis Peters' mediaeval monastic sleuth, Brother Cadfael. In a gathering storm, we drove to the head of Maengwynedd, a remote Welsh valley, to lead the annual pilgrimage to the cairn where Hilda's ashes had been scattered high on the side of a tussocked spur of the Berwyn Mountains. Their summit formed the skyline of an idyllic view up the Tanat River valley from Hilda's weekend chalet Fron Goch, meaning 'Red Bank'. It perched beside the limestone crags of Llanymynech Rocks, straddling the Welsh-English border half an hour's drive northwest of Shrewsbury.

In her last letter to me, Hilda had described what was to be her final visit to those mountains, in September 1983:

> There was a wonderful day three weeks ago when the sunshine was golden all day with soft balmy warmth and a perfectly clear sky as we so rarely see. I cut sandwiches and went to Maengwynedd and parked by the sheepfold… I had lunch sitting against the wall facing the mountain. Then I got into my boots and set off.
>
> I thought I would just go as far as I could and then turn back. I took it slowly but gradually walked up the slope towards the col. I then began to think about what would be visible if I got there, so I kept on. Sure enough, when I got to the top of the pass, there was Tryfan with its bristly hump and the masses of Glydr and Carnedd on each side of it. I went two or three hundred yards to the right and the Snowdon massif came into view… I can't tell you how lovely it was – the whole range blue and clear-cut, a marvellous sight.
>
> The pleasure was increased by the fact that a big finger-stone which had stood on the pass to guide travellers from time immemorial, and fell down about the end of my walking time up on the pass about thirty years ago, had been set up again. It is a splendid stone, eight to nine feet high and slender; I greeted it like an old friend. It was warm to the touch…

An intrepid Central TV News cameraman filmed us clinging together around the quartz cairn, wind gusts howling as the women belted out a Greenham peace song. Later in a parallel valley, I unveiled a commemorative slate stone engraved with 'Hilda Murrell 1906-84' in a birch grove established in her memory in 1994. We planted another fifty seedlings around the flourishing ten-year-old trees before visiting the garden of Fron Goch.

The next afternoon we gathered in the Shropshire Wildlife Trust's lecture room in the old Benedictine Infirmary of the abbey to reminisce about Hilda. Friends gave delightful anecdotes from her life, including 'botanising' holidays with her in the French Alps, and a hilarious, accident-punctuated piano recital by Myra Hess in 1940. The famous Hungarian pianist, who had lifted

Londoners' spirits during the German blitz with free lunchtime recitals in the National Gallery, had accepted Hilda's invitation to come to Shrewsbury to raise funds for Jewish refugee children.

I showed some fine childhood photographs of her with younger sister Betty, my mother. Their father Owen took them in the garden of their Victorian home at the family horticultural nursery founded by his father Edwin Murrell. As I gave verbal snapshots of her upbringing, I revelled in this rare chance to share memories of a fascinating woman.

Hilda was often too ill to attend Shrewsbury Girls' High School. When 13 years old she was absent for a complete term with an overactive thyroid; and migraines dogged her all her life. Yet she thrived at school, developing formidable intellectual abilities and organisational skills. As well as becoming head girl and securing the school's first scholarship to Cambridge University, Hilda honed a precocious writing talent by editing the school magazine and contributing articles.

She also kept nature diaries, in which she expressed her passion and burgeoning expertise on Shropshire's rich botanical and bird life. Her love of mountaineering was kindled by Owen, who often took the family to Snowdonia where they stayed in the famous Pen-y-Pass Hotel. She was thrilled to meet there some of Britain's top rock climbers when the sport was in its romantic infancy, and where mountaineers like George Leigh Mallory trained for the early Everest expeditions.

A lovely photograph of her aged 21 at Newnham College, Cambridge in 1926 showed her already wearing her long dark hair in a demure bun. She revealed only the left side of her face with eyes downcast in almost mediaeval style, because of shyness linked to her blind right eye from an accident in the first weeks of her life. Taking her final English Tripos Section A exams that year, she gained Class 2, Division 1 Honours. In 1927 Hilda became the first female family member to graduate from any university, let alone Cambridge, when she was awarded a Bachelor of Arts with similar honours in the Modern & Mediaeval Languages Tripos (French).

On returning home, her father persuaded her to join the family firm because of his worsening arthritis. Despite her preference for an academic career, she threw herself into learning the skills required of a professional plantswoman. By 1937 she had settled into her twin roles as an unprecedented, 31-year-old unmarried woman director of 'Edwin Murrell Nurseryman & Seed Merchant (founded 1837); Rose and Fruit Trees a Speciality', and as resident carer for her parents.

The rose fields were ploughed up during World War Two to grow potatoes, barley, oats, vegetables and fruit. In 1939 Hilda's compassionate and campaigning side emerged when she found Shropshire foster homes for fourteen Jewish refugee children from Germany and Czechoslovakia. Her financial flair, love of classical music and Cambridge connections enabled her to raise funds for them by persuading not only Myra Hess but top fellow Hungarian violinist sisters Jelly d'Aranyi and Adila Fachiri to give concerts in Shrewsbury.

With peace achieved in 1945, Hilda gained a head start over rival growers of old-fashioned roses when Constance Spry, the world's most celebrated flower arranger, quietly passed her unrivalled collection to her. The golden years of Murrell's Roses followed, with Hilda bringing style, grace and passion to the business. She personally wrote an annual catalogue which became a collector's item in the rose world.

Hilda's clientele read like the aristocratic guidebook *Debrett's Peerage*. Nearly all of them women, they included Lady Eve Balfour, Lady de Vesci, Lady Rocksavage, and the Duchesses of Gloucester, Devonshire and Rutland. On 13 October 1951 she complained gleefully in her diary

> Letter from Dowager Duchess of R. Also one from V. Sackville-West asking to send catalogue to Duchess of Wellington. Am beset by duchesses.

Vita Sackville-West and Harold Nicholson were one of the best-known aristocratic couples in the country at the time. When they started restoring Sissinghurst Castle, Vita invited Hilda to help her design the now famous White Garden. They became firm friends, and Vita promoted Murrell's Roses in her *Observer* gardening column.

In 1960 Hilda sold the old nursery site for housing development and moved the business to the south-eastern side of Shrewsbury, becoming sole managing director. Two years later came the first gold medal at Chelsea Flower Show, for an ingenious miniature rose garden on a large table. Between 1952 and 1969 her 'Shrewsbury Roses' amassed 56 top awards, fourteen of them from Chelsea.

Approaching retirement in 1970, she wanted to sell the business to David Austin, a promising Shropshire rose grower and breeder of new varieties of old-fashioned roses. In his 20th anniversary tribute, he explained he could not afford her asking price. So she sold it to Brian Murphy, a local brewer who brought in Percy Thrower, Britain's first radio and TV celebrity gardener, as his front man. Sadly, Hilda's old rose collection languished in weeds while Thrower focused on the more profitable hybrid tea and new perpetual flowering roses.

Surprisingly, she made no fuss. With retirement allowing her concern for the environment full rein, she refocused her energy, intellect and organising flair on the growing menace of the nuclear industry. For relaxation, she enjoyed applying her plantswoman skills to developing the gardens at Ravenscroft, her new home in Sutton Road, and at her weekend retreat, Fron Goch.

Hilda's diary entry a few weeks before her death read:

> Letter from David Austin proposing to name a rose after me… An old-fashioned warm pink after the manner of Constance Spry…

She accepted with deep pleasure – but never saw it. By the time the first blooms were displayed at Chelsea that May, her murder had upstaged them as a hellish, more enduring legacy.

⁂

Hilda was much more than my only aunt – and I had no uncles. After my mother died in 1964 when I was nineteen, I discovered that, despite my youth and inferior intellect and education, Hilda and I 'clicked'. She was great fun, with an infectious enthusiasm for, and curiosity about, life. From the moment I arrived for a visit we talked non-stop. Deeply interested in me and my career, she never invited any other friends to meet me. Having first helped fill the void left by my mother, she became my trusted friend and mentor. By the late 1970s, ours had become an unusual relationship: she an active anti-nuclear campaigner who voted Liberal, myself an apolitical but typically Conservative naval Commander with nuclear weapon experience and a top security clearance.

A true patriot, Hilda particularly loved the British Isles: their long history and how it had shaped the landscape, architecture and, of course, the gardens. She was seldom nostalgic. On the contrary, she constantly probed the future, always with an eye to protecting our cultural heritage and increasingly polluted environment. Moreover, Hilda introduced me to the political world, of which she had an unexpected understanding.

I first fully appreciated the extent of her awareness and wisdom in 1970 when I was selected to join a junior officers' staff course at the Royal Naval College in Greenwich. An intense three-month introduction to public administration, international relations and current affairs, the aim was to prepare us as 25-year-old Lieutenants for the wider responsibilities of higher rank. I could just about cope, until I had to give a talk on any issue of topical importance. I turned to Hilda, who briskly suggested my theme should be 'the impending oil crisis', outlining a scenario of over-reliance on oil leading to conflict in the Middle East. This had barely been thought of in the corridors of power in Westminster, let alone among a bemused audience of young naval officers and their tutors. When the oil price rocketed fourfold two years later, I reminded her of her prescience in a phone chat. Her response was immediate, and equally baffling: "The next one will be nuclear".

A few months before her murder, Hilda recalled in a letter to John Baker, the anti-nuclear Bishop of Salisbury, her reaction to finding out about plutonium:

> I decided on the spot that such an element should have been banned as soon as its nature and its forever-ness were realised, that we had no right to inflict such a thing on the planet and posterity. That seems to me all that needs to be said. The nuclear thing is totally evil and must be abolished, root and branch.

She tried out her findings on friends and fellow members of several committees, including the Shropshire branch of the Council for the Protection of Rural England (CPRE). She soon discovered most of them did not share her zeal; and unlike her they shrank from challenging experts and Establishment contacts. This drove Hilda to express her indignation in letters to *The Times*, like this extract from one in 1976 protesting at the unaccountable decision-making process to expand nuclear-powered electricity generation:

> [P]oliticians have been making such decisions for the last thirty years, without our knowledge or consent, or that of Parliament… Now, of course, the vested interests both of finance and prestige have accumulated to the point where it would take almost superhuman courage to stop the dreadful process; on the contrary the politicians have again decided that it must not only go on, but increase. Do please publish this ordinary citizen's plea for some moral courage and wisdom, or even ordinary commonsense, instead of so much amoral cleverness.

Unsurprisingly, her request was denied.

Early in 1977, Hilda received a copy of the Flowers Commission's 1976 Sixth Report, *Nuclear Power and the Environment.* Sir Brian Flowers' background as an eminent nuclear physicist and part-time member of the UK Atomic Energy Authority gave it unprecedented weight, and what became known as the Flowers Report had a profound impact on British public opinion. Hilda felt vindicated when the report echoed her fears about the nuclear industry's dream of moving towards a 'plutonium economy':

> We should not rely for energy supply on a process that produces such a hazardous substance as plutonium unless there is no reasonable alternative.

Above all, she latched onto this key recommendation:

> There should be no commitment to a large-scale nuclear programme until it has been demonstrated beyond reasonable doubt that a method exists to ensure the safe containment of long-lived, highly radioactive waste for the indefinite future. We are clear that such a demonstration will require a substantial programme of research.

This was the moment when she committed herself to doing all in her power to oppose the nuclear industry's plans.

On 28 March 1979, a US pressurised water reactor at Three Mile Island, near Harrisburg, Pennsylvania malfunctioned. Equipment failures and operator ignorance led to a major core meltdown, and the plant was written off.

Less than two months later, Margaret Thatcher swept into power as Britain's first woman Prime Minister. I was working in the Ministry of Defence just across the street as a newly promoted Commander. Thatcher coined the phrase 'one of us' to describe those she favoured and trusted. As resentment and resistance grew to her 'conviction politics', anyone who disagreed with her and stood up to her learned that she regarded them as 'the enemy within'. She and some close Cabinet colleagues would narrowly escape death in October 1984 when the Irish Republican Army blew up their Brighton hotel during the Conservative Party annual conference. It was an era when legitimate opposition was considered at best subversive and, at worst, treasonable.

In my position as Personal Staff Officer to the Assistant Chief of Naval Staff (Policy), I was a fly on the wall as my Admiral facilitated the internal debate on replacing Britain's four Polaris nuclear-armed ballistic missile submarines with a scaled down version of the massively expensive, over-capable US successor system, Trident. By then, Hilda had convinced me that radioactive waste was the Achilles heel of the nuclear industry, and Three Mile Island had endorsed her view that nuclear power was unacceptably hazardous. However, the new Prime Minister, an enthusiast for all things nuclear, was determined to introduce an ambitious programme of new nuclear power plants. Worse than this, she forced the British nuclear industry to accept a US pressurised water reactor design similar to the one at Three Mile Island.

Hilda was horrified. The apathetic response to her waste concerns from most of her CPRE colleagues drove her to challenge the false economics and unaccountability of the nuclear industry. Drawing upon her business and financial skills, she set about writing a paper, *What Price Nuclear Power?*. With my naval staff training, I was able to help her with the structure.

She was still revising the draft in 1981 when the government's Department of the Environment published a White Paper explaining its plans for managing radioactive waste. This was needed to deflect opposition to Thatcher's programme for ten pressurised water reactors, of which the prototype would be Sizewell B on the Suffolk coast. Hilda was so incensed by the White Paper's complacency and faulty science that she decided to write a critique.

Around that time, the Thatcher government, desperate to find savings, announced a major defence review. With projected cuts to the Royal Navy's aircraft carriers, destroyers and frigates, I took the plunge and applied for redundancy.

Notification that my application was successful came one week into the Falklands War. In April 1982, Britain suddenly went to war with an erstwhile friend, Argentina, over its disputed claim to the Falkland Islands when Argentinian forces invaded and quickly overpowered a token Royal Marine garrison contingent. The Royal Navy's role proved to be pivotal. By then I was working in the command bunker at Northwood in northwest London as Staff Officer (Intelligence) to the Commander-in-Chief Fleet, in charge of a 40-strong team providing round-the-clock intelligence support to the Fleet. The war was directed from Northwood by my boss Admiral Sir John Fieldhouse. At one point the outcome was in the balance: our ships were being sunk, and some friends and colleagues killed. When I expected to be planning my imminent retirement, I had never worked so hard in my life. After the Falklands capital Port Stanley had been retaken, I was allowed to go on terminal leave in September.

I was 38 years old, with no qualifications except my rank and experience. Tired of weekend commuting to high-pressure naval appointments in London, I decided to try my luck and find local work which allowed me to be home every night with my wife Liz in a newly converted barn in a Dorset village. We had no children, so I could afford to indulge myself. I trained as a roof thatcher, enduring many painful jokes with stunned former colleagues. Hilda was delighted with my new career. For eight idyllic years, I loved working with my hands in the open air on what was essentially restoration of often fine old houses, with a bird's eye view of some of the most picturesque parts of southwest England.

As part of her research for her new paper, in October 1982 Hilda visited Don Arnott, a brilliant retired radio-chemist living about half an hour's drive into Wales from Ravenscroft:

> A lovely Regency country house, rather run-down. Two upper teenage girls were outside, they took me in and yelled for 'Pa'. It was rough and dingy. Pa emerged in due course, doubled-up (polio I learnt afterwards) with a terrific hand grip. We had coffee. He had a streaming cold. We went at it hammer and tongs for 1¾ hours. Of course I learnt any amount of useful things. His knowledge is enormous… We didn't cover anything like all the points I had listed… Sizewell will take all his time.

A consortium of trade unions covering firefighters and health workers chose him as an expert witness at the Sizewell B Inquiry. The Three Mile Island accident had forced the Thatcher government to hold the first public inquiry into a new nuclear power plant. However, shortly after his last meeting with Hilda and before he was due to testify in April 1983, Arnott suffered a mysterious heart attack and dropped out of the Inquiry. He and Hilda met once more, when he gave a talk in Shrewsbury on 8 February 1984. By then, she was heading for Sizewell.

Hilda had sent her draft paper to national CPRE Director Robin Grove-White. Realising this was the only critique he had seen of the government's waste management policy, he told her it was so good she should register as one of very few individual objectors at the Inquiry. Her application to testify received final approval on 9 February 1984.

—— ∞∞∞ ——

Margaret Thatcher, her political career salvaged by the military, began her second term as prime minister in May 1983. She was now determined to tame her domestic 'enemies within': the trade unions led by the coalminers, and anti-nuclear campaigners and their left-wing political supporters.

Tensions mounted between the military, police and women peace campaigners at Greenham Common airbase in Berkshire. The first women had started camping outside the base some three years earlier after the plan was announced to deploy ninety-six US nuclear-tipped Cruise missiles there. Supposedly secret exercises were disrupted when the mobile launch vehicles emerged from the base at night. In December 1982 over 30,000 women 'embraced the base', generating worldwide publicity. A year later 40,000 came. Nonviolent direct action proved increasingly effective. The Campaign for Nuclear Disarmament (CND) thrived from this, with huge demonstrations in London opposing both Trident, Thatcher's replacement for Polaris, and Cruise.

Thrilled by the achievements of the Greenham women, Hilda sent them donations, and attended a packed meeting in Shrewsbury when Lynne Jones, a hospital doctor, spoke on 11 January 1983. Hilda recorded in her diary:

> [She] was very good indeed. Very clear and precise about the effects of the bomb. Greenham woman. Dedicated.

In April, 70,000 protesters formed a human chain between the nuclear weapon factories at Burghfield and Aldermaston. Later that year I was startled to find Hilda's name in a full-page advertisement in *The Times* sponsoring the Nuclear Weapons Freeze campaign. As with Greenham, she did not talk to me about her opposition to nuclear weapons. She was careful to confine our discussions to nuclear energy, because she knew I had recently led the team providing top secret intelligence support to the Polaris nuclear submarine deployed on patrol.

Ten years earlier, I had been a 25-year-old Lieutenant serving in the British aircraft-carrier *HMS Eagle* as back-seat aircrew in its Buccaneer nuclear strike jet squadron. 'Observer' is the Fleet Air Arm's traditional term for bombardier-navigator, whose role is to navigate the aircraft and help the pilot operate its weapons system. As well as practising to attack Soviet warships with conventional weapons, my pilot and I were a 'nuclear crew'. Our task was to be ready to deliver a WE177 ten kiloton tactical free-fall nuclear bomb to detonate above a military airfield on the outskirts of Leningrad – which is now St Petersburg's airport.

Thirty years later, in 1999 I landed there to speak at a conference reviewing nuclear policy and security on the eve of the 21st century. In a television interview, I apologised to the citizens of St Petersburg for having been part of a nuclear mission that would have caused appallingly indiscriminate casualties and long-term poisonous effects from radioactive fallout, and virtually destroyed their beautiful ancient capital as collateral damage. By then I had accepted Hilda's view that nuclear weapons would not save me, or the Russians.

Back in 1972, following a decision by the British government that it could no longer afford strike carriers, I switched to anti-submarine helicopters. The following year, I was appointed Senior Observer of a squadron of Sea King helicopters aboard the aircraft-carrier *HMS Ark Royal*. Our task was to use radar, variable-depth sonar and other electronic sensors, plus a variety of weapons, to detect and destroy enemy submarines threatening our ships. Amongst our armoury was a nuclear depth-bomb, an anti-submarine variant of the WE177 design. This was because our lightweight anti-submarine homing torpedoes could not go fast or deep enough to catch the latest Soviet nuclear-powered submarines. However, my opposition to nuclear weapons was first stirred by the disturbing discovery that, if I ever had to drop one, it would have been a suicide mission: unlike strike jets, a helicopter was too slow to escape the explosion.

It was not until after Hilda's death that I discovered she was a member of the Shropshire Peace Alliance which campaigned against all things nuclear. She also joined European Nuclear Disarmament (END), which differed from the much larger and more radical CND in giving equal blame to NATO and the Soviet Union for 'fomenting the most dangerous decade in human history'. Its manifesto called not just for a nuclear-free Europe, but dismantling the two blocs through 'détente from below'.

Nevertheless, Hilda was an active CND supporter. At the age of 76, on 1 May 1982 she described in her diary joining a local demonstration picketing councillors outside the Shire Hall:

> Several nice small children with non-nuclear circles attached to their fronts. At long last the councillors began to trickle down for lunch. Meanwhile we had been roped off and photographed by the press. Gradually the demo found its voice, and with every 1-2 councillors who appeared, set up the chant: "Make Shropshire Nuclear Free" with a heavy rhythmic beat which was effective. Some councillors had CND badges which drew loud cheers. Others grinned sheepishly. One said "we should be over-run by the Russians" which drew a huge NO!

Eighteen months later she was among over 250,000 marchers in London. The Secretary of State for Defence, Michael Heseltine, had responded by setting up a propaganda unit in the Ministry of Defence called DS19, to counter the arguments of the nuclear disarmers. The unit had direct links with MI5, which was let off the leash. According to whistleblowing agent Cathy Massiter, its F Branch, dealing with 'domestic subversion', was massively expanded to extend surveillance to anti-nuclear protesters. Phone tapping and close collaboration with Special Branch police became widespread, with no accountability. Journalist Duncan Campbell revealed in a *New Statesman* article in August 1984 that MI5's A (Operations) Branch was "free to break the law as it applies to others, with impunity".

In this febrile atmosphere, opposition to government policy had become subversion. Any fearless, eloquent, independent critic was now seen as a threat to the State. This included a 78-year-old former rose-growing environmentalist who loved her country so much she was not prepared to let it be irrevocably ruined and poisoned by the nuclear industry – and whose nephew knew too much about the Falklands War, had left the Royal Navy and dropped out of the 'establishment' to become a roof thatcher.

CHAPTER 2

THE FIRST WEEK

"They've rubbed her out." Above all else that day, I remember my involuntary conviction when the Shrewsbury police phoned at about 2 pm on Saturday 24 March 1984.

At about 7 am, an hour or so after sunrise on Saturday 24 March, Police Constable Edmond Lane parks his patrol car outside the entrance to Ravenscroft, a large slate-roofed Victorian house at 52 Sutton Road, Shrewsbury. He walks slowly into the wide, grey shingle driveway towards the side of the house facing the road. Seeing a door slightly open, he knocks and calls out twice. He goes round to the front porch, and rings a doorbell: again no response. He does not go inside the house, leaves the side door as he found it, and resumes his mobile patrol.

An hour later, PC Lane is back at Ravenscroft: the door is still open. Once again he knocks and calls out, without response. This time he enters through the kitchen where the curtains are closed and a light is on. He climbs the stairs to the landing, and sees a broken baluster. He finds another narrow flight of steps to the attic, and starts a systematic search of each room, finding no-one.

Back in the kitchen, Lane notes the scrubbed table strewn with documents and two handbags. Oddly, wet white bedsheets lie in a heap on the scullery floor. He knows this is the home of a Miss Hilda Murrell whose car has been found abandoned, stuck on a muddy verge in a local country lane three days ago.

By now it is 8.30 am. As he leaves, he sees a key on the inside of the door. He locks it and takes the key to Frances Murrell, the widow of a cousin of Hilda, across the road.

Lane then visits the town's general and psychiatric hospitals to check if they have admitted Hilda Murrell. He radios the police communications room to suggest a dog handler be used to start a search of the area of her abandoned car.

At about 9 am, neighbour Brian George arrives to tend his vegetable plot in Hilda's large garden. He notices the curtains and shutters are partly closed in the downstairs rooms.

David Williams arrives to start his weekly job of helping to keep the garden tidy. Seeing the up-and-over garage door half-open with no white Renault 5 inside, he calls to George. They try the side door which has been locked only thirty minutes earlier by PC Lane. Nearby they find the conservatory door unlocked; surprisingly, so too is an inner door. Tentatively, they enter the house.

In the kitchen, Williams sees the two handbags and documents on the table. George first notices the wet sheets in the scullery, then Hilda's upper denture plate on the wooden draining board of the sink. He knows she would never go out without wearing it.

With mounting concern, George calls out to Hilda as they climb the stairs. The broken baluster is in three pieces: one is on the landing carpet, the other two on an ottoman in the bathroom. They knock and enter Hilda's curtain-dimmed bedroom. The bedclothes are pulled right back, and drawers are open in a dressing table. Curtains are closed across the window facing the drive. Unusually, the window overlooking the back garden is wide open, its curtains only partly drawn back. They check the other two bedrooms: curtains are closed, which is also unusual. A picture with its glass broken lies in the doorway of the smaller back bedroom. On checking downstairs, Hilda is not in the sitting room, dining room, toilet or cellar. In the front porch, they note a pile of Guardian *newspapers and mail on the tiled floor. The chain and bolts are in place across the locked double doors.*

Back in the kitchen, George decides to phone Betty Latter, Hilda's cleaning lady. The telephone is on a small chest of drawers beside a wooden box seat built below a narrow window facing Sutton Road. Concerned that the receiver is partly off its cradle, he picks it up: there is no dialling tone. His eyes follow the thick grey plastic-covered cord from the phone to the junction box: the box cap is loose and unscrewed. Lifting it, he sees that three of the four wires inside are partially disconnected and the spade terminals are intact – so the cord has not been wrenched out.

Meanwhile, two hundred miles south in Dorset, Liz and I stayed in bed until around nine o'clock before enjoying a leisurely breakfast.

At 9.20 am Police Constable Robert Eades, a rural beat officer, is returning to Hunkington Lane, about three miles east of Shrewsbury as the crow flies. He is re-investigating a small white Renault 5 hatchback, seemingly abandoned and stuck on the soft grass verge, hard against a low hedge on a bank. He first inspected it before sunset on Wednesday 21 March with PC Paul Davies, when they established it was not reported stolen, and is owned by a 78-year-old unmarried woman called Hilda Murrell living at 52 Sutton Road.

Eades enlists the help of the local gamekeeper, whose cottage is about a mile away. He is out, but his wife offers to help search with two gundogs. They start in hazel thickets flanking Hunkington Lane about half a mile from Hilda's car.

Back in Shrewsbury, Brian George walks home to phone Betty Latter. She last saw Hilda when she cleaned Ravenscroft the previous Monday, and agrees to meet him there.

George phones Fron Goch, Hilda's weekend retreat. The phone is out of order. He dials 999.

George, his wife Betty, Williams and Mrs Latter then search Ravenscroft together. It takes half an hour before a woman police constable arrives. She makes a call on her radio. PC Lane joins his colleague and neighbours in the drive after no progress at the hospitals. They all re-enter the house where he is shown the disconnected telephone, and is told that Hilda would never leave her home untidy or unlocked.

When Detective Superintendent Needham arrives a few minutes later, he asks to use the Georges' phone to contact his superior officer and meet him out at Hunkington.

Across the road, Frances Murrell watches with growing disquiet. She phones

Carolyn Hartley-Davies, a daughter of Hilda's cousin Leslie Murrell and a frequent visitor to Ravenscroft, who lives ten miles away. Carolyn phones her father.

Liz and I went on our weekend shopping trip to Yeovil. None of Hilda's neighbours would have known how to contact me. I barely knew Carolyn, her father or Frances Murrell.

Shortly before 10 am, PC Eades gives up searching the thickets. He remembers Hilda's interest in birdwatching. The gamekeeper's wife recalls seeing a pair of barn owls hunting along a hedge next to Moat Copse – a plantation of mature poplar trees over 500 yards across a waterlogged field of heavy red Shropshire clay sown with winter wheat. The quickest and easiest way to the copse is around the back via lanes and a cart track through Somerwood Farm.

As they enter it, the dogs point and run to the base of a poplar tree twenty yards ahead where Eades finds a dead elderly woman. At 10.15 am, within an hour of starting to search, he reports his discovery to a police search team assembling near the abandoned car.

Liz and I returned home from shopping. At about 10.30 am my sister rang with the disturbing news that Hilda was missing. On phoning, I got no reply from Ravenscroft, and her Fron Goch phone was out of order. With no contact numbers for Hilda's Shrewsbury neighbours, I phoned two of her friends at Llanymynech. They had not seen her or heard from her since the previous Sunday.

Hilda was a notoriously impatient driver. Anyone who dared to pull in front of her or slow her down would soon hear exasperated toots of her horn and some startling expletives. Could she have crashed and staggered away from the car, maybe suffering from concussion and amnesia?

With no more news, at about noon I phoned Monkmoor Police Station in Shrewsbury to learn that a full-scale search was underway. As next of kin, I asked to speak to the officer in charge of the search; "Sorry, sir, that's not possible".

"In that case, please tell him that my aunt Hilda was writing a paper for the Sizewell Inquiry criticising the nuclear industry, and she may have made enemies." The desk sergeant said he would.

At around 1.30 pm, Detective Chief Superintendent David Cole, head of West Mercia Police Criminal Investigation Department, arrives at the police investigation caravans parked on a root crop storage pad near Hilda's white Renault 5. He examines it. Further back up the lane are muddy tyre tracks which suggest the car went out of control, swerving from side to side before leaving the road. He notices the mud-clogged front offside tyre with a small hardback book lying in front of it. The driver has apparently tried to get the car moving.

DCS Cole enters Moat Copse, where the body of a frail-looking, thin old woman is lying next to a tree. She is wearing a thigh-length, thick woollen brown overcoat. Her right arm is extended in front of her, her left arm alongside her body; her shrivelled white legs are slightly bent and mostly exposed, with severe abrasions and redness on the knees. Only the coat and an underslip cover the top of her thighs; one thick brown stocking is crumpled around her left ankle; she is not wearing knickers. Items of clothing are scattered nearby: the other stocking, a green skirt and cream suspender belt, but no knickers. Cuts to each palm look like classic defence wounds from a knife attack. A bloodstained handkerchief and the keys to her car are in her right coat pocket.

The duty sergeant phoned me at about 2 pm. An elderly woman's body had been found. Any further thoughts of an accident were overwhelmed by that terrible gut feeling: my beloved aunt had been 'rubbed out'.

Liz and I set off immediately to my sister, about an hour's drive away on the way to Shrewsbury. Later I learned the body had been found 1½ hours before I made that first phone call to the police at midday. As Hilda's next of kin, I should have been told then.

Next to arrive in Hunkington Lane, at 4.45 pm, is Birmingham pathologist Dr Peter Acland. He supervises removal of the body to Copthorne General Hospital in Shrewsbury. The two undertakers need his help to carry it out of the copse. Shortly after 6 pm, Carolyn's husband formally identifies the body as Hilda. Dr Acland begins the autopsy, which takes three hours and produces as many questions as answers.

At around 6.30 pm the police phoned the family to confirm that Hilda was dead. A further police call at around 10.30 pm confirmed she had been murdered.

Next morning, Sunday 25 March, my brother-in-law and I set off on an apprehensive three-hour drive to Shrewsbury. My first priority was to find out what had happened to Hilda's Sizewell paper.

On our arrival, the police said they could not see us that day. Alarmed, I insisted on meeting the detectives in charge of the investigation the next morning. At Monkmoor Police Station, we were led through a large, crowded open-plan incident room where we could see the huge effort and resources already being devoted to the case. For the West Mercia Police, who had a 100 per cent success rate in solving murders, it was fast becoming their most extensive investigation.

In a side room we met DCS David Cole and his right-hand man, Detective Chief Inspector Chris Furber. Cole refused to let me see Hilda's body until later that day. Disbelief and outrage welled up as I demanded to know why. Unmoved, he warned it might not be released for months, possibly years, because of the "very unusual" circumstances of the case. He drew parallels with the 1979 murder in Saudi Arabia of English nurse Helen Smith: her body had been preserved for five years. The realisation that Hilda's funeral would have to be shelved indefinitely came as a major new shock.

I told the two detectives about my instinctive feeling that the murder was linked with Hilda's anti-nuclear work. Both looked at me blankly. When reminded, Cole confirmed he received my message, adding dismissively: "I had no idea what you were on about". I asked if Hilda's Sizewell paper had been found. They gave me a copy of a version corrected in her handwriting. Later, they let me have a photocopy of her 1984 diary, in which her final entry confirmed she was working on the paper the night before her abduction.

Hilda had sent me an earlier draft with a letter dated 15 October 1983, which had a disturbing postscript:

> I am now seriously thinking of going to London on Saturday. Just in case of 'anything happening', as they say, could you see that the paper goes to Gerard Morgan-Grenville... I don't want to be melodramatic but I have put a lot of work into this thing and I want it to get to the target.

She did go, to support a massive CND demonstration.

In Shrewsbury, the police invited me to make a statement about my relationship with Hilda, my recent movements, and how I learned she was missing. I outlined the close bond between us. Then came the next jolting, unmistakably hostile exchange:

"When did you last see your aunt?"

"About fourteen months ago."

"And you claim to be close?"

Grief-laden anger welling again, I tried to explain our closeness was not dependent on frequency of meeting. We kept in touch through monthly phone calls and occasional letters. I had last stayed overnight at Ravenscroft on 7 January 1983 when I helped Hilda brainstorm the first draft of her critique of the Government White Paper on radioactive waste management, which became her Sizewell paper. It was the last time I had seen her.

On the Monday afternoon I was finally able to pay my respects, in Copthorne Hospital's Chapel of Rest. In front of a modest altar and wooden cross, Hilda's body lay in a coffin with only her head exposed. Staring with horror at a face discoloured by terrible bruising, I began to grieve. Traumatised and naively trusting the police, I did not question why her hands were hidden, let alone the details of her other injuries. Years later I learned that, among several organs, her brain had been removed. I suspect what was left of her in the coffin was probably in a body bag.

———— ❧ ————

Later that day the story filled three pages of the county's evening newspaper, the *Shropshire Star*, beneath the front page banner headline 'ROSE EXPERT IS MURDERED'. Readers learned sixty police officers were looking for 'a savage killer'. For nearly three days the police had treated Hilda's car as just an abandoned vehicle. Now it seemed she had been abducted in her own car, before somehow ending up with multiple stab wounds and other injuries in Moat Copse.

Reports of Hilda's movements before she was abducted were coming in to the police.

At around 11.30 am on Wednesday 21 March, George Lowe parks just ahead of Hilda's car which he recognises because she is a relative and, until recently, a neighbour. He sees her in Safeways supermarket, but has no chance to speak to her. Ten minutes later Lowe returns to his car and sees Hilda sitting in hers. As he greets her, he notes she is wearing an unusual, wide-brimmed, floppy brown hat. She drives off.

Lowe drives to his previous home almost opposite Ravenscroft, to collect mail. On leaving, he notices that Hilda's car is not in her drive. He then passes her waiting to turn into Sutton Road: she spots him and waves. It has been 15-20 minutes since they spoke – so she has been somewhere else.

Soon after, a woman cleaning the front room of a house opposite Ravenscroft watches Hilda walk slowly, nursing her arthritic feet, out of her drive, across the road towards her, then out of sight to the witness's left. Hilda visits her neighbour Mary O'Connor to pay for a raffle ticket. The cleaning woman notices Hilda is dressed smartly in a large wide-brimmed felt hat, matching brown coat, pleated tweed skirt, patterned thick stockings and shoes. Some minutes later she watches Hilda re-enter her house through the side door. She does not see Hilda's car in the drive, but notices the garage door is shut; so she assumes the car is inside.

Hilda did not tell Mary O'Connor she had a lunch appointment with friends of twenty years, Drs Alicia and John Symondson, half an hour's drive away. The invitation was for 12.45 pm. She never arrived. If she was about to go out, why did she put her car in the garage?

DCS Cole speculated publicly that Hilda unpacked the vegetables and fruit she had bought before going upstairs to change, where she surprised a burglar. For some crazy reason he decided to abduct her, and the baluster was broken as she resisted. He probably knocked her unconscious to get her through the front door into her own car, which Cole assumed she had left parked in the drive. This ignored the evidence of the cleaning woman. His second assumption, that Hilda had been taken out through the front door, was because it was not directly visible from the road. But would her abductor have left her free to escape from the car while he went back in through the side door to chain and bolt the front door, then locked the side door facing the road, risking discovery?

Witness reports indicated that, bizarrely, Hilda's abductor apparently drove with her slumped in the front passenger seat into town past the police station, then out on the Newport Road to Haughmond Hill. There he swung right into a back lane leading through the cover of woods where he could more easily have dumped her. Yet he drove on into open country, before seeming to lose control of the Renault and getting it stuck against a hedge and bank about 400 yards short of Hunkington Farm.

A woman's hat was found near a hedge beside a heavy clay field some 300 yards from the car. Hilda's smashed spectacles, her moccasin style house boots, and a large kitchen knife lay nearby. Cole concluded her abductor frogmarched her at knifepoint on a fine spring afternoon across the field to the hedge. Somehow, despite severe injuries, she then crawled or was dragged a further 300 yards to the copse. Later, a large man vaguely resembling the driver was seen running back into Shrewsbury by the same route.

Hilda had been hit in the face, and possibly strangled because her hyoid bone was broken. Her broken right collar bone had probably been stamped on. There was a knife wound through her right upper arm and several more shallow ones in her abdomen. Pathologist Dr Peter Acland's assessment was that she had died of hypothermia. Cole decided her killer was probably local, despite his admission that it was "an odd area" for an assailant to take his victim.

When Cole first briefed me, he added that in Ravenscroft there were signs of a struggle in a back bedroom as well as on the landing. However, no bloodstains were found anywhere in the house or car. I was shown the footwear found some twenty yards apart between the hedge and the copse. They were Hilda's old beige quilted cotton house boots, which she would only go out in to fetch coal from her backyard. They were bloodstained. This implied Hilda was stabbed while upright after leaving the car, but before reaching the copse.

My sister joined us the next day, Tuesday 27 March. After another meeting at the police station she, her husband, Carolyn Hartley-Davies and I were asked to visit Ravenscroft. We donned white protection suits and gloves, as the house was still being examined by forensic experts.

My immediate reaction was the house was untidy, but not "ransacked" as reported by police and media. In the kitchen, I noticed a large dark area of damp rush matting where the wet sheets had been. They had been removed by the police, who seemed uninterested in them. Hilda would never have left them like that – she always took her bed linen to a local laundry. I saw the telephone receiver partly off the hook, the end of its cord and an extension cable lying clear of the junction box. On the table, two handbags – which none of us recognised – were open beside a man's empty wallet, an empty purse and, to my surprise, Hilda's watch, cheque book and bank card. Also, her dental plate was on the sink draining board. She would never have gone out without this or her watch. The downstairs toilet was stained by liquid faeces on the bowl rim, which Hilda would never have left. In the sitting room, partly closed curtains and an open door of the drinks cupboard were the only unusual aspects.

Upstairs, apart from the broken baluster and picture glass, there were no obvious signs of violence. Hilda would meticulously close drawers and doors of cupboards, some of which had been left open. An almost full can of lager was found in the toilet in the bathroom.

However, during our brief tour I was preoccupied with shock and grief in a house previously associated with happy memories and stimulating conversations. It was impossible to tell what might be missing. Nonetheless, I did not see four familiar items: Hilda's current purse and handbag; a leather music satchel she used to carry important documents; and a large, brown wooden-handled carving knife she used to cut bread which usually lay on a big plate with a bold flower pattern on the kitchen table.

Hilda's cleaner Mrs Latter also did not recognise the handbags on the kitchen table, nor the wallet or purse. She recalled Hilda using a "free-standing, dark brownish handbag possibly made of leather with two handles". Carolyn agreed, adding that Hilda told her she had difficulty opening certain types of clasps due to her arthritis, so her everyday handbag had an easy one.

When the police asked us to identify the Totes rain hat with a narrow stiff brim found in the hedge halfway to the copse, none of us could. We were shown a second, wide-brimmed hat made of canvas, which we did recognise. Only later did I realise that the wide-brimmed floppy brown felt hat Hilda was wearing when George Lowe, Mary O'Connor and the cleaning woman saw her, and apparently worn by the passenger in her car, was never shown to us or returned to the family.

Months later, for some reason the police asked Mrs Latter to review the state of the house. She made some interesting fresh observations. She said three pieces of clothing, found on the bed in the small back bedroom where a struggle with Hilda was supposed to have taken place, had been there for several weeks. One of these, a green jacket left on the pillow, matched the old skirt found near Hilda's body. Although some things were out of place, the bed looked undisturbed. It was where Hilda often sorted old clothes and materials for mending or jumble sales. Mrs Latter thought the bandages, rags and old ironing board cover found on the bed had come out of a drawer in that room.

Mrs Latter also commented on the box seat below the kitchen window where Hilda stacked her anti-nuclear papers. The front panel of the seat had two recent marks, possibly made by a crowbar to prise it open as part of a search. The police seemed dismissive about this.

As news of the murder spread, I cleared Fron Goch with the help of a resourceful removals firm. Workers had to cope with the steep, stepped paths and tortuous cart track below. The property seemed untouched. I found no anti-nuclear papers. Instead, I made a thrilling discovery: two loose-leaf binders and a large envelope full of notes and sketches. They were from her expeditions along the Welsh Borders, and her holidays in Mallorca, Anglesey,

Ireland and the Scottish Highlands over thirty years. Hilda kept a daily diary, but these were her nature diaries. A wonderful blend of botanical observations, romantic musings and accurate sketches of plants and flowers, they revealed an artistic talent I had no idea she possessed.

∞

A week after Hilda's abduction, the forensic experts announced they had completed their examination of Ravenscroft. It meant Liz and I could start clearing it. Responsibility for the house was formally handed over to me by the police, while a constable kept guard at the drive entrance.

During the handover, they pointed out two microphones taped crudely to the walls of the kitchen, plus pressure pads on the floor inside the side and front doorways. Apparently these devices were "for security". Only later did I wonder just whose security they had in mind... At the time I had too much else to worry about. Clearing Ravenscroft was a massive, distressing task; and sorting through Hilda's possessions made us feel we were violating her hitherto intensely private life.

While we were doing this, the police suddenly trumpeted a discovery supporting their idea that the crime was committed by a petty burglar for cash. Hilda had withdrawn £50 from Lloyds Bank the morning she was abducted, and it had not been found. She had supposedly been killed for about £47, left after she had bought a few vegetables and fruit at Safeways. The police said nothing else was taken. They dismissed the complicating suspicion that her everyday handbag and purse were missing, along with her documents satchel. No-one could prove if any of her anti-nuclear papers had disappeared; but the house had clearly been searched.

The police also reported the telephone at Ravenscroft was "torn out". On reading this in a newspaper report, Brian George was furious. He sought me out while I was clearing the house, to recount what he first saw on the Saturday morning. He was adamant the phone wires were only partially disconnected, not ripped out. What was going on?

∞

The crazy journey of Hilda's car through Shrewsbury as she was apparently abducted was the only part of the crime to be witnessed.

Rosalind Taylerson joins traffic on the Column roundabout when, suddenly to her left, a white Renault 5 car speeds across in front of her. She brakes violently to avoid a collision. However, she gets a good view of the right-hand side of the male driver's face. He is in his late 20s-early 30s, with short light-brown hair and a clean-shaven, tidy appearance.

Pamela Bird is standing on the pavement next to the Monkmoor Road junction lights. She sees a Renault car swerving into the right-hand lane. It is a controlled, confident manoeuvre across three lanes of traffic. The car stops, giving her a chance to look inside. The driver is a man in his mid-to-late 20s. His shoulders are broader than the seat. Someone slumped in the front passenger seat appears to be an elderly woman because she is wearing a broad-brimmed, floppy hat, but the head is hidden. The car speeds off up Monkmoor Road before the lights turn green, skilfully avoiding on-coming traffic.

William Moseley and his wife are in a car in Monkmoor Road about to turn right on a green traffic light into Abbey Foregate. Suddenly, a small white car crosses in front of them from left to right, having jumped the lights. Moseley sees two occupants: the driver is stocky with big shoulders, and looks quite odd in such a small car. He is aged 35-40, with dark shortish hair and neat sideburns, and is not wearing a seat belt. A small woman passenger seems to be leaning to her left.

The route taken by the "running man", between 1.30-2.30 pm on the Wednesday, was becoming clearer to the police. He had apparently retraced the car's route in reverse. Almost fifty witnesses made statements that they had seen the man. Most agreed he was in his early to late thirties, tall and well-built, dressed in greyish, mudstained clothing and trainers, and he seemed tired and distressed. The last sighting was not far from the police station.

———— ∞ ————

A key witness was the farmer who first reported Hilda's car abandoned in Hunkington Lane – but his story was not being released.

Between 2-2.30 pm on Wednesday 21 March, John Marsh is driving to his farmhouse in Hunkington Lane when he spots a small white Renault which appears to have crashed into a low bank. Even though he was accustomed to abandoned cars there, he walks back to examine it. He notices the front offside wheel is covered in soil. Further along the lane he finds where tyre marks have left deep ruts on the opposite verge. Marsh feels very uneasy about this car. He goes home and reports it to Shrewsbury police station. Concerned by the lack of response, at 5.20 pm he phones his local policeman in Upton Magna.

Marsh was corroborated by his neighbour, John Rogers, who rode his horse past the car that afternoon. Rogers was adamant the offside was close enough to the bank to prevent the driver's door from opening. Therefore the driver's only exit was via the front passenger door – after pushing the semi-conscious passenger out?

———— ∞ ————

Liz and I were exhausted and mentally drained after clearing Ravenscroft. One of the last items we packed was a small handmade calendar, hung above the telephone. Beneath '21 March' Hilda had written: '12.45. Symondson'. If the police had taken prompt action by sending officers to her house after Marsh first reported her car around 2.30 pm, they would have seen the calendar. If they had checked with the Symondsons – whose phone number was in Hilda's address book close by – the search for Hilda could have begun well before nightfall. With help from dogs, she could have been found alive – as Cole admitted in a briefing to police at the time.

∞

From the many letters and cards of condolence arriving to pay tribute to her, I was learning more about Hilda. Until then, I had never known the extent of her friendships with a wide variety of people from the different eras and interests of her life, stretching back to her schooldays and Cambridge.

Joan Tate, a local friend whom I got to know well, provided an antidote to media reports of Hilda with this vivid, forthright portrait which punctured the stereotypical descriptions of her:

> Seventy-eight years old (ancient and tottery), ex-rose grower (as if she spent her whole life growing roses), spinster (hmm), above all old. Hilda Murrell was younger and more alert than many people half her age. Nor was she a tweedy old thing in sensible shoes. She had a great flair for attractive and original clothes and wore them with style. She had a great sense of humour, a sharp wit and an independence of mind... She was single all her life, uncluttered you might say, so was able to concentrate on what she considered important to the world, not just to herself.

Ruth Sinker reduced me to grateful tears with these observations:

> Dear Robert, Hilda always called you that to me: she talked of you so often, & you obviously meant more to her, and gave her more happiness, than anyone else in the world. I hope this may be a help to you. What would have horrified her is that you should be the one to bear the main burden of this appalling business.
>
> Among other things, when I was utterly lost after my husband died, she came & forced me to make a garden, dug most of it herself, & stocked it with plants... we had a real, & rare, communication of thoughts & ideas.

Ruth's son Charles Sinker was a distinguished botanist and former director of the Field Studies Council, who later edited Hilda's nature diaries for publication in 1987. In his obituary of her for *The Times*, he described her thus:

> ... a rose-grower of international repute, and an ardent conservationist. A highly intelligent and charmingly eccentric woman of strong opinions, she was loved and respected by a wide circle of friends. She was an authority on rose species, old varieties and miniature roses.
>
> Her deep love and concern for the countryside and wildlife of the Welsh Marches made her an active founder-member of the Shropshire Conservation Trust, and she also

worked with vigorous dedication for the Shropshire branch of the Council for the Protection of Rural England.

Her close friends remember her as a fierce but fundamentally gentle warrior, a Bunyan-like soul on a lonely and constant quest for the real path of the spirit. She was valiant for truth.

She died in tragic circumstances, alone in the empty countryside. It is an almost intolerable irony that a life so dedicated to peaceful pursuits, and to the pursuit of peace, should have been terminated by an act of mindless violence.

Charles' text as sent to *The Times* also included this paragraph, which was omitted from the printed version:

In recent years she became involved in the campaign against what she saw as the unacceptable hazards of nuclear power generation… Because she did her homework and was unswervingly honest, her spoken and written arguments commanded respect. When she chose to deploy her charm as well as her trained intellect, the toughest chauvinist expert might well beware.

Joan and Clive Tate, who lived in a comfortable old town house in the mediaeval heart of Shrewsbury, were our wonderful hosts for this and many of my subsequent visits. Together they made a formidable intelligence-gathering team in my absence.

By the weekend the police had come up with an artist's impression of the car driver and running man, considered to be the same person. Described as between 25 and 40, powerfully built with broad shoulders, he had medium brown to dark-coloured hair, neatly groomed with a slight fringe, clean-shaven with a narrow face and sallow complexion. He was wearing either a grey suit or grey trousers with a grey-blue jacket and training shoes.

However, my growing concerns were now being openly voiced by others. Why had there been such a delay between the first report of Hilda's abandoned car at 2.30 pm and finding her body in the copse? Police statements glossed over what caused the delay.

At 6 pm on Wednesday 21 March, PC Paul Davies comes on duty on his rural beat in the village of Upton Magna, about two miles south of Hunkington. He follows up a phone call forty minutes earlier from local farmer John Marsh. His fellow rural beat officer, PC Robert Eades, picks him up in their shared police vehicle.

By 6.20 pm, around sunset, they reach the reported Renault 5. Eades finds the car is unlocked and opens the front passenger door. There are no keys in the ignition and no sign of any loose wires. In the boot he finds a bag of peat and a large grapefruit.

Meanwhile, Davies checks the identity of the car's owner from the Police National

Computer. Within minutes they know it is Hilda's, that she is 78 years old, and where she lives. In the gathering dusk they briefly check over the hedge, see no-one in the field, and assume she has gone for help. They decide the car is not causing an obstruction or danger to other vehicles; so they leave the scene at 6.30 pm. A duty officer in Shrewsbury police station phones Hilda's home: there is no reply. No further action is taken.

John Marsh was making no secret to friends that he reported the car twice that afternoon and again on Thursday and Friday. His cleaning woman remembered hearing him angrily berating the police on Thursday: "Get that car off my land!"

In April Joan Tate tipped me off that Marsh reported his farmworkers also saw two strange men in the field near the car on Thursday. Much more disturbingly, he added "**on the Friday, the place was swarming with police**" and they told him " it was a murder hunt". Did they know, as recently confirmed by Marsh's son, David, that no workers would be working there that day? Were these Special Branch, working independently of West Mercia Police who always claimed they did not begin searching for Hilda until the Saturday morning? However, an officer apparently visited Ravenscroft on Friday evening.

At 6 pm on Friday 23 March PC Davies phones Shrewsbury police station from Upton Magna to be told that Marsh has made yet another call about Hilda's car. He tries phoning her home, but there is still no reply. He returns to the car: it is as he left it on Wednesday. Taking the initiative, he decides to visit 52 Sutton Road.

By the time he arrives at 7 pm, it is almost dark, and raining. He reverses his patrol car into the drive, and gets out. He sees a light through curtains across a downstairs window, then notices the side door facing the road is wide open. He knocks: no answer. Walking round to the front of the house, he rings the bell: silence. He notes curtains and shutters are closed across windows either side of the front porch.

He enters the kitchen through the open side door. He calls out but there is no response. The light is on and he sees the table covered in papers, and also a handbag. Deciding nothing is suspicious he concludes Miss Murrell must have "popped out" to the shops.

Without her handbag or purse, leaving her door wide open, and on foot because her car is still stuck out at Hunkington?

Davies decides not to go further into the house and retreats to the side door, which he first thinks has been blown open by the wind. He sees no key in the lock. Then he has to pull the door hard several times before it closes properly.

He checks the garden by torchlight but finds no-one. As he drives away, he radios Shrewsbury police station at 7.20 pm, requesting that someone contact the house again. Several phone calls are made until midnight, with no reply. The station duty officer decides it is too late to persist in case the occupant has returned. He arranges for an early shift officer, PC Lane, to visit at first light the next day.

Police reluctance to explain their actions prompted suggestions they were "instructed" to do nothing. I was ready to believe these early conspiracy theories because of my initial instincts and Hilda's last letter to me. It was increasingly difficult to accept that the murder had been committed by a local burglar. The police theory seemed to raise too many questions:

- Would a burglar not escape immediately he heard a car on the shingle drive – especially as Hilda had briefly entered the kitchen to leave her basket before visiting Mary O'Connor?
- Would a burglar abduct an elderly woman in her car?
- Would a burglar not have taken jewellery and other valuables, or at least her cheque book and card – as well as the £47 cash?
- Would a local burglar have taken a busy route through town and past the police station? The quickest and quietest way to open country was a right turn, not left, out of the drive.
- Would an assailant who had beaten and stabbed an old but articulate woman not make sure she was dead before abandoning her? Or far more likely, would he not simply do so in her house?

The Shrewsbury underworld was equally incredulous. Micky Bridgewater, one of nearly a hundred burglars questioned by the police, said publicly he was convinced that a local thief was not responsible. A burglar would never normally abduct his victim, nor stay in the house if he disturbed the owner: "I'd be through the window and gone as fast as I could". He was confident that, had it been a Shrewsbury man, he would have heard about it through the local criminal grapevine. He would have been straight on the phone to the police and "grassed on him – because you don't hurt an old girl living on her own".

⚬⚬⚬

I was thoroughly alarmed by the next story I heard via Joan and Clive Tate – not from the police.

On Thursday 22 March at around 3.30 pm, local landowner Ian Scott is in Moat Copse at Hunkington with his dogs – just over 24 hours after Hilda's abduction. He wants to fell most of the poplars. He inspects each tree – 170 of them – before returning to his home at Somerwood Farm nearby.

On Monday 26 March, Scott contacts Shrewsbury police station. He is concerned about reports that Hilda has died in Moat Copse the previous Wednesday afternoon. He tells the police "categorically" that she was not in the copse when he was there 24 hours later. He explains that he must have walked within a yard of where her body was found – yet he neither saw her nor any item of clothing. He says he would have seen a dead rabbit, let alone a body.

Scott's report convinced me that this was a much more complicated and sinister case than the police were admitting.

After an exhausting and traumatic week in Shropshire, Liz and I had to go home and back to work.

CHAPTER 3

MORE THAN A BURGLARY GONE WRONG

When Gerard Morgan-Grenville phoned on 2 April 1984, I recognised his name from Hilda's last letter in which she asked me to get her draft Sizewell paper to him 'just in case of anything happening' to her.

He told me he had made a statement to the police about a half-hour phone call with Hilda "a few weeks" before she was murdered. "Hilda phoned me late one evening, and seemed unusually agitated and anxious – to the extent that my wife summoned me out of my bath. I recall getting very cold standing dripping wet with just a towel round me." Her last words were: *"If they don't get me first, I want the world to know that at least one old woman has seen through their lies."* He had never heard her speak like that. For the first time, she sounded "rather desperate".

Was this confirmation of my gut reaction when I first heard Hilda was missing, that "they" had "got" her? The police dismissed this disturbing evidence because he could provide no corroboration other than his wife's, and there was no mention of the call in Hilda's diary. Morgan-Grenville agreed to meet me the next day at his home in Wales. My return to Dorset had lasted all of two days.

I pulled up outside a magnificent old fortified manor house overlooking the market town of Crickhowell in the southern Welsh Black Mountains. Morgan-Grenville had all the qualifications for membership of the British 'establishment' – old Etonian, former Guards officer, Countryside Commissioner with friends in high places, including cabinet ministers who were regular weekend house party guests. Despite this, it seems he experienced something of a similar mid-life crisis to mine, committing himself to admirable ecological causes.

Our meeting was affable. Although he could not specify the date of Hilda's last, agitated phone call to him, her 1982-84 diaries record that they were communicating intensively. For example, between the end of June and July 1983 they phoned each other nine times, and exchanged seven letters. On 12 March 1984 Hilda complained in her diary:

```
      Tel. bill £52.90 - the largest I have ever had. Must
   limit talk with Robert, Gerard...
```

For February her diary records two long calls to me – but only one to him, on 11 February:

> I tel. G.M.-G. & told him about reading papers. He said it would be much more effective if I were to read it (this is clear enough). He thought I would find it "encouraging". That's about the last view I take of such an enterprise.

Her concern about her record phone bill offers circumstantial evidence that she must have made more calls to Morgan-Grenville later in February, but chose not to mention them. She recorded that a letter from him arrived on 16 March – about a week before her body was found, and two weeks before he heard of her death. The entry reads:

> Nice letter from Gerard Morgan-Grenville, he has discussed my paper with Peter Bunyard, it will stand up on its own and will make a greater impact if it comes from an individual than if it were part of say, the Ecoropa case. This was always my point. Wishes me good luck. I shall need it.

Earlier entries suggest she often phoned him in the evening after receiving a letter. Did she not write about her final, distressed phone conversation with him because she wanted her diary to survive?

During my meeting with Morgan-Grenville, my naval career inevitably came up in conversation. He casually drew my attention to a review copy of a book on his desk, *Sink The Belgrano*, by Arthur Gavshon and Desmond Rice. It became a best-selling account of how, on 2 May 1982, in a hiatus in the Falklands War, the Argentine cruiser *General Belgrano* was torpedoed by the British nuclear submarine *HMS Conqueror*, with the loss of 321 Argentine sailors. This controversial attack gave Thatcher the full-blooded war she desperately needed to salvage her political career.

Morgan-Grenville, aware I had worked for Naval Intelligence during the war, offered the unpublished book to me and asked, "Would you like to borrow this, and let me know what you think of it?" Curiosity overriding my judgement, I accepted his dangerous invitation.

I was still bound by the Official Secrets Act. The smallest secret detail about my work during the conflict could have been used to discredit me or even prosecute me. When I called on Morgan-Grenville again a week later, I unwisely gave him some written comments. Fortunately, they went little further than suggesting "such things happen in war". However, I had dropped my guard. This episode gave me an important wake-up call about my political naivety and vulnerability.

Morgan-Grenville died in 2009, aged 77. His most enduring legacy is the Centre for Alternative Technology in Machynlleth in mid-Wales, which I enjoyed visiting with Hilda soon after it opened in the 1970s. He also ran the British branch of the European ecological action group Ecoropa. In 1983 they co-ordinated the distribution of seven million anti-nuclear energy leaflets. Hilda hand-delivered hundreds. Dangerously for me, she then distributed another Ecoropa leaflet which accused Thatcher of fomenting the Falklands War, ordering the sinking of the Argentine cruiser *General Belgrano* to scupper a peace plan, and alleging anti-submarine nuclear depth bombs had been deployed. After Hilda joined Ecoropa and started making donations in March 1982, Morgan-Grenville thanked her, and let her know she had supplied roses to his mother who held Murrell's Nurseries in great esteem. This gave Hilda the confidence to contact him directly.

Morgan-Grenville was the first of several influential anti-nuclear lobbyists to encourage and help her with her critique of the Government's White Paper on radioactive waste management policy. After he read her only copy of an early draft, which she unwisely posted to him because of photocopying difficulties, she wrote in her diary on 23 June 1983:

> Letter from G M-G – deeply impressed by my paper, it is a 'tour de force'. If I will send him 2 or 3 copies, he will send it to members of the government.

Morgan-Grenville also told her he would arrange for the paper to be vetted by Dr Ross Hesketh, a nuclear scientist working as Research Head Solid State Physics in the research laboratories of the Central Electricity Generating Board (CEGB). He was risking his job by helping Ecoropa and CND with their submissions to the Sizewell Inquiry.

A week later Hilda was alarmed to receive another letter from Morgan-Grenville asking her to "send back the document so that we can send it to Dr Hesketh". He had wrongly assumed his secretary had returned it – because it had disappeared from his office.

Hilda decided she had no choice. She started retyping her paper, and sent it to him a few days later, keeping a carbon copy. Then she recorded in her diary that she went to Fron Goch:

> Found door on to balcony wide open. There was a very small warbler fluttering in the window. At 5 pm tel rang: GM-G's secretary has found my paper. "It must have blown off the desk"!! (13 very long pages stapled together??). Told her an up to date top copy was on the way, not to worry, it was better.

Six weeks earlier she had had a similar scare:

> Was going to send my paper [to Morgan-Grenville] but can't find it! Searched high and low. The large envelope that Harry [Bury] gave me when he returned the copy has both copies, the TCPA paper and Cmnd 8607, none of them to be seen. The box of carbon paper has also vanished from the typewriter…

She would have been shocked when she found them two days later, completely out of place in a dining room cupboard. Hilda was not absent-minded or disorganised, especially over something so important. Did she suspect an intruder had been in her home, removed her papers to photocopy them and check the used carbon sheets for other typing, and deliberately put them back in an unexpected place to intimidate her?

Further disturbing news followed from Morgan-Grenville. As Hesketh's *Times* obituary in 2004 explained,

> Hesketh suspected that plutonium from British civil nuclear-power reactors (Magnox reactors) was being supplied to the USA for use in nuclear weapons… Hesketh began publicising his suspicions, starting with a letter to *The Times* on October 30, 1981. This publicity greatly embarrassed the British Government. In 1983 Hesketh was sent on leave for a few months and then fired by the CEGB, a publicly owned body. But he continued to expose the diversion of plutonium produced in British civil reactors to military use and its export for the same purpose.

Morgan-Grenville wrote to Hilda:

> Dr Hesketh confirmed my worst fears about the goings-on inside the CEGB and likened it to the Orwellian stoats and rabbits. He, personally, has been threatened in many subtle ways and has been the subject of many pressures to prevent him blowing the whistle. He has also had a written confession put in front of him to sign. Really the only difference between the treatment of dissidents in this country and, for instance, in Czechoslovakia is quantitative and not qualitative. But, I fear that the people of this country will awake to the reality too late. For every Hesketh, there are 1,000 non-Heskeths who just fall in line and soon learn the arts of professional apathy.

Soon after that, Hesketh wrote to Hilda commenting on her paper:

> Yours is a powerful indictment of the state of affairs we are now in… but when you speak of "somebody at the top who could put a stop to it" you reveal the great difficulty: no one wishes to put a stop to it, at the top. There's the rub!

The episodes with the missing papers provide circumstantial evidence that, nine months before she was murdered, both Hilda and Morgan-Grenville were under surveillance and harassment as she gained support for her critique from anti-nuclear organisations and prominent scientists. Her correspondence with Hesketh would have especially alarmed the nuclear industry security and State security authorities. Also, back in March 1983 she had written to Dr Patricia Lindop after reading a controversial article by her on the catastrophic consequences, including genetic health effects, for Europe if the high level radioactive waste tanks at Sellafield were attacked in a nuclear war. Early in 1984, Morgan-Grenville alerted Hilda to the work of Dr Rosalie Bertell, an American nun and expert on radiation-caused illnesses and genetic deformities, who later testified for Ecoropa at the Sizewell Inquiry. Hilda sent donations towards her travel cost to give evidence at Sizewell, and to help publish her book *No Immediate Danger*, which became a best-seller when it appeared in 1985.

In addition, on 30 July 1983 Hilda wrote in her diary that Morgan-Grenville was proposing she should send copies of her paper to some major figures:

> I should come out in the open and write covering letters saying who I am and about the nursery etc. They really don't like it when the respectable oppose them and they tend to answer, whereas they just ignore the wildcats. He suggested John Baker CEGB, Sir Peter Hirsch AEA [UK Atomic Energy Agency], Sir Kelvin Spencer [former Chief Scientist to the Ministry of Fuel and Power in the 1950s] and the Minister of Energy. I asked him please to deal with Sir Dennis [Denys] Wilkinson [Chair of the Radioactive Waste Management Advisory Committee]... I shall write to Sir Kelvin Spencer first...

Throughout this period, Hilda and I were conferring closely. When I visited her in October 1982 to tell her I had taken up roof thatching, she briefed me about Don Arnott, the retired nuclear scientist who was advising her. On 12 October 1982 her diary records:

> I read the thatching book and R read the Arnott papers. Then I read my paper. R urged the inclusion of several bits from Gowing [who wrote a definitive history of the early years of the British nuclear industry] and Arnott. To bed eventually, unwashed, after a very good day of talk such as I could hardly have with anyone else.

On 2 July 1983, Hilda wrote that when I phoned her, she told me "about the paper, GMG and Hesketh".

Six weeks later, she had just decided, following encouragement from CPRE Director Robin Grove-White, to submit her paper to the Sizewell Inquiry. Her diary records us discussing an incident which would have rung more alarm bells for anyone intercepting the call:

> Tel R. There is a Winfrith worker living 100 yards away – he had a talk with him in the pub one night and mentioned that I was working on the subject but not that I had written anything. R would like to show it to him. R's idea I think was that he might produce points. I said not till I have thought about it. I want it to spring

on them from nowhere without any prewarning. Danger of
photocopying. Promised to let him know developments.

At a subsequent pub meeting with the worker from the secretive reactor research centre near the Dorset village of Winfrith, the man understandably got cold feet and nothing more came of my proposal. Only eight months earlier I had left the Navy and dropped out of the 'establishment' as a thatcher. Now, convinced and empowered by Hilda's research, I had tried to incite a nuclear industry worker to whistleblow. Also, Hilda, Morgan-Grenville and I were often naively indiscreet on the telephone. Only on reading Hilda's diary did the chilling realisation dawn on me that around this time she was leafleting her neighbourhood with Morgan-Grenville's allegations about possible nuclear weapon deployment during the Falklands War. I must have already been under surveillance, suspected of being his possible source.

❧

After meeting Morgan-Grenville again, I decided to make a pilgrimage to where Hilda's body was found. I parked on the concrete pad used as the police field HQ, and gazed across winter wheat to Moat Copse. The leafless branches of its ranks of mature poplar trees which witnessed Hilda's tortured death were now softened by sprouting catkins. Farmer John Marsh knew it as Funeral Field because so many horses died trying to plough the waterlogged red Shropshire clay. Since then, it has been converted into a water storage lake.

Incredulity seeped in about the police theory as I absorbed the scene. From where the car had crashed to the copse was over 400 yards in a straight line, let alone following the hedge. The muddy field was wide open to view from surprisingly frequent traffic, and was overlooked by Marsh's farmhouse and workers in adjoining fields.

❧

Unable to have a funeral, the family held Hilda's thanksgiving service on 18 April, almost a month after her murder. Hundreds of mourners packed into the maze of curving pews inside the unique Georgian circular nave of St Chad's Church in the mediaeval heart of Shrewsbury. Instead of Hilda's coffin, we placed a small wreath of roses in front of the altar.

The principal eulogy was delivered by the Bishop of Shrewsbury, Leslie Lloyd Rees. His participation reflected her distinguished place in the wider community rather than her support for the Church of England. Hilda was deeply spiritual, but without the need of organised religion.

The Bishop captured the mood well: "We all feel caught up in it, and diminished by it; and yet in a strange way we are brought close to one another in our revulsion and sorrow. In the darkness of the circumstance, however, there is something which penetrates and transforms it – and that is the thanksgiving which we are offering together for Hilda herself."

He concluded: "Yes, a remarkable person; a pilgrim on the way, a constant seeker after truth, responding to the hints of ultimate reality as she perceived them; a person of the spirit, and as her obituary notice said, a fierce but fundamentally gentle warrior. It seems to me highly significant that, although Hilda would not have claimed to be an orthodox Christian, we are thanking God for her in a Christian church and within the most holy week of the Christian year, a week dominated for us by a Cross on a green hill outside a city wall…"

∞∞∞

Emotionally drained, we left St Chad's Church to discover, via the *Shropshire Star*, that two young men had been prosecuted for stealing the vehicle licence tax disc from Hilda's car on the afternoon it crashed. Charles Bevan, aged 21, and 18-year-old Christopher Watton admitted stealing the disc, worth £42, at about 4.30 pm on 21 March – nearly two hours before the police first inspected the car. When the youths heard about the murder they panicked and burned the disc. We were astonished the police had not told us about the theft or the court case, especially as one of Cole's deputies attended the thanksgiving service. He could also have warned us about the shocking revelations they were about to make the next day, after we returned home. As the victim's next of kin, living hundreds of miles away, I expected to be kept informed of all significant developments. This never happened. It meant I had to rely on reports from Joan Tate, who became the hub of a growing network of local contacts. Why were the police excluding Hilda's family?

At a press briefing on 19 April, Cole announced that Hilda had been sexually assaulted. Apparently the 'sex attack' happened at her home before she was abducted. He described it vaguely and disquietingly as "sexual activity", not rape. Family and friends were left to fret about the exact extent of this added violation of Hilda.

Why had this particular moment been chosen to release the sexual angle? Cole must have known about it within days of Acland's autopsy. Was it because they wanted to put the murder back on the front pages, which it did, and deflect attention away from mounting murmurs that the real motive was political?

The question of when the police discovered the sexual angle would receive a disturbing twist nine months later. In January 1985, journalist and author Judith Cook and Member of Parliament Tam Dalyell revealed they had met a professional counsellor from Shrewsbury who was occasionally called on to assist investigations into sex crimes. He was troubled because, he claimed, two Shrewsbury police officers had visited his home at 6.30 pm on the *Friday night before Hilda's body was discovered.* (This was soon after Marsh reported police "on a murder hunt" on his farm, and just before PC Davies visited Ravenscroft).

The officers asked if he could think of anyone who might have a sexual hang-up about elderly ladies. Did he know a man who would be turned on by going into a woman's bedroom and interfering with her clothing? Someone who might be violent? When Hilda's murder was reported, he was shocked to discover some of the details matched the scenario outlined by the two detectives. Before anyone officially knew there had been a murder, were the police already aware of it, including the sexual component?

In addition to the sex attack sensation, on 19 April the *Shropshire Star* reported that DCS Cole was appealing for information about two cars 'which may be connected' with the case. A red Ford Escort had been spotted in Sutton Road at about 10.30 on the morning of the abduction. Cole did not add that a similar car was seen several times around Hunkington while Hilda was missing.

At about 2.30 pm on Thursday 22 March, tractor driver Bryan Salter is spreading fertiliser on the field next to Hilda's car. He thinks nothing of a red Escort driving by – until he sees it again, and then a third time in a period of an hour and a half. It is always travelling in the same direction, as if the driver is patrolling the area.

The Escort was not the only suspicious car Salter saw in Hunkington Lane that day.

At about 3.45 pm, shortly after Ian Scott has checked the Moat Copse poplars for felling, Salter again watches curiously as a large, dark saloon car drives slowly along the lane. It stops and reverses onto the verge opposite a double gateway into a field next to Funeral Field. A man in a suit gets out, crosses the lane, and walks through the gateway. He follows the far side of the hedge between the two fields, where the police later find the large kitchen knife, Totes rain hat, broken spectacles and house boots. The mystery man returns along the hedge to the car about twenty minutes later and drives off.

After Hilda's body was found on the Saturday, farmer John Marsh made a point of watching out for vehicles. On the Sunday afternoon, he noticed a two-door red Escort saloon drive past his farm. Half an hour later the same car passed again travelling in the same direction – so it would have driven past the police post on the concrete pad twice.

Recently I learned that, after the young men had stolen the tax disc from Hilda's car on the Wednesday, they had to brake sharply when a red Ford Escort Mk II with a CB aerial on its boot suddenly pulled out in front of them. It had been parked in a gateway some 300 yards further along Hunkington Lane. Driven by a man in his late twenties, it sped away ahead of them before they lost sight of it. The next afternoon a yellow van was seen parked in the vicinity – about two hours after Salter watched the mysterious man in a suit walk to the copse and back. The van, with two men in it, was close to the spot where Hilda's driving licence and AA membership card were subsequently found. Police enquiries about these suspicious vehicles came to nothing. Also, they made no attempt to update me about all these developments.

Through her anti-nuclear work, Hilda became close to Harry Bury, a retired doctor, and his wife Gladys, a former social worker. They shared a passion for the countryside and revulsion of all things nuclear. Hilda lent them her latest research papers, and discussed her Sizewell draft with Harry. One month before her murder she told them she thought both her phones were tapped. Harry was not surprised as he was sure their phone was also being monitored. It was also probably bugged.

Six weeks after the murder, Harry went out campaigning for local council elections, and shut but did not lock the front door. Gladys was resting when she was disturbed by noises downstairs. On investigating, she was confronted by a man and a woman, both smartly dressed, standing in her hallway.

When Gladys challenged them with her usual feistiness, they claimed to be plain clothes police officers wanting to talk to her about Hilda. Ignoring her demands for identification, they hurriedly left. Gladys immediately phoned Shrewsbury Police Station to ask if anyone had been sent to question her: they had not. She was confident she had rumbled two security agents who, assuming the house was unoccupied, wanted to search for papers which Hilda might have left for safekeeping – because they had not been found in Ravenscroft?

Like Joan Tate, Gladys told me that Hilda always dressed stylishly when she went out, even to shop. She found it very odd that, when Hilda's body was found she was in an old jumper, underneath a rough brown coat which she only wore for fetching coal. The old green moth-holed skirt found nearby was not the smart, brown pleated tweed one she was wearing to visit Mary O'Connor. Her stockings were heavily darned, and her suspender belt was tattered and missing a rubber grommet. Now why would a panicking lone burglar have wasted time dressing her in different clothes?

Gladys also confided that the Hilda she knew would not have been intimidated by a thief. She may have been in her late seventies, but she was fit and spirited enough to kick and scratch any assailant – especially a short teenage boy. Three incidents recorded in Hilda's 1969 diary support this:

[11 July] Found 2 boys in kitchen garden, couldn't catch them but threatened them with imprisonment in cellar and starvation!!! They had been in strawberries and this was 2nd time.

[27 July] ...arrived just in time to storm at 8-10 boys... They went out again at remarkable speed...

[15 August] Went down garden for lettuce - 3 boys, 1 up plum tree, another under it & another just getting over the fence. 2 of them were back over fence in a flash, the third just stood and I hit him several times. He thought of retaliating but saw the knife and decided against it.

From top left: Betty Murrell (2), Lily Murrell, Hilda Murrell (5). (Photo: Owen Murrell)

Hilda, 1966.

Robert Green (far right front row) Royal Navy Staff Course 1978. (Photo: Royal Navy)

Commander Robert Green 1982 at Northwood. (Photo: Royal Navy)

Robert Green thatching at Milborne Port 1988.

From top: Front of Ravenscroft.

Ravenscroft with large garden, alleyway, Millmead flats and surrounding houses.

Kitchen door of Ravenscroft facing the road.

Back of house showing Hilda's bedroom window wide open upstairs.

(Photos: West Mercia Police)

Millmead Flats

Alleyway

Sutton Road

From top left: Kitchen table with handbags, purse, papers, watch and wallet.

Back kitchen with unexplained wet sheets.

Telephone cord and cable near Hilda's anti-nuclear papers on kitchen window seat.

Junction box above kitchen window seat.

Hilda's homemade calendar hanging above the phone showing Symondsons' lunch date at 12.45 pm on 21 March 1984.

Fresh crowbar marks in window seat under phone.

(Photos: West Mercia Police)

From top left: Small bedroom where Hilda was purportedly sexually attacked, with ironing board cover, picture and old clothing on the bed.

Broken baluster upstairs in Ravenscroft.

Bolted and chained front door through which Hilda was supposedly abducted.

Drinks cabinet in sitting room where a can of lager was taken from.

Downstairs soiled toilet where Andrew George's handprint was found.

(Photos: West Mercia Police)

Mrs Latter was surprised and impressed by Hilda's physical strength and determined tenacity, and felt that, if Hilda found anyone in her house up to no good, she would have shown no fear as she was used to dealing with staff and workmen. She would have curtly challenged them and tried to phone the police.

Olga Evans, a magistrate friend of Hilda, recounted an incident to me. On 13 January 1984, when she returned Hilda from a lunch party, Hilda confided that her spare house key was missing from its hiding place. When the subject of possible burglary came up, Hilda declared: "I would never fight over my possessions – only my papers".

In another attempt to show the investigation was making progress, a police photograph was released of the large kitchen knife found in a ditch alongside the hedge which was "believed" to be the murder weapon. Soon after, DCI Furber and a Detective Constable Nick Partridge visited Liz and me at home in Dorset with the knife, which I recognised came from a set of three beside Hilda's kitchen sink. Its blade was eight inches long, broadening from the tip to more than an inch thick at the hilt. Detailed forensic tests had been carried out, with no mention of results. Why had they taken so long to go public when the knife had been photographed within a week of the murder? I took the opportunity to enquire if the bread knife had been found – it had not. Also, they were now downplaying the sexual assault as only "incidental" to the motive for the murder.

Early in July the police invited ridicule when they released a second, very different, artist's impression of the wanted man. In the first image, based on Rosalind Taylerson's evidence, the driver had been depicted as a fit-looking man with light brown hair. We were now asked to believe he was also thin-faced with staring eyes and unkempt, longer dark hair. As journalist Paul Foot observed in the satirical weekly *Private Eye*, 'Here are two artist's impressions of the man the police don't want to find in the Hilda Murrell case.'

In early August, the inquest was postponed for a second time – and Hilda's body was suddenly released to the family. We were furious; and suspicions grew. Apparently there were no facilities for long-term storage of bodies at Shrewsbury's Copthorne Hospital. The decision had therefore been taken to hold a second autopsy by a Dr Gower. He confirmed the body was so badly decomposed that it should be disposed of as soon as possible. Why had Hilda's body been allowed to get into such a state if it had been so important to preserve it? Was this more incompetence, or something else?

Dr Helen Payling Wright, Hilda's friend and a former pathologist, later told me, "The most extraordinary thing was that they did a second post-mortem. You get nothing out of them." She was appalled Hilda's body had been allowed to deteriorate because Birmingham medical school could have kept the body deep frozen.

We abruptly had to re-arrange summer holidays and organise a funeral. On 25 August we were joined by close friends for a short service at Emstrey Crematorium in Shrewsbury. The police made no effort to pay their final respects, or update us. Three weeks later – and two days after I presented her anti-nuclear paper at the Sizewell Inquiry – we carried Hilda's ashes up the flank of Bwlch Maengwynedd in the Berwyn Mountains. We chose a grassy knoll strewn with chunks of quartz crystal, and built a glittering white cairn to mark the spot where we scattered the ashes, while a solitary raven soared and tumbled in aerial salute above us.

I had not publicised my conviction that her murder had been connected with the nuclear industry. Instead, I had concentrated on tidying and presenting Hilda's paper at the Sizewell Inquiry.

On 13 September 1984, I found myself seated at the front of a large stage with my back to an 800-seat auditorium. The sides of the stage, accustomed to operatic divas, choirs and musicians, were now lined with lawyers behind tables; and the auditorium seats, normally packed with lovers of classical music and opera, were empty apart from a few towards the front taken by anti-nuclear campaigners. I was in Snape Maltings in Suffolk – a picturesque old white weatherboard-clad building originally designed to turn barley into beer, converted in 1967 into a lofty concert hall for the Aldeburgh Music Festival, instigated by Benjamin Britten in 1948. Because of its size and proximity to the proposed site for Britain's first pressurised water reactor (PWR) on the North Sea coast, now it was the incongruous setting for the Sizewell B Inquiry, which had been sitting since January 1983.

The Burys, who were now two of my strongest supporters, had travelled across the country from Shrewsbury to witness the culmination of Hilda's anti-nuclear project. At rear centre stage, facing me with an encouraging expression, was Sir Frank Layfield, the Inspector in charge of the Inquiry. To my right sat a phalanx of impassive barristers representing the nuclear industry, led by the wily, diminutive Lord Silsoe at a reputed cost to the taxpayer of £1,500 a day.

It took me about an hour to read *An Ordinary Citizen's View of Radioactive Waste Management,* given an Inquiry code number HM01. Hilda's conclusions reverberate poignantly for the victims of the 2011 Fukushima nuclear power plant catastrophe in Japan:

> The inescapable burden now inflicted on posterity imposes a straight moral choice, which was not faced in the beginning but which must be faced now. Even a desperate need for energy would not justify creating these worst of

all pollutants, whose control for merely a few centuries (in the case of High Level Waste) we cannot guarantee…

This is a failed and dying industry, which is a major liability and should be closed down. The fact that plans can be made for adding to it shows an unbelievable degree of irresponsibility and stupidity in all concerned.

The Ordinary Citizen implores the Inspector to urge the right moral choice on the government, which should redirect all its spare billions towards energy conservation, cleaning up fossil-fuelled power stations, and developing alternative energy sources.

Because I was not the author, I could not be cross-examined about it. Nevertheless, nearly six months after her murder I had fulfilled Hilda's request in the postscript of her last letter to me. It was my initiation as an anti-nuclear campaigner.

That evening, in a prime-time BBC TV programme called *Crimewatch*, the West Mercia Police revealed that, for the first time in a British murder investigation, they had been assisted by the United States Federal Bureau of Investigation. The FBI had taken three months to come up with a profile of the suspected killer. The next day, the *Shropshire Star* reported excitedly beneath a headline 'America's FBI boffins join murder hunt':

Data... was sent to the bureau's behavioural science research department where experts drew up a picture of the man they want.

And the information backs up what murder chiefs from the West Mercia force had already agreed.

The man police want to interview – and they believe he could strike again – is:

- Between 30 and 35, with medium to large build with broad shoulders, dark hair and deep set eyes.
- He is a loner and a withdrawn individual who either lives or works locally, has an intimate knowledge of the area and or who has lived locally.
- He is unsociable, likely to be an unskilled worker and often visits local pubs.
- Someone locally is probably shielding the person and they should contact the police immediately.

The underwhelming, and somewhat self-contradictory, outcome of this dramatic collaboration fell into a similar desperate category as reports that the police had resorted to hypnosis of key witnesses of the crazy last journey of Hilda's car. These merely fuelled my suspicions regarding the police's blundering and ineffective handling of the case. I was ready to turn my attention to pursuing the truth.

The possibility that Hilda had been the victim of a political conspiracy made no national impact until November 1984 – when I was confronted with a second theory.

Judith Cook, an experienced investigative journalist, author and regular contributor to *The Guardian* and the *New Statesman* magazine, had followed up the conspiracy rumours. She visited me in September, when I briefed her on the discrepancies in the police investigation and my own theory. I carefully made no mention of my role in Naval Intelligence, and she did not ask me about it.

I was therefore surprised and alarmed by Cook's feature article in the *New Statesman* on 9 November. She raised good questions about the bizarre route taken by the attacker through the town centre, and the police delay in acting on the abandoned car. She also mentioned Hilda's agitated phone call to Morgan-Grenville, and Ian Scott's categoric statement that there was no body in the copse the day after Hilda's abduction. The shock came towards the end of the article. After speculating that Hilda's house was broken into by somebody who was interested in her Sizewell paper, Cook abruptly introduced a novel twist and punchline:

> [D]id somebody somewhere think Miss Murrell had access to even more sensitive information because of her close links with her nephew in naval intelligence and the very sensitive work on which he had been engaged? Is it possible, in the current climate of paranoia, that it was thought – quite wrongly – he had passed on information to his aunt?

Cook must have spotted a framed citation from Admiral Sir John Fieldhouse, Commander-in-Chief Fleet, commending my work during the Falklands War. The main impact of her article was to establish a disturbing link between me, Hilda's murder and the Falklands War – and specifically the sinking of the Argentine cruiser *General Belgrano*. It also stimulated renewed media interest in the case, and the inquest when it was finally held on 5 December.

The inquest took place in an oak-panelled upstairs chamber of the Elizabethan Market Hall in the heart of Shrewsbury. At the last minute I arranged for a solicitor to represent Hilda's family. I had put the police on written notice that I wanted answers to a whole range of questions. Their response was for DCI Furber to try to reassure me about my concerns over the phone. He did not succeed.

I was surprised there was no jury for such a controversial, high-profile murder. I was then alarmed to learn that neither John Marsh nor Ian Scott would be called. The Shrewsbury coroner, Colonel David Crawford-Clarke, permitted just two witnesses to testify: DCS Cole, and the pathologist Dr

Acland. Neither Cole nor Furber greeted me and my sister as the victim's next of kin; all Cole could manage was a nervous nod in our direction as we arrived.

Acland took the stand first. I had not been allowed a copy of his autopsy report, and the police had never briefed us about the full extent of Hilda's injuries. Now, I listened with mounting horror as he read it dispassionately. "Hypostasis was faint in the right lateral position... On the right side of the face was a diffuse bruise over the right forehead, around the right eye and across the right cheek measuring ten centimetres by six. There was a split to the skin just below the right eye." Acland said the face injury was probably caused by a broad, blunt instrument. Hilda had probably been kicked. There was also a bruise measuring 3.5 centimetres across on the left side of her chin, from a punch or falling. On Hilda's right shoulder there was more bruising where her collar bone had been broken. He offered no cause for this; later I was advised Hilda's shoulder had probably been stamped on.

He described the knife wounds in excruciating detail: "On the right arm 12 centimetres below the point of the shoulder in the region of the biceps muscle was a penetrating incised wound..." There were five shallower stab wounds in Hilda's right upper abdomen. "The first was three centimetres away from the umbilicus and was a small incised wound measuring 0.6 centimetres in length..." Two had reached the liver: in his opinion they were disabling but not fatal. I was struck by how small the wounds were. If Hilda's large kitchen knife had inflicted them, it would have needed considerable control to keep them so shallow. What he was describing was deliberate, skilfully applied torture – by a lone, panicking petty burglar? Cuts on her palms showed that poor Hilda had tried to fend off the knife.

According to Acland, large abrasions on Hilda's knees were consistent with her crawling around, which probably led to her losing her "lower clothing". However, he did not rule out the possibility that she had been dragged. There were apparently no marks on her back, "but soiling by earth and debris was noted over the buttocks".

His choice of words at one point was so unintentionally inappropriate that I jotted them down. "The brain weighed 1415 grams and appeared unremarkable." With a shudder, I realised he had removed it.

Acland added that the hyoid bone in her larynx had been broken, but there was no evidence of asphyxia. This suggested being held in an armlock. To my relief, there was "no indication of sexual assault". After all the police fuss and lurid media reports, this was his only reference to the sexual aspect. He concluded that "death was due to hypothermia, plus penetrating wounds to the abdomen with multiple bruises to the face".

In response to a question from the coroner, Acland said there was some evidence Hilda had been crawling, but not more than 100 yards from where her body was found. He estimated that "in very cold weather" she would have died between five and ten hours after being left in the copse.

Questioned by the family solicitor about the sudden second autopsy, he replied that Dr Gower "entirely agreed with all my findings and conclusions". Acland admitted that, had she received medical treatment within 5-10 hours after the attack, "she may have survived". This was the only question raised about the consequences of the police delay in following up the abandoned car.

Despite advising caution about drawing too many conclusions, Acland then speculated: "Miss Murrell may have been trying to escape from the car and was pursued and possibly frogmarched with an arm across her neck and the knife held towards her... The evidence suggests she had been stabbed through her clothing."

On the need for a second autopsy, the coroner explained: "I was advised after a period of time that the natural processes were reaching a stage when it would shortly thereafter be quite impractical for the second post-mortem to be subsequently carried out if somebody was charged...", so that the body could be made available to the defence. He offered no explanation for how it had been allowed to decompose.

DCS Cole began his testimony by refusing to disclose all evidence in his possession. "This is in no way an attempt to conceal anything. I must be in a position to put evidence to a suspect which has not been previously released so that the accuracy of any confession may be tested."

Outlining his initial enquiries, Cole exonerated his officers from any negligence regarding the three-day delay in finding Hilda's body. He made no mention of the state of Hilda's telephones. He summarised Hilda's last known movements, and five reports from the 69 witnesses to the car's strange journey.

He emphasised that Hilda's character and lifestyle had made it a difficult investigation – for example, none of her friends reported she was missing. He surmised: "Once inside her house Miss Murrell apparently had time to change from her outdoor clothing and put away some of her shopping." Questions erupted in my mind as he claimed there was evidence of a struggle upstairs. Why? A broken baluster and a picture which had fallen off the wall did not automatically mean Hilda was even present when this damage occurred. There was no blood, and the clothing found on two of the beds had been there, undisturbed, for some time.

Cole confirmed Hilda was subjected to "sexual activity". "It then appears that either because of further violence or under extreme duress, Miss Murrell was abducted and driven away from her home in her own vehicle, a distance of approximately six miles, to the scene of her death." He omitted to mention witnesses noted that the woman slumped in the front passenger seat looked either "unconscious", "handicapped", or "asleep". This raised another question: had she been knocked out – or drugged? Yet Acland had made no mention of any alcohol or toxicology tests.

Cole confirmed there was also no blood in the car, which suggested she was stabbed somewhere between the lane and the copse. His only reference to the knife found near the hedge was that it probably came from a set in Hilda's house. Neither man mentioned any forensic results. Despite the huge forensic effort at Ravenscroft, Cole also made no mention of fingerprints or footprints. When the family solicitor asked why farmer John Marsh was not giving evidence, Cole replied he was too ill after a heart attack. The absence of Ian Scott was more difficult to explain. Regarding Scott's dramatic claim, Cole said: "This has been carefully considered and researched. He may be mistaken. The body was in a slight hollow and dressed in clothing which matched the undergrowth."

To convince the coroner Scott had been wrong, we were suddenly shown police colour photographs of Hilda's body lying in the copse. Apart from the shock of seeing it for the first time, what struck me was how obvious her long, thin, starkly white naked legs looked lying on the flattened brown winter undergrowth. Scott had said: "I would have seen a dead rabbit, let alone a body, had it been there." A fresh wave of horror and revulsion swept over me as I flicked through the rest of the photographs of the body, including some from the autopsy. Seconds later they were retrieved.

As for conspiracy theories, Cole claimed police inquiries had failed to find any evidence. He had come to "the inescapable conclusion that this was an offence of burglary and that the offender was, in the main, after cash."

He had not finished. In a brazen attempt to establish a link between police effort and results, he reeled off a stream of statistics to illustrate the scope of the investigation: "4,404 lines of enquiry have been pursued, 1,361 telephone messages received, 2,162 statements taken; 4,800 houses have been visited, 11,900 residents interviewed, 1,570 vehicles checked…"

For me the figures simply begged the question: why, after so much effort, had the police still failed to find a house burglar who was seen by so many witnesses behaving in such a bizarre way?

Why, after so many vehicles were checked, had Cole said nothing about the various sightings of a red Ford Escort car – let alone the episode of the strange, suited man walking from a large dark car to the copse and back soon after the landowner had checked the trees for felling?

What about fingerprints and footprints? I had been told some had been found; but we were still waiting to hear any results. Very few of Hilda's friends who had often visited Ravenscroft in the previous year or so had been fingerprinted or checked for what shoes they wore.

Why was there no mention of the state of Hilda's telephones?

Were there any forensic findings from the sexual activity? I had to assume that these were the details being withheld by Cole for cross-examination of any suspect.

One other figure Cole listed was 491: the number of potential suspects who had been interviewed and eliminated. Nearly twenty years later, I would discover that one of them had been 16-year-old Andrew George.

Colonel Crawford-Clarke refused to let the family's solicitor question Cole. Summing up, he agreed with the police view of events, and concluded: "The only verdict that I can record in such a case is that the deceased was killed unlawfully." Again, the police made no attempt to meet us.

As I emerged dazed into the winter sunshine, suddenly Paul Foot introduced himself. A celebrated left-wing journalist with a weekly column in the *Daily Mirror*, he said that as a Shrewsbury School old boy he always enjoyed an excuse to return. He had recently published a bestselling investigation into the mysterious death in Saudi Arabia of Helen Smith which bore the hallmarks of a British diplomatic cover-up – the case cited by Cole for delaying Hilda's funeral. Foot's outrage at what he had just experienced was a great comfort to me, and he promised from then on to follow the case closely.

I instructed the family's solicitor to write to the coroner requesting a copy of both autopsy reports. Crawford-Clarke replied that their release was entirely at his discretion – and refused.

Subsequently, I received independent legal advice that "it is not within the coroner's lawful discretion to withhold the post-mortem report from a person who is entitled to examine witnesses at an inquest".

Years later, I learned of an extraordinary episode after the inquest. That evening in the Horseshoes public house near Uckington, three miles south of Hunkington, a woman neighbour who had known Hilda overheard six men chatting about seeing "our Hilda, and that son of hers that's in the Navy" on TV. An older one among them with a Welsh accent warned them to keep their voices down. Another asked if any of them had been questioned by the police. A young man replied he had expected them earlier that evening: "They didn't turn up." The questioner advised that, with an alibi, they had nothing to worry about. One admitted he had been questioned twice. Then another bragged: "Norman knows who knocked her off." Ignoring a more urgent plea to shut up, a third man added: "That car was put there before she was dead." The older man commented: "I daresay we all know who's done it." Two of them volunteered that they had been to Hilda's house.

I was looking forward to relaxing over Christmas. Two weeks later, however, in the early hours of 20 December 1984, Labour MP Tam Dalyell stood up in the House of Commons and declared that "British intelligence had been involved" in Hilda's murder.

CHAPTER 4

DALYELL'S EXPLOSIVE ALLEGATION

'Secret Service Killed Navy Man's Aunt' screamed the headline across the front page of the London *Evening Standard*. The *Shropshire Star* more nervously chose 'Hilda Death Probe Shock'. On 20 December 1984, her murder erupted into one of the biggest ever British stories of political conspiracy and intrigue. During the final all-night sitting of the House of Commons before the Christmas recess, Opposition backbench Labour MP Tam Dalyell accused "men of the British Intelligence" of being involved in Hilda's murder. The sensation went worldwide.

I had just a few hours' warning of Dalyell's allegations via the MP for Yeovil, Paddy Ashdown. A former Royal Marine officer, he would become leader of the Liberal Democratic Party from 1988-99 and subsequently a member of the House of Lords. An advance copy of the speech was delivered to me after Dalyell asked Ashdown, whom I knew quite well, to tip me off.

It was a fair summary of events surrounding Hilda's murder, exposing many of my concerns about the case. However, Dalyell claimed her murder was directly linked with my work during the Falklands War. Worse, he implied that I left the Navy because I was disillusioned by the war, and that I was responsible for sending the signalled order to the nuclear submarine *HMS Conqueror* to attack the Argentine cruiser *General Belgrano*. Ashdown failed to find Dalyell in time to correct these serious errors.

Sir Thomas 'Tam' Dalyell of the Binns, 11th Baronet, was something of a maverick. His education at Eton was in keeping with his aristocratic ancestry. However, when called up for National Service in 1950, he insisted on serving in the ranks of the Royal Scots Greys – founded by one of his forebears. At King's College, Cambridge he studied history and economics, and ran the students' Conservative Association.

It was the 1956 Suez crisis, while he was teaching in Edinburgh, which convinced him to join the Labour Party. Six years later he won the West Lothian seat, which he held comfortably for the next 43 years, when he retired from politics. He was highly unusual: a fearless politician who tenaciously pursued the truth no matter how unpopular his stand might be. Furthermore, he took up controversial causes, and developed a formidable network of contacts and knowledge of the Westminster system.

Dalyell was determined to uncover the facts surrounding the sinking of the *Belgrano* on 2 May 1982 with the loss of 321 lives. For almost two years after the Falklands War, he received a steady trickle of top secret and politically dangerous information about the sinking from several sources. For obvious reasons, he steadfastly refused to identify them. However, one source's clear access to raw signals intelligence and intimate political knowledge of Thatcher's reaction to each leak strongly suggested he worked in the Cabinet Office, risking his career to provide these details.

This convinced Dalyell much more was at stake than Thatcher's need to hold her line that the attack was justified and in accordance with the laws of war. His information implied that a military response to the Argentine invasion was essential if her political career was to survive. In a hiatus following initial skirmishes in South Georgia, therefore, she needed to scupper a US-Peruvian peace initiative and provoke full-scale war. A negotiated settlement would have raised too many questions about her failure to prevent the invasion, and her insistence on the scrapping of *HMS Endurance* as part of the 1981 Defence Review despite minimal savings. Removal of this symbol of British resolve to protect the islands effectively gave Argentine President Galtieri a green light to invade. I had been so concerned by the *Endurance* decision that I had written a formal memorandum placing it on record.

Since the end of 1982, Dalyell had asked a series of increasingly probing questions which had forced the government to admit the *Belgrano* was not in the exclusion zone imposed by Britain around the Falklands, and therefore should not have been attacked under the prevailing rules of engagement. However, Thatcher was still insisting it was a direct threat to the British Task Force. The source of the top secret leaks had still not been found and stopped.

On 19 March 1984 – *two days before Ravenscroft was broken into and searched, and Hilda abducted* – Dalyell hand-delivered a letter to Michael Heseltine, the Secretary of State for Defence. In it he asked nine new questions about the *Belgrano*'s exact position and movements, indicating it was steaming away from the Falklands. These threatened to expose what really happened in the South Atlantic, and the ensuing cover-up.

Dalyell's latest letter must have been the last straw. As Heseltine explained to a House of Commons Foreign Affairs Committee Inquiry on 7 November 1984, just two days before Judith Cook's *New Statesman* article about Hilda's case appeared,

> On 19 March Tam Dalyell wrote to me asking nine detailed questions, including changes in the *Belgrano*'s course… that led me to take a view that the whole question that arose in connection with the *Belgrano* had got to be subjected to the most detailed scrutiny… So on 22 March, I then began the investigation which led to the documents which are now known as the 'Crown Jewels'…

Civil servant Clive Ponting, at the extraordinarily young age of 37, had just been appointed Head of DS5, a section in the Ministry of Defence responsible for Naval operations and policy matters. In 1980 he received an OBE for helping identify dramatic savings in the defence budget, during which he impressed the new Prime Minister in a Cabinet briefing. As part of Ponting's introduction to the project, he was given the book *Your Disobedient Servant*, chronicling waste and mismanagement in Whitehall. Seldom could there have been such an example of the law of unintended consequences.

In early March 1984, Ponting was instructed to collude with Government deception in response to questions to the Prime Minister from Labour's defence spokesman, Denzil Davies. These were prompted by publication of the Gavshon and Rice book, *The Sinking of the Belgrano*, which finally persuaded the Labour Party leadership to back Dalyell's lonely campaign.

On 22 March, Heseltine ordered Ponting to write a comprehensive review of the situation, "to be quite sure that there is not a Watergate in this somewhere". Ponting completed the 'Crown Jewels' within a week. Heseltine then met his advisers to decide how to reply to both Dalyell and Davies. My former boss Admiral Sir John Fieldhouse, by then First Sea Lord, was present.

Heseltine's reply to Dalyell ignored a draft proposed by Ponting with specific answers to questions, and instead stonewalled. Ponting was appalled by this deliberate attempt to conceal information showing that Ministers had misled Parliament for the previous two years. On 24 April – a week after Hilda's thanksgiving service – he sent an anonymous note to Dalyell which included the following:

> For what I hope will be obvious reasons I cannot give you my name but I can tell you that I have full access to exactly what happened to the Belgrano.

He recommended specific questions to ask. He knew it had reached Dalyell on 2 May 1984, the second anniversary of the *Belgrano* sinking, when the MP was suspended from Parliament for calling the Prime Minister a liar during question time. Dalyell was not deflected. His next letter to Heseltine in July listed questions exposing the most dangerous issue for the Government: its Ministers were no longer accountable to Parliament.

By then, the Foreign Affairs Committee was inquiring into the future of the Falkland Islands and prospects for a negotiated solution to the conflict. Ponting found what he needed in *Your Disobedient Servant*. He would not breach the Official Secrets Act if he passed any classified information to the Foreign Affairs Committee.

On 16 July, Ponting sent Dalyell an explanatory memorandum with a copy of the previous reply Heseltine had rejected. Dalyell delivered both documents to the Chair of the Foreign Affairs Committee – who promptly sent them to Heseltine. Heseltine launched a Ministry of Defence police investigation into the source of the leak. On 10 August Ponting was questioned, confessed, and tendered his resignation. He was charged under the Official Secrets Act a week later. Dalyell immediately released details of the cover-up in the *Observer*.

Ponting did not know another consequence of the 19 March Dalyell letter. Elsewhere in Whitehall, one of Dalyell's sources told him it caused a "tremendous flap in Downing Street". A meeting was hastily arranged between Thatcher and Heseltine. Following this, the order was given to find Dalyell's source at all costs.

I would have come under suspicion soon after Dalyell began his campaign in late 1982, when I was on leave before ending my Naval career. I was one of only two officers at Northwood with access to top secret intelligence signals relating to the *Belgrano* sinking who had taken redundancy. Six months later, Hilda started distributing the Ecoropa leaflets making sensitive allegations about nuclear weapons being deployed in British warships to the Falklands War.

Shortly after Ponting was charged, Dalyell received the following typed note, reproduced here complete with errors and indecipherable words:

```
Dear Mr Dalyell

I rtust you won't send this to the Select
Committee. Please understand why it is not signed.

You should know that you are getting much closer to the
truth. They have been turning overfiles and intelligence
desperately to see who has been talking to you and the New
Statesman and the Observer.

The Prime Minister is very angry.

Clive Ponting probably didn't tell you about Heseltines
decision to have a full (but secret) internal investigation of
the Belgrano affair. The Secretary of State didn't want to get
caught out by it. The study has all the secrets in it, and is
inches thick. Very few people have ever seen it. Some call it
the crown jewels. [3-4 unreadable words] Heseltine has one. I
don't know who are the others. The documents in the crown jewels
are stamped with almost every classification the Ministry has.

Parliament should assert its right to get these things
out into the open. Deep throats and journalists can
only do so much but will never get the whole story.
```

```
You can tell the press about this, but carefully. Paraphrase
it. Keep at it.
```

It was clearly not from Ponting. The indecipherable words in the copy in my possession were caused by the original having been crumpled up. The poor typing strongly indicates someone who had never been without secretarial support. This is reinforced by the typist's remarkable inside knowledge, including the mood of the Prime Minister.

At 3.50 am on 20 December 1984, Dalyell told the House of Commons that an anonymous caller alerted him to Judith Cook's *New Statesman* article. After reading it, he contacted one of his "numerous sources" who confirmed the involvement of the intelligence services looking for *Belgrano* information I might have left with Hilda. He summarised the case, raising several questions for the West Mercia Police. Although like Judith he repeated several errors and false rumours, he did cover my main concerns.

Reminding MPs of his many dealings with the nuclear industry's leaders, he said he could not believe for "one mini-second" that they would "authorise minions to search the house of a 78-year-old rose grower who had elegantly expressed, but unoriginal views on reactor choice and nuclear waste disposal". Having shown his pro-nuclear bias, he continued: "The story I am told is as follows. In the early spring, the Prime Minister and Ministers close to her were getting very nervy" about his incessant questions about the *Belgrano*. Emphasising "this was pre-Ponting", he pressed on: "Because Commander Robert Green was known to be unhappy about certain aspects of the Falklands War, and was known to have wanted to leave the Navy, he came under a cloud of suspicion – wrongly, to the best of my knowledge, but certainly under a cloud of suspicion. It was thought that he might have copies of documents and raw signals that incriminated the Prime Minister, some of the originals of which had been destroyed on instructions from a very high level by the intelligence services.

"Just as those of us who have had certain documents have taken the precaution of keeping them in friends' or relatives' houses while we have them, so it was thought that some of Rob Green's supposed records might be in the home of the aunt to whom he was close... suspicion fell on Rob Green, as he was one of the officers at the very heart of the Falklands operation. He was one of the very few to have left the service, although I understand that he had decided to go before the Falklands crisis blew up...

"I am also given to understand that – and I quite accept it – there was no pre-meditated intention of doing away with Miss Murrell; only a search of her house when she was out. Alas, on Wednesday 21 March she returned unexpectedly to change. The intruders either arrived while she was dressing or were disturbed by her…" Apparently, they had not been after money or nuclear information, but had been checking the house for any *Belgrano*-related documents. "Things went disastrously wrong. They had no intention of injuring, let alone killing, a 78-year-old ex-rose grower. Yet, being the lady she was and in her home, Hilda Murrell fought and was severely injured. She was then killed or left to die from hypothermia, and the cover-up had to begin; because I am informed that the searchers were men of the British intelligence."

Dalyell wanted to know who had ordered their involvement. He speculated that agents could have been acting on their own initiative, reflecting increasing concern at the time that elements within MI5 were out of control in connection with the coalminers' strike.

Towards the end of his speech and almost as an afterthought, he said: "I ought to add that Commander Rob Green was, I am told, the person who physically sent the signal to *Conqueror* that sank the *Belgrano*…" When I read this in all the leading national newspapers, my heart sank. Back on 2 April 1982, with intelligence reports of the Argentine invasion pouring in, I had worked non-stop for 36 hours. My intelligence team was therefore reorganised and expanded into a four-watch system, in addition to the separate cell providing 24-hour intelligence support on Soviet deployments.

I was watching TV at home on 2 May when I learned *HMS Conqueror* had torpedoed the *Belgrano*. From my previous time on watch, I knew the obsolete cruiser was being trailed by *Conqueror* – but not allowed to attack while it stayed outside the exclusion zone, which it did. I immediately realised the implications, and that repercussions would be serious.

Dalyell's final howler wrongly implied I had been closely involved in the attack. It also showed his ignorance of the fact that intelligence support was entirely separate from operational control of the war. Moreover, that signal was the most important operational order of the war to date. It would therefore have been authorised by Admiral Fieldhouse himself before being sent personally by Flag Officer Submarines, Vice Admiral Peter Herbert, for onward transmission to *HMS Conqueror*. The impression Dalyell gave to my former colleagues, from Admiral Fieldhouse down, was that I had ridiculously inflated my role. Even more serious was the renewed suggestion – now stated under Parliamentary privilege and recorded for posterity in *Hansard* – that I could have been disloyal and stupid enough to have taken top secret documents and given them to Hilda for safe keeping. His inference that I might have been disaffected, a potential traitor, and willing to endanger Hilda was not only extremely offensive, but very dangerous for my credibility.

I was therefore grateful to Paddy Ashdown when he opened his response to Dalyell's bombshell with a robust expression of support for me. However, he spoiled this somewhat by claiming I agreed with all Dalyell had said. No doubt sensing the danger for me, he quickly added that I had in no way collaborated with Dalyell.

Ashdown challenged the Government: "If what the Hon. Member for Linlithgow says is true, it is inconceivable that it could have occurred under normal circumstances other than with agreement at the very highest level. But if that did not happen, there must have been a significant breakdown in the way that our intelligence services are controlled... There are many people, including me, who, because of friends and contacts, have reason to worry that the traditional and appropriate control of this country's intelligence services has become much looser than appropriate and much less regulated than is necessary within a democracy..." He warned that in the absence of satisfactory answers, there was only one way forward: "A full inquiry in front of a High Court judge."

Giles Shaw, Minister of State for the Home Office, had listened intently to these speeches. When he rose to reply at 4.33 am, he announced that because he had been given no warning, he was unable to answer Dalyell's "numerous and far-reaching" questions. However, Shaw made the curious observation that "it may be considered odd, if there were a British security element involved in the investigation, or occasioning the crime for which the investigation has been set up, that it should continue without those involved being able to ensure that the police and the security services are sharing common knowledge". A Home Office Minister was admitting in Parliament that, if MI5 was involved in Hilda's murder, it would have no difficulty staying ahead of the police, and therefore covering its tracks.

Despite his claim of lack of notice, Shaw was well-briefed on the main facts of the case. He even regurgitated the smokescreen of statistics from DCS Cole's inquest testimony about the police effort put into the investigation. No evidence had been found to link the murder with Hilda's anti-nuclear activities. Repeating the inquest findings, he noted Dalyell had expressed substantial criticism of the Home Office. He assured him that "the debate and the questions will obtain full consideration and a proper and comprehensive reply..."

Nine days later, Shaw's written reply amounted to twenty words:

> I am now able to state unreservedly that your allegations about the Intelligence services being involved are totally without foundation.

Yet the police had not even met Dalyell! He told the media: "I think Giles Shaw has simply gone through his officials to the Security Service and asked them, and they've said: 'There's nothing in it, old boy'."

───── ∞ ─────

Dalyell's allegations gained credibility when it emerged that the Hatfield flat of a former colleague of mine was broken into and thoroughly searched within hours of his speech. The day after the break-in, I bumped into Lieutenant-Commander Peter Hurst in a shop in Yeovil. Until then I had no idea he lived little more than five miles from me. He, too, had carried out top secret work in the Northwood command bunker. We were the only two with that security clearance to have left the Navy since the war. However, unlike me he was on watch during the exchange of signals leading to the attack on the *Belgrano*. What was more, he worked in operations, and was closely involved in communications with the nuclear submarines.

His flat contained valuables including solid gold cufflinks in full view, hi-fi equipment, two video recorders and televisions; yet nothing was stolen except a bottle of gin. All his personal papers in a filing cabinet were rifled through, and an electric typewriter was moved to near the door. The other three flats in the same block were not touched, which was odd because his was the most difficult to access as the only one on the first floor. Hurst believed he had also been placed under surveillance, because later that day the phone started behaving strangely at this flat, his family home and at another London flat he rented out to tenants who complained about it. Later I learned from a reliable media source that another officer doing high security work at Northwood and living in lodgings nearby believed his belongings were searched. Two hold-alls, left secure in a cupboard, had been opened.

Hurst and his wife were a timely comfort to me and Liz. The first former colleague I discussed Hilda's case with, he gave me desperately needed affirmation that he did not question my loyalty. After their experience, they had no doubt our fears about the *Belgrano* connection were justified.

West Mercia Police issued a statement that inquiries had revealed no evidence of involvement by intelligence officers, and refuting claims of a cover-up. However, the police had no choice but to investigate the allegations and seek an early meeting with Dalyell.

His speech ensured that the run-up to Christmas in Dorset was far from peaceful, as Liz and I were besieged by national and international media. The pace was set by Stuart Prebble, producer of Granada Television's flagship national investigative programme, *World in Action*. It was no coincidence that he had arranged to visit us on the eve of Dalyell's speech. Naively, we invited him to stay the night. That evening he told me he had also discovered *HMS Conqueror*'s logbook was missing. I did not sleep well.

Over breakfast the next morning, Prebble challenged me. "Rob, if you know the facts about all this, and you suspect Mrs Thatcher was ultimately responsible for the abduction and assassination of Hilda, then you now have the opportunity to bring her down. What's more, it's your duty to do so." I felt like a rabbit caught in headlights. Aghast and horrified, I retorted: "Bulls..t. Even if I wanted to, I don't have all the facts. Besides, you know better than I do that Thatcher would have layers of bureaucratic defences around her."

Later that day, when BBC Midlands TV interviewed Dalyell, he said, "Sources that have proved reliable in the past have a track record and my track record from these sources and other sources is so far 100 per cent accuracy in relation to the *Belgrano*. No, I can't say [who it was] because I would never be trusted again to be a receptacle for information that they didn't want to be identified." When challenged that it was a long stretch to link Hilda to the Falklands War, he replied: "Not if one has the kind of information given anonymously, and then not anonymously."

——⁕——

I had mixed feelings about Dalyell's bombshell. After the suppression of evidence at the inquest only a fortnight before, it was gratifying, and heady stuff, suddenly to find my concerns not only front page news in the national media, but debated in the House of Commons. On the other hand, I felt profoundly uneasy that Dalyell had become a self-appointed political champion of Hilda's case. I was also appalled that the most sensitive part of my Royal Navy career had been publicly dredged up just when I had been settling into rustic obscurity. Most disturbing of all was to come under suspicion of being a traitor – and, the ultimate nightmare, that I could be personally implicated in the murder of Hilda. Nearly twenty years would elapse before my research confirmed the deadly significance of Dalyell's 19 March letter to Heseltine. Until then, I remained in denial that the *Belgrano* connection was the trigger for the British state security apparatus to move against her. I simply could not cope with the possibility that my work had caused Hilda's death.

Feeling an urgent need to distance myself from Dalyell, I decided to challenge him publicly that he might have been set up. I reasoned that blaming Hilda's murder on Thatcher's embarrassment over the *Belgrano* was almost too convenient a distraction from the nuclear industry.

Dalyell's obsession with the *Belgrano* controversy meant he could not resist going public about the link with Hilda's murder. Moreover, his fascination with science – for years he had written a parliamentary column called 'Thistle Diary' in the *New Scientist* – had laid him open to cultivation by the nuclear industry. Thus he could be relied on to exonerate it – which he had.

Meanwhile, I was gaining media traction as a serious critic of the police handling of the case, and for my suspicion that the nuclear industry was somehow involved. The state security machine, therefore, would have wanted to flush me out and neutralise me, and head off any suggestion of nuclear industry dirty tricks.

The risk of tempting Dalyell to run with the claim of MI5 involvement would be worthwhile if it drove me to speak out against the war – whereupon I could be impaled upon the Official Secrets Act. Ponting was on remand awaiting trial for a similar offence, so MI5 would have been confident. My decision to become a roof thatcher provided enough circumstantial evidence to convince a jury that I had become disaffected.

Now Dalyell had indeed run with it. The break-in to Hurst's flat a few hours after the debate made me take Dalyell's claim seriously; and I did come under enormous media pressure to discuss my views on the war.

I urgently needed to shore up my loyalty to the Navy. On 29 December, therefore, I wrote to Admiral Fieldhouse to set the record straight. I wanted him to know I had never contacted Dalyell, and had tried to correct his errors:

> ...namely that I did not make the signal to sink the Belgrano(!), and that I did not resign because of my dissatisfaction with the war but had applied for voluntary redundancy three months before the invasion for reasons totally unconnected with it.

Journalists continued to repeat the inaccuracies almost every time they wrote about the murder. A myth was widely spread that I had been a nuclear submariner, not back-seat aircrew in carrier strike jets and anti-submarine helicopters, and even that I was the commanding officer of *HMS Conqueror*!

I also let Fieldhouse know I had been reliably informed that some documents had gone missing from Northwood at about the time I left on terminal leave in early October 1982, and that I had come under suspicion. I assured him that 'such a stupid and irresponsible idea never even entered my head', and asked to meet him because DCS Cole wanted to interview me again. The First Sea Lord reassured me he needed

> ...no persuading that you did not mislead Mr Dalyell into concluding that you stored classified information in your Aunt's house, or that you sent the signal ordering the sinking of the Belgrano. Thank you also for restating your reasons for your resignation...

Though happy to see me, he thought it would serve no purpose. His letter was enormously comforting.

A few days later, I found myself suspected of murdering Hilda.

CHAPTER 5

CONSPIRACY THEORIES STRENGTHEN

I had tried to trust the West Mercia Police to conduct an objective investigation. As Hilda's next of kin, I expected updates with every major development, and reasonable responses to my requests and concerns. After the inquest, my faith in them evaporated.

DCS Cole phoned me on 27 December 1984, a week after Dalyell's intervention, wanting to question me as soon as possible. He was under intense political and media pressure. On 6 January 1985, the *Sunday Times* ran a full page feature article entitled 'Who killed Hilda Murrell?'.

Two days later, we met in my local police station in Sherborne – exactly two years after my last meeting with Hilda. Liz insisted on accompanying me with our solicitor. The icy weather matched the atmosphere inside the interview room, during what turned out to be a three-hour hostile interrogation. DCI Furber, playing 'good cop', accompanied Cole. I had not met Cole since giving him my original statement.

Neither detective attempted small talk, or expressed any sympathy for the situation I found myself in. There was no effort to update me about the latest developments. Instead Cole set the tone, aggressively launching into a line of questioning as if I were a suspect. "Were you aware of the contents of your aunt's will before she died?" What had my Navy salary been? How much was I now earning thatching? "Tell me again why you claim you were close, when you last saw her on 8 January 1983?" They had checked Hilda's diary. As I tried to describe the nature of our relationship, outrage welled up that I was having to do so again.

I seized my chance to educate the two officers about Hilda's research into the economics of nuclear energy, and the dangers of radioactive waste. When I mentioned I had used my naval staff training and experience to help her with her Sizewell paper, this triggered questions about my security clearance, and whether I had told her anything of a classified nature. Cole seemed to know a lot about my involvement with Naval Intelligence, and the top secret electronic espionage work at Government Communications Headquarters in Cheltenham.

Probing the circumstances of my departure from the Navy, Cole tried to discover if I had been disaffected by the Falklands War. I explained that for career reasons I had applied for voluntary redundancy before the war. Later, I realised with some shock that, far from dismissing Dalyell's allegation, he had almost certainly been interrogating me about whether I was one of

Dalyell's sources, or had helped Dalyell's close friend Morgan-Grenville with his inflammatory Ecoropa leaflet about the Falklands War.

Cole's next thrust was to question me about Morgan-Grenville's statement. I outlined why I visited him; but I chose not to mention Hilda's last letter to me with its ominous postscript, in case it was dismissed as an old lady's fears about simply being knocked down by a London bus while attending the CND rally in October 1983.

As I recounted my gut reaction on hearing Hilda was missing, Cole cut me off with another dangerous question. "When you were in Naval Intelligence, did you ever have any contact with the civil power?" By this he meant MI5. I replied that my work was in military intelligence about other countries. Had he hoped I might be indiscreet about that?

Both he and Furber then accused me of breach of confidence about sensitive details of Hilda's case in press reports. I retorted that they never briefed me about these or distressing developments like the sexual activity, but I learned of them from journalists. Judith Cook's *New Statesman* article misquoted me. Were they hoping to scare me into doubting my integrity, and show that I could not be trusted with sensitive information after having the highest security clearance? I told them Dalyell and I had never communicated with each other until I tried to correct damaging errors in his Parliamentary statement. I had no evidence relating to his allegation of British intelligence involvement. However, I accepted there might be something in it – especially after learning about Hurst's burglary. I was certainly not satisfied with the dismissive responses from the police.

I had been on the defensive long enough. I hit back: "I don't believe the police are deliberately involved in a cover-up, although they may be unwitting victims of one." Cole recoiled, saying he had investigated the nuclear angle, but with no evidence he could not take it any further.

The interview reverted to suspect interrogation mode. Cole demanded detailed evidence of my movements, not just on the day Hilda was abducted, but the day before as well. I had to send them a photocopy of my thatching diary for those days, a photo of me working and a signed statement from Liz corroborating this. They also took a second set of my fingerprints. Later I learned they made the secretary of Leigh Village Hall Committee give a statement confirming I attended the annual general meeting on the Tuesday evening. In light of the fact that, with a beard at the time, I bore no resemblance to the driver of Hilda's car, such treatment of the victim's next of kin amounted to vindictive intimidation. Not only was I rattled and alienated; inevitably my suspicions grew that MI5 was indeed involved, and the police had something to hide.

Around that time, it became obvious our phone was tapped. When trying to phone us, a neighbour heard instead a conversation between two men discussing my movements. This reminded us of another strange incident early in 1983. Just days after I left the Navy, we came home from a shopping trip. As Liz opened the front door, she exclaimed, "Someone's been in here." With no signs of forced entry or anything disturbed or missing, I dismissed her intuitive suspicions. This was soon after Dalyell began his campaign. Now I realised MI5 could have searched our house for any *Belgrano*-related documents over a year before Hilda was murdered – and only a day or two before my final visit to her, which would have been arranged by telephone.

Corroboration emerged following my meeting with Cole, when *World in Action* producer Stuart Prebble said he was told that I and some colleagues were investigated. Presumably all searches drew a blank. The net, therefore, would have been widened to catch not just potential sources such as myself, but also my trusted friend, Hilda.

———— ✎ ————

By bizarre coincidence, another suspect was making the headlines as we left Sherborne police station that day. Hilda's photo was on the front page of London's *Evening Standard* newspaper, beside a banner headline: 'I WAS PRIME MURDER SUSPECT – Burglar tells of questioning by police over case of the Navy officer's aunt'.

Robert Higgins, who had admitted to five burglaries within a mile of Ravenscroft, had faced an identity parade in which one witness picked him out as the 'running man'. He told the paper: "They were under pressure to find someone and I just didn't have an alibi… I didn't even know about the murder until they told me." Higgins' biggest worry was he might be framed. His lawyer, former Conservative MP Delwyn Williams, told Shrewsbury magistrates Higgins had been extensively interrogated by detectives hunting Miss Murrell's killer: "He has been through hell." He was not charged.

———— ✎ ————

The day after my interrogation, the West Mercia Police escalated their aggressive strategy. Beneath a front page headline 'MURRELL COVER-UP IS DENIED', the *Shropshire Star* on 9 January reported on a major press conference, reinforced by a centre-page exclusive interview with Chief Constable Robert Cozens. Negotiations were continuing with the BBC for a reconstruction of the murder on the *Crimewatch* programme around the first anniversary. So *World in Action* would have competition.

The next morning, in an extraordinary letter in *The Times*, pathologist Peter Acland dismissed the notion that he, or anyone else, had been influenced by "any Secret Service organisation". He concluded:

```
I don't know who killed Miss Murrell, but I have a
strong suspicion that some twopenny halfpenny thief is
gloating over a pint of beer in a pub not many miles from
Shrewsbury about all this media interest.
```

Acland received widespread publicity, including an interview on peak-time national breakfast television. It was highly irregular for a pathologist to go public after an inquest, and would have needed approval from the coroner and Cozens. Probably aware that his pro-police speculation had damaged his impartiality, in the letter he offered to 'discuss the case with any other pathologist nominated by the family'. I decided to call his bluff.

The first television programme to examine the murder in any depth was screened two weeks later from Cardiff. On 24 January, Harlech TV's current affairs series *Wales This Week* highlighted some of the mysteries surrounding the case and ended with a live interview with Dalyell. I declined an invitation from producer John Osmond to take part. Instead, I suggested they should ask Dalyell whether he might have been set up when told the murder was linked with the *Belgrano*, to distract attention from the nuclear industry and tempt me to be indiscreet about the Falklands War. Dalyell replied that, although he did not believe he had been duped, it was something he had not considered and could not rule out.

Dalyell then said this for the first time in public: "Francis Pym [Foreign Secretary during the Falklands War] publicly complained in June 1984 that in March 1984 his room in the House of Commons was rummaged through, if you please; his papers were gone through... Obviously, the authorities were going absolutely berserk at the time to try and find where those leaks were coming from". He confirmed that the same source who alerted him to Hilda had recently alerted him to look at what Francis Pym said in June 1984.

Thirty-six hours after the programme, Hilda's weekend retreat Fron Goch caught fire. The cedarwood chalet would have been destroyed in minutes but for the prompt action of a neighbour. On seeing smoke at 8 am, he ran up to find flames around the back door. A nearby rainwater storage tank and bucket enabled him to put out the fire before it could take hold.

The police sealed off a wide area around the chalet and brought in forensic experts, but never publicly revealed what was found. Welsh Nationalists were suspected, because they were targeting second homes owned by people in England. However, this arson attack did not match their usual, highly effective methods. Also, they invariably took responsibility for their attacks, but had not done so in this case.

The West Mercia Police dismissed the incident as a dangerous prank by children. They hid behind the fact that, as Fron Goch was on the Welsh side of the border, it was the responsibility of Dyfed-Powys Police to investigate. It took me until April the following year to meet with the detective in charge of the investigation, DCI Dai Rees.

Rees told me there was no attempt to break in, ruling out a tramp. The fire had no detonator or accelerator, eliminating Welsh extremists. Unusually, it had been lit in damp newspaper in a tea chest laid on its side filled with logs beside the back door, and had probably smouldered for 12-15 hours. He agreed this showed both cunning and malice. However, he refused to consider it was intended to bring family pressure on me to stop pursuing the case.

By then I had tracked down the fireman who was first at the scene. He remembered how defensive the senior Shrewsbury police officers were. "We were quickly asked to retreat from the incident. This was very unusual. Also, we were expecting to hold a routine press conference, but it was clamped on." Like DCI Rees, he reckoned the fire was odd, and could have been lit up to 12 hours earlier. In his opinion, neither a nationalist nor a child was the culprit. Welsh Nationalists used diesel-soaked rags lit by candles left on all the windowsills. This was the work of someone who knew how to burn down a building using a technique leaving few clues and plenty of time to get away. He agreed it looked like a heavy warning to me to "get off the grass".

At the time Fron Goch was unoccupied and vulnerable. I had no doubt the attack was another vindictive reaction by the State security apparatus to the fact that the spotlight had been thrown back onto conspiracy theories. Two days after the fire, on 28 January the trial of Clive Ponting opened in the Old Bailey in London.

On 27 January, the *Observer* newspaper broke a story headlined 'Private eyes spy on objectors to Sizewell probe'. It revealed that monitoring had been organised by a private detective agency with links to British intelligence. Zeus Security Consultants, run by a former military intelligence officer, had been hired to:

> ...ascertain identities of principal objectors at the Sizewell atomic power station inquiry at Snape Maltings. If possible, obtain list of objectors, their connections with media, political leanings, etc.

Zeus refused to name who commissioned the operation. I later learned its 'private client' was a firm of London solicitors which, in turn, took instructions from a large corporate client whose identity was never confirmed. However, it built nuclear power stations and therefore had a keen interest in the Sizewell Inquiry.

The *Observer* had obtained a list of some of the people targeted for surveillance. Hilda's name was not on it because it was dated January 1983, before she decided to become an official objector. Nevertheless, she was in frequent contact with some people on the list. These included CPRE Director Robin Grove-White; Colin Sweet, an economist who testified for the National Union of Mineworkers; Peter Bunyard of the *Ecologist* magazine, and members of the Stop Sizewell B Association and Ecoropa.

Hilda often phoned Maurice Telford, a retired teacher living near Sellafield. He kept her updated about what was going on in the troubled headquarters of British radioactive waste management. A month before her murder, they had a long phone call discussing his meetings with Sellafield workers. She offered to buy them a Geiger counter to measure radioactivity levels along the fence, linked to new evidence of clusters of child cancers and deformities around the site.

The *Observer* scoop proved for the first time that surveillance was carried out on opponents of the nuclear industry. It also opened up the murky world of private investigators. Zeus sub-contracted the work to another agency, Sapphire Investigation Bureau, which then enlisted the help of Contingency Services. This was run by Adrian Hampson, alias Victor Norris. His criminal record and background were uncovered by Paul Foot in the *Daily Mirror* in an article headed 'Satan, Sex and the Sizewell Snooper'. Norris had six convictions for sex offences involving his young daughters, was the leader of a devil-worshipping sect called the Anglian Satanic Church, and had founded the Nazi Phoenix Society.

The *Observer* article led to wider claims that private investigators were regularly employed by the Security Service. Norris himself explained: "We have a couple of very good imitation lefties. They know the score: they know the patois these people use. They can drop names; they've got connections. We can infiltrate alright. I do the work the Home Office don't want their people to do."

My network of local informants in Shropshire, journalists and TV producers had developed to the point where I was beginning to conduct my own parallel investigation into the case. Pre-eminent among these was Don Arnott.

We first met following Hilda's thanksgiving service. Looking like a bent-over, bearded gnome, Don's rich, deep voice, clear diction and marvellous use of words reminded me of the actor Leo McKern. I immediately warmed to him and his puckish sense of humour.

On 3 May 1984, I tried to avoid the worst of the potholes in the long tree-lined drive into Rhiewport Hall, his home on the outskirts of Berriew, near Welshpool. Hilda had last visited him for advice about the nuclear industry just over a year before. He shared the massive, rambling Regency country house with his extended family. I needed his help with Hilda's paper before I presented it at the Sizewell Inquiry.

Don was head-hunted in 1941 as a brilliant young radio-chemist for Amersham International, which became the UK Atomic Energy Authority (UKAEA) after World War Two. However, on hearing about Hiroshima, he resigned from a secure post which would have involved working on Britain's Bomb. Instead, he devoted much of his life to developing techniques in radio-medicine. He contracted polio at the age of 38, leaving his spine permanently locked in a severe stoop. This did not prevent him from working for the International Atomic Energy Agency, and writing their first handbook on radioactivity. In 1978 he retired and bought Rhiewport Hall.

As opposition to Thatcher's nuclear schemes grew, local anti-nuclear campaigners discovered Don was a major asset. He was a precious rarity: a high-calibre nuclear scientist who was prepared not only to advise them but to speak and write publicly against any new nuclear power plants, and the problem of what to do with their radioactive waste. Don guided a campaign called People Against Nuclear Dumping On Rural Areas (PANDORA), which headed off proposals to bury waste in the Welsh mountains.

Curiously, Hilda never told Don she was writing a critique of the Government's White Paper on radioactive waste management, and he never probed her motive for seeking his advice. He answered her questions without revealing the evidence he planned to present at the Inquiry. Also, he never told her that he knew he was under surveillance.

Don was to be an expert witness for a consortium of trade unions – anathema to Thatcher – representing fire fighters and health workers who would be called upon to deal with any emergency at the planned power station. His evidence included his concerns about a fundamental flaw in the safety system of the US pressurised water reactor design on which the Sizewell plant was modelled. He had stumbled across it while studying the official report into the nuclear near-disaster at Three Mile Island in March 1979.

He spotted that the control rods, designed to drop into the reactor core and stop the nuclear chain reaction during an emergency, were made of an alloy of 80 percent silver, 15 percent indium and 5 percent cadmium. His chemistry expertise enabled him to calculate the melting point. To his horrified disbelief, it was the lowest of any material in the core; yet the control rods should be the last to melt. Then he discovered the control rods melted at Three Mile Island. Moreover, the Sizewell design would have the same alloy in its control rods.

The UKAEA learned of Don's discovery soon after Sir Walter Marshall, Thatcher's front man for the nuclear programme, took over as chairman. Don and Marshall first met during World War Two at Amersham International. Don told me he alluded to the control rod problem in the last PANDORA newsletter, which he always sent to Marshall.

When the arrangements for the Sizewell Inquiry were published, Don wrote to Marshall complaining about the mismatch in Government funding between the nuclear industry and objectors. To Don's surprise, Marshall invited him to UKAEA headquarters in London, and sent a limousine to collect him. For their meeting Marshall had summoned two other heavyweights: Lewis Roberts, then head of Harwell, the birthplace of the UK nuclear industry, and Ron Flowers, the top scientist at Nirex, the body set up to deal with the waste problem. There was little talk about funding objectors; instead, the three of them questioned Don closely on what he knew about the control rods.

He received more unexpected attention at a pre-Inquiry meeting at Snape Maltings in Suffolk. While staying overnight at an inn, he found himself in a scene out of a third rate spy thriller. In the bar, a man sidled up to him and whispered that he should be careful, as he was being watched. Apparently, the spook had been hired by the Central Electricity Generating Board who opposed the UKAEA's push for US-designed reactors, which spelled the end for British designs.

Far from troubling Don, the warning intrigued and encouraged him. He was annoyed, however, when a file containing his correspondence with Marshall disappeared during the visit. He was left in no doubt that he was seen as a threat to the Government's nuclear energy plans.

Don was not deterred; but he failed to testify at Sizewell. On 13 April 1983, with the Inquiry into its fourth month, he was invited to speak at an anti-nuclear conference organised by the Greater London Council. Before he could do so, he collapsed from a heart attack shortly after a coffee break. This put him in intensive care for five days and forced him to withdraw from the Inquiry. No-one else raised the control rod problem. He had been under intense stress preparing for the Inquiry; but when he eventually died in 2000, it was not from heart problems. Had his coffee been spiked, perhaps with an overdose of caffeine, to induce cardiac arrest?

Because of his heart attack, Hilda left Don alone for a few months. They met once more, on 8 February 1984, six weeks before she was murdered. Harry Bury invited her to hear Don speak at a Shrewsbury meeting of the Medical Campaign Against Nuclear Weapons. Describing his talk on the anatomy of a nuclear bomb as 'riveting', she chatted to him afterwards – without mentioning she had written her paper, and had applied to present it at Sizewell. If Hilda herself was under surveillance by then, their rendezvous under cover of such a subversive meeting, where she was not a member of the group, would have rung more alarm bells in MI5. They would have suspected Don briefed her to raise his concerns about the control rod design when she testified.

At our first meeting in May 1984, Don was shaken to read Hilda's draft paper, because it was so good. He suggested I should ask the Secretary to the Sizewell Inquiry to be allowed to read it into the record. This was approved by the Inspector, Sir Frank Layfield. A long working partnership with Don ensued, through which I took up Hilda's torch against the nuclear industry and investigated her murder with him.

I sent her paper to Anthony Tucker, the *Guardian*'s science correspondent. On 18 August 1984, a front page article by him appeared headlined 'Murder victim's Sizewell scorn'. A lengthy supportive review, with her main points quoted verbatim, continued on an inside page under 'Ministers "hiding facts on nuclear waste"'.

Having finally had Hilda's funeral, on 13 September 1984 I presented Hilda's paper to the Inquiry. However, it was no threat to Thatcher's plans for the nuclear industry. So, why had she not told Don at their final February meeting she was about to testify at Sizewell? Could it have been that by then she was into something far too dangerous to risk his safety? If so, MI5 and the nuclear industry would have been further agitated by the prominent media coverage of her Sizewell paper.

⚬⚬⚬

It was after Don read about the inquest in the *Shropshire Star* that I accepted his offer to help me pursue the truth. A stream of closely typed assessments of the case, which I dubbed 'Dongrams', followed. By mid-January 1985 we had exchanged seven rounds of questions, comments and responses as Don teased out what I knew.

He analysed the extraordinary coincidences in the case. The Oxford English Dictionary defined coincidence as a 'concurrence of events or circumstances without apparent causal connection'. However, in Don's scientific experience 'genuinely random coincidences are rare, and the Universe would be impossible were it otherwise'. He went on to select three apparent coincidences from the case:

- Both Hilda's telephones, in separate houses, faulty.
- The break-in and search of papers in Peter Hurst's flat after Dalyell's speech.
- The arson attack on Fron Goch.

He argued that the probability of three separate coincidences actually being random was far lower than any single one of them. I found this really helpful, while not accepting that any of these was coincidental.

⚬⚬⚬

Questions about Hilda's telephones were first publicly raised by Derek Woodvine during interviews for both *Wales This Week* and *World in Action*. Woodvine was a Labour councillor on Shropshire County Council. He was also a member of West Mercia Police Authority, a committee which acts as a police watchdog – but hitherto had rarely shown any teeth.

A British Telecom employee contacted Woodvine following the police press conference the day after my interrogation in Sherborne, and the headlines about the questioning of Higgins over Hilda's murder. Chief Constable Cozens wanted to refute claims made by Dalyell, including the MP's contention that "the police version of the burglary did not tally with what was obviously a sophisticated break-in, in which the telephone had been cut, leaving it so callers could ring in but not out."

Woodvine's whistleblower had not examined Hilda's telephone himself. He was in British Telecom's Shrewsbury depot when an engineer returned from inspecting the phone at Ravenscroft. While the police were saying the phone had been ripped out, the engineer disagreed. The main phone in Hilda's bedroom was still working, and the kitchen extension had been disconnected carefully – as Brian George had told me. The effect was that a caller would have heard the normal ringing tone, but there would have been no sound in the house. Such a 'silent ring' would have led callers to believe no-one was at home rather than suspect a fault, which might have prompted a personal visit or a call to British Telecom.

Former Conservative MP and Higgins' solicitor, Delwyn Williams, corroborated Woodvine in the second *Wales This Week* programme on the case, broadcast on 7 February. Williams, who like Woodvine had two engineer sources, made the following remarkable comment: "I believe that the Secret Service should have been looking at this house bearing in mind the connection with the *Belgrano* affair; and I would be surprised, and in fact upset, if they were not…". He challenged the police to admit that a Secret Service presence might have interfered with their enquiries: "The truth will never hurt anyone".

At the end of the programme, Woodvine revealed that two members of the West Mercia Police Authority intended to initiate a discussion to resolve the questions. Williams added that, if this was unsatisfactory, "then the Home Office should set up an Inquiry which should be made public". The same evening, London's *Evening Standard* broke the story of the telephone engineer under a headline 'Murder mystery of a silent phone'.

Three days later, Clive Ponting was sensationally acquitted at the Old Bailey. This must have sent shockwaves through the State security authorities. No longer could they rely on a jury to convict anyone, including me, with a public interest defence.

Soon after the *Wales This Week* programme, the West Mercia Police Authority met. Woodvine told me that Chief Constable Cozens made a "savage attack" on him. "It was… like someone lining up to thump you. It was that sort of situation, gunning for me; an intimidatory, 'I am the authority' attitude." He was all the more shaken because hitherto Cozens had been seen as a liberal, reasonable Chief Constable. Yet when Woodvine challenged him about the telephone, "he became hard and tough and was after me".

Crimewatch was a popular BBC TV programme. Its reconstructions of crimes and appeals for witnesses had proved effective in eliciting fresh information from the public. It also helped the police by broadcasting only their version of events. Nearly a year after the murder, the programme producers made it a special feature. Not to be outdone, Granada TV's *World in Action* programme decided to get in first.

Producer Stuart Prebble asked the police whether he could film Hilda's car. He was told this was not possible as it had been dismantled in the search for evidence. The police instructed him not to divulge that the killer had taken a can of lager from Hilda's drinks cabinet; and a stabbed grapefruit had been found in the car, plus stab marks in the dashboard. This evidence was sensitive as it was known only to the killer and the police, and was needed to cross-examine any suspect. For the same reason, Prebble was denied a photograph of the telephone in the kitchen at Ravenscroft.

On 4 March 1985, the *World in Action* programme 'Death of an English Rose' faithfully complied with these strictures and reconstructed the police version of events. However, it also explored the Sizewell and *Belgrano* theories, the condition of Hilda's telephones, and suppression at the inquest of Ian Scott's sensational evidence that her body was not in Moat Copse when he checked it twenty-four hours after it was supposed to have been there.

Prebble had secured an extraordinary filmed interview with Assistant Chief Constable Bernard Drew. Unfortunately, lack of time excluded from the programme the following exchange about how the investigation would have acquired a completely different dimension if the police had believed Scott.

Drew: "Certainly we don't consider that that's a possibility worth pursuing."
Prebble: "Why not?"
Drew: "I don't have any evidence to suggest that that is in fact so."
Prebble: "Well, there's Mr Scott's evidence... Isn't it extremely unlikely that this person [Hilda's abductor] would have taken the body across the field in broad daylight where any number of people could have seen it?"
Drew: "Certainly so far as the latter point is concerned, that is one of the most unusual aspects of the case. For anybody who has been to the scene, clearly it is open land there; and it remains quite remarkable that nobody saw Hilda Murrell and her assailant anywhere in the vicinity of that car, but that's the position as it is." Prebble should have retorted: was it not far more likely that Hilda was not seen because she was not yet there, with all the associated implications?

In the unscreened interview, Prebble then asked Drew what was done once the owner of the car had been identified. Drew replied: "Well, the officers checked out with the house to find out whether the person concerned was there; and as you are already aware of course, there was no reply from the house."

Prebble's researcher Jenny Rathbone: "Are you saying they then went to the house on the Wednesday?"
"No."
Prebble: "That's what you did say."
"Well perhaps. I don't know how detailed you want to be." Drew then tried to hide behind his claim that, in the first three months of 1984, over 250 cars were reported abandoned in the area. Prebble riposted that local farmer John Marsh knew this, but felt this one was unusual enough to warrant reporting three times. Drew could only lamely agree.

The obvious next step would have been to visit Ravenscroft immediately. Failure to do so at that crucial moment was suspiciously negligent.

After Drew's disastrous interview, the West Mercia Police must have realised that some dramatic diversion was needed to quash talk of conspiracies and cover-ups. Their desperate solution was to bring in another police force to conduct an 'outside' review of their handling of the case.

A few hours before the *World in Action* programme was broadcast, Cozens announced that the review team would also investigate the credibility of "various theories and speculations" surrounding the murder. This 'independent' investigation would be carried out by Peter Smith, an Assistant Chief Constable of Northumbria Police. Headlined as a 'killer hunter' with a 100 percent success record, Smith declared: "I am coming in with a totally open mind".

The *Crimewatch* programme followed ten days later. Prebble watched bewildered as a reconstruction showed Hilda's abductor stabbing a grapefruit and the dashboard with Hilda's large kitchen knife. The police pointed out the can of lager, and showed a close-up colour photograph of the telephone, with both the receiver cord and extension cable apparently ripped out.

I was stunned when I saw the actress playing Hilda wearing the actual Totes rain hat found in the hedge – but which none of her close family or friends had recognised. After Cole's outrageous accusations against me in Sherborne police station, I was angered that he had allowed such key pieces of evidence to be used and contaminated by the *Crimewatch* actors and himself. He, too, handled items with no gloves on. No mention was made of the significant fact that, on returning home, Hilda had crossed the road to pay Mary O'Connor for a raffle ticket. When I next saw Mary, she told me the police had warned her not to talk to me.

The BBC reconstruction had Hilda escaping from her assailant while he was trying to put her bird book under the offside front wheel to gain traction. After grabbing the ignition keys from the car, she implausibly trotted off up the lane until her shouting, knife-wielding abductor caught up with her; whereupon he put her in an arm-lock and started stabbing her. This farcical speculation was to try to explain why the keys were found in Hilda's coat pocket, and why her assailant risked taking her across an open field. The *Belgrano* and Sizewell theories were dismissed as ridiculous. The programme prompted 120 calls from the public. The team of thirty officers still working on the case followed up every new lead – but there was no breakthrough.

One call the police did not welcome was from a mysterious man claiming to have worked for MI5, who later identified himself as Gary Murray. He drew attention to private investigator Barrie Peachman, who apparently phoned him three days after Hilda's murder threatening to kill himself, and shot himself three weeks later. In 1963 Peachman had formed the Sapphire

Investigation Bureau, one of the agencies involved in collecting information on Sizewell objectors.

Obliged to investigate, the police concluded Peachman was nowhere near Shrewsbury on the day of the abduction. Apparently he was depressed because of a failed relationship and tax arrears. However, Murray heard that, shortly before he took his own life, "Peachman said his back was against the wall" and "people were out to get him".

Crimewatch had backfired, merely creating more speculation.

Taking up Acland's offer in his *Times* letter to discuss his findings with a pathologist of my choice, I secured the services of highly respected Professor Bernard Knight. Soon after the first anniversary, he met Acland and Cole, and examined both autopsy reports and photographs of the body in the copse and mortuary. While I had no illusions that he would seriously challenge a fellow pathologist, he came to some significantly different conclusions.

The police and coroner had accepted the time of Hilda's death as between 5-10 hours after she was abducted on Wednesday 21 March. Knight revealed that the pathology about time of death was imprecise. Hilda could have died at any time between the Wednesday evening and Friday evening. This clearly supported Scott's evidence. It would have raised huge complications for Cole, all of them leading away from his simplistic hypothesis and towards the conspiracy theories.

In his report to me, Knight also concluded that Hilda's large kitchen knife was not the murder weapon (my emphasis added):

> ...[I]t could not have caused all the wounds on the body, especially that on the right arm. The blade is too wide to have caused such a narrow track at the required depth of insertion, and this applies to several of the abdominal wounds which have penetrated the liver. **The view is shared by Dr Acland and indeed the police. No blood was detected on the blade** by the forensic laboratory, though of course it had lain in the rain for a considerable time...

At the inquest, Acland and Cole had said nothing about this embarrassing forensic finding. So what was the knife doing in the ditch by the hedge, close to Hilda's broken spectacles and hat? And where was the one which had been used?

In Knight's view, Acland had been under pressure from the coroner to give a more exact time of death for the sake of putting a date on the death certificate. 'Dr Acland readily admits the lack of any firm basis for this time' of 5-10 hours from abandonment to death. When Acland was interviewed soon afterwards for another *Wales This Week* programme on the case, he conceded this. The uncertain nature of hypostasis, the settling of blood in a dead body, meant Hilda could have died later in the week; and yes, she even might not have died in the copse.

These facts opened up other scenarios for the murder. Acland's letter to *The Times*, aimed at quashing speculation about what happened, had backfired.

∽∾

Northumbria's Assistant Chief Constable, Peter Smith, and his assistant, Detective Superintendent Cecil Hall, interviewed 45 key witnesses and protagonists as part of their 'independent' review. When they met me at my home, they listened politely as I outlined my belief that the murder was linked with the Sizewell Inquiry.

Smith and Hall insisted on visiting Judith Cook at her home in Newlyn, Cornwall at 10.45 pm on the eve of the first anniversary. She had just returned exhausted from a big TV interview in Manchester. They interrogated her until after midnight about her sources for her *New Statesman* article, and also for her imminent book *Who Killed Hilda Murrell?*. Smith warned Cook that, by pursuing her own unsubstantiated line while refusing to reveal her sources, she was hindering the police investigation. She insisted she could not break confidences.

Cook had anticipated problems as soon as she discovered Hilda was a nuclear objector with a nephew who had recently been in Naval Intelligence in the Falklands War. While researching her *New Statesman* article, she became so worried that she phoned Tam Dalyell to warn him: "I think I'd better tell you what I know just in case something happens to me..."

From the moment she agreed to write the book, "strange things began to happen". Cook and her husband Martin Green returned home after several days in London to find every letter in a pile of mail had been slit along the bottom. They reported this to the Post Office, whereupon letters arrived badly stuck down. After Cook's story about the intimidation was published in *The Guardian* the post resumed arriving undamaged.

However, instead the harassment changed: "I began to get really nasty telephone calls." A man with a Scottish accent said: "Hilda Murrell didn't take any notice of the phone calls either, and look what happened to her." Another in the middle of the night warned she would "end up like Hilda Murrell". Variations on this theme followed several times. If Martin picked up the phone, the man would ring off. These calls stopped after she phoned Dalyell and Ashdown about them. The book manuscript, which she had sent carefully packaged by recorded delivery to her publisher, did not arrive. Following a formal complaint and Post Office investigation, it turned up out of its packaging with pages torn. This echoed my own experience a year later, when a copy of Chris Martin's eponymous drama documentary about the case arrived from him in similar condition. Later she had a break-in when only her papers were disturbed. Undeterred and angry, Cook rang *The Guardian*

Dear Mr Dalyell

I trust you won't send this to the Select Committee. Please understand why it is not signed.

You should know that you are getting much closer to the truth. They have been turning overfiles and intelligence desperately to see who has been talking to you and the New Statesman and the Observer.

The ~~Prime Minister~~ is very angry.

Clive Ponting probably didn't tell you about Heseltines decision to ~~ve~~ a full (but secret) internal investigation of the Belgrano affair. The Secretary of State didn't want to get caught out by it. The study has all the secrets in it, and is inches thick. Very few p⸱ have ever seen it. Some call it the crown jewels. ⸱⸱ ⸱ ⸱⸱ ⸱⸱ Heseltine has one. I don't know wh⸱ the others. The documents in th crown jewels are stamped with a⸱ most every classification the Ministry has.

Parliament should assert its right to get these things out into the open. Deep throats and journalists can only do so much but will never get the whole story.

You can tell the press about this, but carefully. Paraphrase it. Keep at it.

Top: Crumpled note from Tam Dalyell's primary source. (with permission from Paul Rogers)

Tam Dalyell. (Photo: Press Association)

Judith Cook 1986. (Photo: Watermans Arts Centre, Brentford)

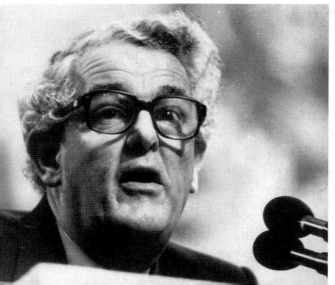

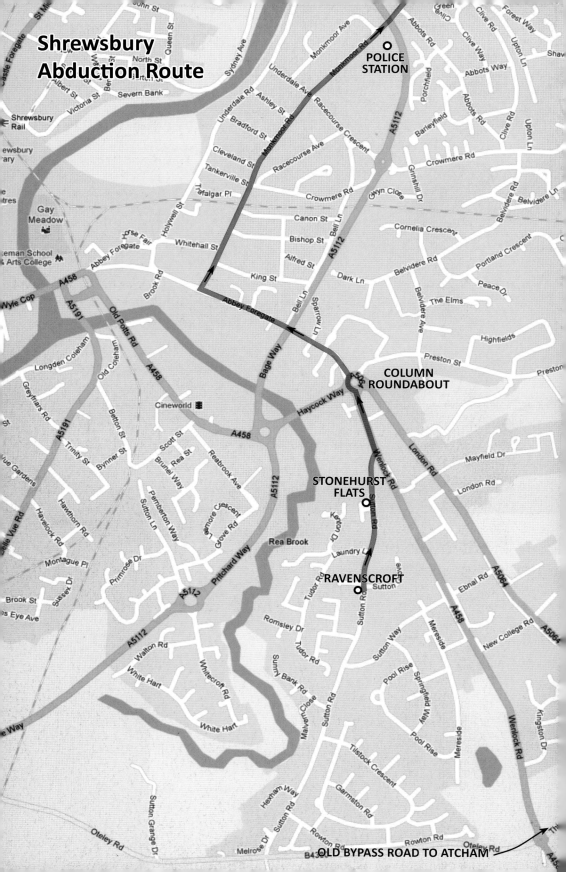

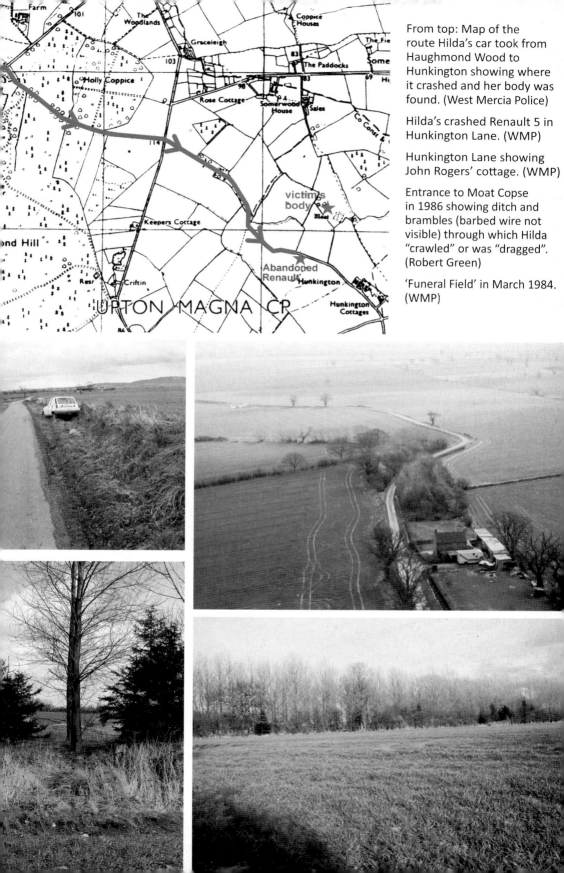

From top: Map of the route Hilda's car took from Haughmond Wood to Hunkington showing where it crashed and her body was found. (West Mercia Police)

Hilda's crashed Renault 5 in Hunkington Lane. (WMP)

Hunkington Lane showing John Rogers' cottage. (WMP)

Entrance to Moat Copse in 1986 showing ditch and brambles (barbed wire not visible) through which Hilda "crawled" or was "dragged". (Robert Green)

'Funeral Field' in March 1984. (WMP)

From top: Hilda's body in copse showing trees which Ian Scott counted on Thursday afternoon.

Hat (not recognised by family and friends) found in the hedge by Funeral Field.

Hilda's body in the copse.

Hilda's Death Certificate.

Hilda's kitchen knife (too large to be the weapon) found near the hedge.

(Photos: West Mercia Police)

who published a report of her experiences.

Dora Russell, the 91-year-old ex-wife of the famous philosopher and anti-nuclear campaigner Lord Bertrand, lived near Cook and knew her. Lady Russell wrote a supportive letter which *The Guardian* published. Soon after it appeared, her home was broken into and she was beaten up by an intruder. Then she received an initialled postcard in the mail with the following written in an educated hand:

> We broke into Hilda Murrell, we broke into the Woolf's, and if the Guardian continues to be puzzled, we'll break in wherever we want to! But lots & lots of people will think differently.

The Northumbria detectives left with a smug warning that Cook was going to make a fool of herself as "some kind of Cornish Miss Marple", because they would "almost certainly find the killer by the time her book was in the shops". 20,000 copies of her book sold out in ten days. Her publishing editor told her that their biggest author, Jeffrey Archer, who was Conservative Party Chairman at the time, prevented any more being printed. When a friend of mine requested a copy from her local library within a week of publication, the library reported that this was impossible because all remaining copies had been withdrawn from sale and pulped.

Smith and Hall also interviewed Graham Smith, author of the first book on the case, *Death of a Rose-Grower*. On 19 February 1985, he called Cook to tip her off that he was also writing a book. After discussing it at length, they decided not to collaborate. The next morning, his publisher Cecil Woolf found his London home had been broken into through a kitchen window overlooking a snow-covered back lawn. Nothing was stolen – not even a gold watch in full view on his desk – and footprints in the snow had been carefully swept over. Woolf had recently published two outspoken short books by Dalyell about his findings from the *Belgrano* controversy.

After eight weeks what became known as the Northumbria Report was presented to West Mercia's new Chief Constable, Tony Mullett. Cozens had raised eyebrows by leaving to become a special adviser to the Home Secretary. However, the report designed to dispel accusations of a cover-up was never published.

A few copies were circulated among senior officers and politicians, excluding Dalyell. Even members of the West Mercia Police Authority were denied access to it, apart from the Chair, a Tory Councillor. The rest of us had to rely on information from a long overdue press conference at West Mercia Headquarters on 26 June. The police carefully arranged for it to be held two days after Cook launched her book on national radio. The press conference did not go well.

The press were told the report had not been published because it contained key pieces of evidence which the police could use to identify Hilda's killer.

However, they refused to release even an abridged version. Peter Smith announced that, apart from some minor niggles, he had found the handling of the case had been exemplary. His report fully supported Cole's opinion that the murder had been "a burglary which went tragically wrong". No other motive had been found, and no evidence had been suppressed. Smith assured reporters that, though he could give no details, he had asked questions in the "highest echelons" of the Security Service to eliminate any conspiracy theories.

Admitting it was one of the most bizarre cases he had ever encountered, he highlighted the number of coincidences. Then came his most memorable observation. "Looked at collectively, these coincidences could appear – as journalist Judith Cook said in a new book – like 'a can of worms'. But taking them individually, and holding them to the light, there is no evidence of any involvement of British Intelligence." There were three mild rebukes for the West Mercia Police: the failure to find Hilda's body for three days; shortcomings in how the police followed up the alleged connection between her murder and the death of Barrie Peachman; and the media should have been handled better.

Journalists smelt a whitewash. Smith and Mullett quickly found themselves under pressure over police inaction. On discovering that Hilda owned the car, apparently the police telephoned her number but got no reply.

Question: "That night?"

Smith: "Yes."

"It was two days later before the police called at her house?"

"Oh yes, exactly – I agree with you; and that's my criticism, and..."

"If they had acted promptly they might have found Hilda Murrell alive?"

"I don't think there are sufficient grounds for you to say 'if they had acted promptly'... Let's take the 250 abandoned vehicles...", launching into Drew's bluster with Prebble. Years later, I was astounded to watch DCS Cole, in a videoed briefing for other police forces shortly after the murder, admit: "The wounds alone wouldn't have killed her... It is my belief that her assailant never intended to kill her up until the time the car crashed. When he did decide to do so, he made a pretty inept attempt. If she hadn't laid [sic] out in the open on a freezing night she'd probably still be alive."

At the press conference Mullett tried to argue there was nothing unusual about the car – with stab marks in the dashboard? Contradicting the earlier police line, he suggested the marks were "nothing more than wear and tear", even though they had featured prominently in the *Crimewatch* reconstruction. "I don't know whether you have seen any of the photographs. I am unable to detect any stab marks in either the dashboard or the grapefruit. It is an old car. It's full of scratches, bumps and grazes; and I would defy anyone seeing those photographs to identify them themselves." The Renault was three years old. The media were unimpressed. Dalyell demanded in the House of Commons that the Northumbria Report be published, and wanted answers to more questions. He was brushed aside by Home Office Minister Giles Shaw.

The following evening, Dalyell told a packed public meeting near Birmingham he would not reveal the name of his 'deep throat' source. "Police would give it to the Home Secretary, Leon Brittan, who would prosecute the source for leaking official information, even if his identity was given in confidence to detectives." He added that he would not be asking his source for any answers to the questions raised by the Northumbria review, because "any more information would identify my source".

Nonetheless, on 5 March after the *World in Action* programme was broadcast, a TV interview with Patrick Burns on BBC *Midlands Today* included the following exchange.

Dalyell: "I have to be exceedingly careful not to go beyond what I was told that British intelligence were involved."

Burns: "In a contract sense possibly?"

Dalyell: "That would certainly cover it."

Burns: "Mr Dalyell is not alone in his suspicion that Miss Murrell may have been the subject of a clandestine surveillance operation here. I myself have been told the same thing on an unattributable basis."

CHAPTER 6

INCONVENIENT EVIDENCE

When I first heard the name Laurens Otter, I was basking in morning sun working on a thatched cottage in a little town in Dorset. It was Monday, 24 June 1985 – two days before the police press conference about the Northumbria review of the case. Judith Cook's live interview on BBC national Radio 4 about her new book *Who Killed Hilda Murrell?* boomed out from my pick-up truck. The whole street therefore heard the next bombshell to hit the case.

Cook revealed that, just three weeks earlier, she had received incendiary new information from Otter. In 1960 he was a member and Secretary of the Committee of 100. Formed by philosopher Lord Bertrand Russell, this more militant group within the fledgling Campaign for Nuclear Disarmament had practised civil disobedience following the Gandhian model, such as sit-ins and marches against nuclear weapons. Otter lived in Wellington, ten miles east of Shrewsbury, where he continued campaigning and organising local peace groups.

He had sent Cook three closely typed pages, which she later copied to me, describing what happened to him on the day of Hilda's abduction. An edited extract follows:

> At about 11 am I received a phone call from a woman who sounded elderly and well-educated. I deduced that she was in a public phone box, because she had trouble connecting the call at first, as if unused to the instructions.
>
> She did not give her name, but told me she had asked me a question after a meeting of the Shropshire Peace Alliance. She then asked if I was coming to the Alliance meeting that night. I said "Yes".
>
> She explained she was working on a paper objecting to Sizewell: "I've found glaring errors in the official case. I want to make sure these reach the Inquiry – but I'm certain the authorities are going to use any means to prevent my material reaching it. My telephone is tapped; I am being followed; my house is being watched, and there has been an attempt to break in. I have received threats, and my post is being opened."
>
> Then she asked: "Where would you publish something that the Government would not want published?"

"I would suggest *Peace News*." I added that I would deliver it personally to the office in Nottingham.

"Can you come into Shrewsbury and get the papers immediately?"

"I'll get the timetable and look up the time of the next train."

"Oh, I can't wait that long. I have an appointment at midday to meet an Inspector Davies – he's coming up from London to see me. I'm not sure what it's about. It's a bit of a difficulty, as I'm due to have lunch with the Symondsons – do you know the Symondsons?"

"I don't."

"Oh well, I won't be able to see you until this evening, will I? Bring a stout bag; there are a lot of papers. You will be coming tonight, won't you? You won't forget? It's very important. I don't know what the interview's about – it's not just about Sizewell."

Aware that Tam Dalyell was making headlines with his increasingly effective campaign over the Belgrano sinking, I blurted back: "Is it the Belgrano?"

The phone had gone dead. She had probably run out of money.

Otter duly turned up for the peace meeting with a large bag, and stayed with two other men for an hour and half. When no old woman appeared, they went home.

This was the sort of information I had been waiting to hear. Unusually, Hilda declined to give him her name, which suggested she was concerned about surveillance. However, why had this man apparently taken 15 months to come out with such an explosive story? I hurried north to find the answer.

Otter was a caricature of the veteran peacenik, complete with shock of white hair, goatee beard and wearing an anti-nuclear T-shirt and knee-length shorts. I knew at once he had a credibility problem, not least with me. Listening to him was hard work, as he frequently launched into labyrinthine, pedantic digressions. Nonetheless, he was quite sure the elderly woman caller mentioned the Symondsons. This impressed me, because it identified her as Hilda. This fact had not appeared in any media report.

Otter was clearly highly intelligent and well-educated. He seemed disarmingly sincere in his regret and self-reproach at not making sure his evidence had emerged sooner. Above all, he did not have the vindictive, calculating, ego-driven character to have fabricated such a dangerous tale. For if he was telling the truth, he and his family, and any witnesses prepared to corroborate him, were now at risk.

Two days later I spent over an hour with DCI Furber in Shrewsbury Police Station. We had not met since my Sherborne interrogation in January. He said when he personally interviewed Otter the day Cook broke his story, he dismissed him as an unreliable witness because, like Morgan-Grenville, he could not corroborate his story. "If Hilda had been so concerned, and you and she were so close, why had she not contacted you?" I decided not to remind him of the ominous postscript of her last letter to me in October 1983, which I had revealed on *World in Action* in March. I shot back: "If she had been under heavy State harassment, Otter would have been the best local choice to collect her sensitive nuclear papers and get them published. He was used to surveillance and intimidation, and had edited *Peace News*. And she would have avoided involving me at all costs."

Furber had not checked Hilda's diaries for corroboration that she questioned Otter at a previous Peace Alliance meeting. After a tense search together, we found she recorded attending meetings on 12 November 1982 and 18 March 1983. I reminded Furber that George Lowe saw Hilda turning into Sutton Road about twenty minutes after setting off from shopping. So she went somewhere else, and had time to make such a phone call.

Otter told me Furber had revisited him the day after the June 1985 police press conference for a final, hostile meeting, threatening to prosecute him for wasting police time. Afterwards Otter recalled that on Saturday 24 March 1984 – when Hilda's body was found – he was at a peace meeting in Birmingham, where he mentioned the phone call to some friends. After Cook broke Otter's story, one of them recalled the conversation and offered to travel to Shrewsbury to make a statement. Otter thanked him, but "decided that everyone would assume it was a put-up job and advised against so doing".

He kept me updated with local news about the case. Over the next few years, he gained enough confidence in our relationship to reveal he had acted much earlier. Close examination of Hilda's diaries revealed two other peace meetings she attended, on 24 May and 13 October 1983.

It took until 1987 before I found someone else prepared to support Otter's claim that Hilda had wanted to meet him. It was Brian George; and he was prepared to sign a statement for me. By then, I had talked to Brian many times about Hilda, the state of the house and the telephone wires, and had confidence in his integrity. Apparently, during 1983 she began to worry about going out alone in the evenings, and driving at night. So she asked Brian to take her to meetings, which he did on at least three occasions, although he was not involved with CND.

We had made no mention of Otter, when Brian suddenly said that, several weeks before the murder, Hilda told him she wanted to meet "a gentleman by the name of Laurens Otter who was involved in support of CND activities in the Telford area". She had read his numerous letters to newspapers which she had found to be very supportive of her views, including Sizewell B.

She asked if Brian would take her to Telford to meet Otter at one of the peace meetings. However, Brian declined as he did not want to travel outside Shrewsbury. She also mentioned that she hoped to ask Otter to come to Shrewsbury by train as he did not drive a car. She would collect him from Shrewsbury railway station, and bring him to Ravenscroft "to enable her to learn first-hand his views on her Sizewell paper, which she was about to finalise".

Otter first wrote to the police offering information about Hilda's phone call within two weeks of the murder, but received no response. He then sent the police a postcard inside an envelope after reading Anthony Tucker's *Guardian* article on Hilda's Sizewell paper in August 1984. The police still ignored him. In a third attempt, he wrote to Cook after reading her *New Statesman* article. The letter never reached her, like some of her mail at the time.

On 14 May 1985, Otter heard Dalyell speak in Shrewsbury about Hilda's case. This spurred him to write a fourth letter, to him. Dalyell immediately phoned him and passed a copy to the police, and to Cook who also phoned Otter. The police took a month to contact him; and only a junior detective visited to take a statement. Nothing more happened until the day after Cook broke his story.

Initially, Furber had been pleasant to Otter, to find out how much he knew, and admitted he had found his postcard. On it, Otter referred to his first letter sent only two weeks after Hilda's murder. Furber's feeble excuse was they could not find the earlier letter, without which "it didn't mean much".

Laurens Otter made a major impact on the case. If his story was true, here was circumstantial evidence for both conspiracy theories.

———— ∞ ————

Soon after the second anniversary, Don Arnott and I conducted field research in and around Moat Copse when conditions would have been similar to those at the time of the murder. Don's scientific approach led us to start where the body was found.

We went to Hunkington equipped with a *Shropshire Star* photograph of DCS Cole helpfully crouching at the spot. By matching the trees and ground behind him, we refined to within a tree or two where he was photographed. The trees in that position had been felled, so Ian Scott must have walked directly over the ground where Hilda's body was found two days later. There was almost no ground cover, and I recalled how starkly obvious her body looked in the police photograph produced at the inquest.

Don timed me walking from where Hilda's car had crashed across Funeral Field to the copse. With heavy clay clinging to my gumboots, I was struggling by the time I reached it. The experiment became even more arduous, and took twice as long, when I followed the hedge where the knife, hat and spectacles were found.

We had satisfied ourselves on two crucial aspects of the evidence. No abductor would have succeeded unobserved in frogmarching Hilda across Funeral Field's impossibly waterlogged clay on a fine weekday lunchtime in full view of Hunkington Farm and the lane. In the hour we were there Don noted nine cars passed the crash site. Also, Scott could not have been mistaken when he stated Hilda's body was not where the police said it was in Moat Copse. As we absorbed these deductions, a thought struck Don. "Rob, did you realise the only circumstantial evidence that Hilda was in her car when it crashed is that the keys were in her coat pocket?"

I spent several days interviewing as many local residents as possible, and kept a record. Some were never approached by the police. Almost all were unhappy about the investigation, which they said was mechanical, incomplete, and conducted "between 9 am and 5 pm".

I found John Marsh's tractor driver Bryan Salter, who saw the large dark car and its suited driver walk to the copse and back soon after Scott had been there. I also heard about another mysterious visitor to the copse. Nick Waters, who lived in Drury Lane behind the copse, was walking his dog at about 9 pm on the Wednesday evening when he spotted a torchlight for about five minutes in the copse near where Hilda's body was later found. His first thought was that it might be a rabbit 'lamper' – a poacher with a torch to dazzle rabbits which are killed by a dog – but the beam was too dim and steady. Also, if Hilda had been there that night, a poacher's dog would have found her.

On the second anniversary in March 1986, DCS Cole issued a renewed appeal to the public. He complained that witnesses were being frightened off by talk of State crime and conspiracy, for which "not one shred of evidence" had been found. Coincidentally, an old friend of Hilda came forward with disturbing new information.

Aged 85, Constance Purser was still running a small farm museum called the White House in Aston Munslow, twenty miles south of Shrewsbury. She was interviewed by police shortly after the murder, because Hilda was a longstanding friend, a trustee of the museum, and a regular visitor. Con was worried about what she said in her original statement, and wanted to see me urgently.

Over coffee in her rustic kitchen, Con recounted she first told the police that on Hilda's last visit about a week before she died, she seemed her usual self and just talked about gardening. However, so soon after her dear friend's brutal murder she was too grief-stricken, frightened and confused to remember Hilda visited her again, only about three days before her abduction. Arriving unexpectedly in the afternoon, Hilda was "taut and trembling" as she entered the kitchen carrying a basket filled with plants, their roots wrapped in newspaper.

Hilda told her she had taken her Sizewell paper to London sometime in January, and "shown it to some people who were very pleased with it". She was also concerned about the security of Ravenscroft. A man had recently called on her, claiming to be a new neighbour, and told her that "if ever she felt nervous about anything, she should let him know". Far from reassuring Hilda, she felt intimidated.

Hilda produced what looked like an "exercise book covered in brown paper" from beneath the plants in her basket. When Con realised Hilda wanted to leave it with her for safekeeping, she fearfully declined. Looking dismayed, Hilda quietly hid the book again. They then walked slowly in silence across the farmyard to Hilda's car.

Encouraged when I told her about Cole's appeal, Con now felt strongly that she should make a new statement. I asked her to wait while I made some enquiries. If I could find some corroboration, here was important support for the nuclear conspiracy motive and Laurens Otter.

In Hilda's diaries, she last went to London on 21 October 1983 for the CND rally. Not to have recorded a further visit placed it in the 'sensitive/threatening' category. I requested another meeting with DCI Furber.

On 10 April 1986, during a tough three-hour discussion I gave him Con's information along with her request that they interview her again. Furber was well-prepared this time. Producing Hilda's 1984 diary, he smugly pointed out that her last recorded visit to Con was on 8 March – not 15 March as stated by Con in her first police statement. Another unreliable witness.

I countered: "You should hear what she has to say, now that she has cleared her mind." Furber retorted: "In my long experience, what people say first is normally the truth." I exploded: "How can you say that equally for a man reporting a broken window and an old lady whose best friend has just been brutally murdered? Now you're being offered new and potentially important information by one of Hilda's friends, you have a duty at least to take a second statement from her – even if you then dismiss it, as you did with Otter." Furber said he would consider it. I tipped off John Osmond of Harlech TV, who quickly filmed interviews with Con and Otter.

Two days later, Furber told me they had decided not to take another statement from Con. Furious, she repeatedly phoned Shrewsbury Police Station, undeterred by their tactic of leaving her hanging on the line and then telling her no-one was available. After Furber realised she was not going to give up, he sent two detective constables.

Instead of simply taking Con's statement, they interrogated her. "Has Rob Green been here? Has Harlech TV interviewed you?" They then produced her first statement and leant on her to stick with her original evidence. They even tried to make her say I had put her up to all this. Exhausted and frightened, she signed a statement which did not accurately reflect what she wanted to say.

Con's ordeal was not over. One evening about ten days later, she was in her kitchen when her old black Labrador started barking violently at the locked back door. Someone was trying to open it. After a few minutes the intruder seemed to go away, and the dog calmed down. Next morning, she opened the door to find a wooden plug lying on the ground outside. It had been prised out of an old finger-hole through which it used to be possible to lift the original wooden latch. As Con arranged for new locks and chains to be fitted, she had no doubt that the intruder was linked to Hilda's case.

Twenty-one years later, Kate, my second wife and skilled researcher, trawled through Hilda's 1984 diary for every reference to Con – and struck gold. On Sunday 18 March, three days before her abduction, Hilda had written:

> Arr R. 5.40. Got good fire going, had 2 of Con's scones
> warm for tea…

Kate pounced. Scones go stale and hard after a few days. After her final, desperate visit to Con, Hilda would have enjoyed the comfort of them as soon as she got home – and certainly not ten days after her last recorded visit on 8 March. She had left subtle, poignant corroboration for Con's claim in her diary. Paradoxically, this supported Furber's assertion that part of what Con had said first was nearer the truth. On 18 March, Hilda recorded she went to Fron Goch that morning. Leaving after lunch, she called in at neighbours. She would then have had time to drive home via Con: a major detour, but taking only an extra hour or so.

Con's story supported Otter's. Here was circumstantial evidence that Hilda did have sensitive nuclear documents which she needed to leave with a trusted friend – and if that failed, then with an experienced activist. The remoteness of Con's farmhouse, the plethora of hiding places there, and the fact that Con was not involved in the anti-nuclear movement, made her a shrewd first choice. Close anti-nuclear friends like Harry and Gladys Bury would have been too obvious – witness the two 'detective' intruders in their house in May 1984.

After first hearing Con's story, I checked with Diana Moss, Hilda's neighbour and secretary of the local CND branch. She clearly recalled Hilda saying she had "attended another CND event in London" on 22 January 1984. Hilda's diary that day made no mention of any journey, but it was the shortest and most anodyne entry for that year. Could Hilda have used the 'CND event' as a cover? These two claims, from two of Hilda's friends who never met each other, provided mutual corroboration that she went back to London sometime in January 1984. Only some major discovery relating to her anti-nuclear campaign would have persuaded her to make the huge effort again in the middle of winter.

<hr/>

As I extended my investigations to Sutton Road, several of Hilda's close neighbours told me of suspicious activities they witnessed during the week of her murder.

Around mid-morning on the day before Hilda's apparent abduction, Mary O'Connor had worried about a young man smoking an ornate pipe sitting on the footpath outside her house, and another strange older man dressed like a tramp nearby. Early the next morning, Brian George noticed an unusual man and woman walking fast near the junction of Sutton Road and Wenlock Road. Both acted as if they did not want to be recognised. The woman, in her mid-twenties, wore a long heavy fawn tweed coat with the collar up around her face. The man was aged about 30, in a smart light grey suit – but was wearing white, well-worn trainers.

At 11.10 am on Wednesday 21 March 1984, Ursula Penny was standing chatting to a friend on the footpath opposite her house in Sutton Road. Hilda drove by into town, "wearing a brown hat". Seconds later a man emerged from the garden in front of a large Victorian house converted into flats almost opposite, jumped over a low wall onto the footpath and walked rapidly towards Hilda's house. He was about 40 years old, medium height and athletic build, with a clean-shaven weathered face and fairish short-cropped hair, wearing a grey lapel-less windcheater zipped up and grey slacks. She did not recognise him as a resident. Along with key witnesses to Hilda's apparent abduction, in the next few years Penny would attend several identity parades, but would never see the man she and her friend witnessed.

These neighbours made statements to the police because they felt it was unusual to see four strangers not far from Hilda's house that week. The man seen by Penny matched the features described by many witnesses of Hilda's car driver. The one spotted wearing a suit and trainers in Wenlock Road looked like the 'running man'.

Years later, I also learned of changes to Hilda's house between her abduction and discovery of her body. Her friends Lucy Lunt and Hana Bandler had visited without warning on the Thursday morning. They saw curtains closed across an open rear window in her bedroom, and closed shutters and curtains in her sitting room, out of sight from the road. Thinking she might be unwell, they called out and tried to open the front and side doors, but found them locked. Then they realised Hilda's car was not there. Hana was worried enough to want to contact the police; but Lucy dissuaded her, suggesting Hilda had probably gone to Fron Goch. Tragically, they took no further action.

On the Friday morning at about 9 o'clock, Brian George was waiting for a lift outside Ravenscroft. He saw the kitchen door was open, kitchen curtains closed, and the light on. At that moment his lift arrived, and could not wait.

For six years the postman had delivered Hilda's mail, arriving regularly at about 9.45 am. Everything seemed normal on the Wednesday and Thursday. However, on Friday he noticed the kitchen door was ajar; and the kitchen curtains were closed, which he had never seen before. Also, overnight two twenty-foot long, half-inch deep tyre scuff marks had appeared in the shingle drive curving away from the kitchen door towards the gateway – as if a vehicle had left in a hurry.

The milk lady regularly delivered two pints a week to Ravenscroft. On the Friday at 10.30 am, 45 minutes after the postman, she noticed the kitchen door was wide open. As usual, the conservatory door was unlocked for her to put the milk inside, out of sight from the road. The inner door between the conservatory and house was kept locked. An hour and a half later, at noon, a woman delivering leaflets corroborated the milk lady's report. She dropped a leaflet inside the kitchen doorway, noticing that the open rain-swollen door was scuffing on the linoleum.

At 7 o'clock that evening, PC Davies confirmed the kitchen door was still wide open, the kitchen curtains closed and lights on when he made his half-hearted search for Hilda. He needed a few pulls to shut the door before leaving. Three hours later, a retired fireman who regularly walked his dog past Hilda's house noticed the side door was half open again and the house was in darkness when his dog ran into the drive. The next morning, PC Lane found the door ajar, but with the lights back on. The police were silent about all these anomalies.

Jane and Mick Gilmore, two younger anti-nuclear friends of Hilda, told me she seemed depressed when they met around Christmas 1983. At one point, she suddenly said: "The nuclear industry will be the death of me". Daphne Phillips, a long-time family friend, remembered a strange conversation early in 1984 when Hilda had told her: "I am walking on dangerous territory..."

—❦—

While Don and I were doing our research in 1986, an unusually committed and resourceful freelance producer/director in TV and radio, Christopher Haydon, interviewed Hilda's friends and key players in the case on audiotape. To Haydon's surprise, Dr Peter Acland agreed to an interview, in which he made some highly contentious statements.

The pathologist asserted that on the Wednesday "it was below freezing in the daytime". He stressed this to support his claim that, in such conditions, Hilda would have become hypothermic within five to ten hours, and died that evening. However, records at RAF Shawbury, the nearest official weather observation site just five miles north of the copse, show it was sunny with temperatures between 3 and 6 degrees C during Wednesday afternoon. They did not dip below freezing until 2 am on Thursday.

Also, Acland insisted Hilda's leg injuries showed she had been crawling before dying. Yet he knew she had a broken right collar bone, which would have made it impossible for her to support herself on her arms. She suffered other debilitating injuries, including a penetrating wound through her upper right arm, deep cuts in both her hands and stab wounds to her stomach. He undermined his inquest conclusion by admitting he could not exclude the possibility that Hilda had been dragged. He even said: "I can't rule out that people came along later and moved the body."

Acland made another extraordinary admission, about Hilda's body being allowed to decompose in the Copthorne Hospital mortuary. Acknowledging "it was only kept in a 4 degree fridge", he confirmed that the pathologist and mortuary technicians complained about the smell. He said it should have been taken to deep freeze facilities within two to three days after he performed the first autopsy – but the decision was Cole's responsibility. Deep freeze facilities were available in Hereford and Birmingham.

⨯⨯⨯

On Easter Day, 30 March 1986, the *Observer* published a short article headlined 'Commander accuses State over Hilda Murrell murder'. It was based upon a paper I had written and distributed to the media called 'Some Reflections Two Years On'. I suggested the murder was linked to the State through its need to hide the truth about the *Belgrano* sinking where it was beginning to lose the argument, and to protect the nuclear industry. When BBC Radio Shropshire interviewed me, I encouraged those who knew what had happened to Hilda to contact me because I would believe them – and could help protect them with publicity.

Less than two weeks later, I again drove 200 miles north from Dorset to Don. He wanted to meet before being interviewed about the murder and the Sizewell Inquiry for HTV's *Wales This Week* at 2 pm before the film crew went on to interview Con and Otter. Ten minutes after midday, I parked outside Don's front door to be greeted by his daughter Alison and two grand-daughters, Arabella and Abigail, aged twelve and nine. Don and I started to go through the main points of his interview in the sitting room.

At about 12.40 pm Alison drove off on a routine errand, leaving us alone in the house while the children played outside. Five minutes later I saw Arabella leading a pony ridden by Abigail past the bay window; my car was out of sight to the right of the window. Soon afterwards, Arabella knocked on the door and announced breathlessly that my car's front tyre was flat. We hurried out after her. Abigail had heard hissing as she passed the car. The sidewall of the front nearside tyre had clearly been cut.

I changed the wheel, and took the damaged tyre to the local garage, whose owner Ray Heath knew Don. An experienced mechanic, Heath confirmed the tyre was an almost new, tubeless radial design with steel reinforcement. It had definitely been slashed: "Probably a Stanley knife with a hacksaw blade." Noting two cut marks close together, he reckoned it had taken two attempts by a strong man to puncture it.

Berriew was a quiet, friendly village. Don was a popular and respected resident of some ten years' standing, a Parish Councillor, and a regular at the Lion Inn. Why would a local vandal walk 200 yards up his drive and damage a car, which was not Don's, parked outside his house?

Though not visible from the road, Rhiewport Hall could be watched from a lane across the valley. Continuous shrubbery gave cover from the road to the edge of the drive directly in front of the house. From there a professional intruder would have taken ten seconds to cross to the parked car, slash the tyre and escape. However, he would have needed to know I was coming, have observed my arrival, and chosen a moment when most of the family members were at work or on regular errands, and the children out of sight. This meant Don's home must have been under sustained surveillance.

If we were right, then Con Purser's new information must have rattled those who knew how and why Hilda was murdered. Perversely, the incident gave us enormous encouragement. We quickly realised it could be linked with the arson attack at Fron Goch on 26 January the previous year. I used this as a lever to gain access to DCI Dai Rees at Dyfed-Powys Police HQ in Newtown, who had led the investigation into the fire at Fron Goch and in whose area of responsibility Don lived.

Coincidentally, I was meeting DCI Furber later that day to discuss my second anniversary paper, and his refusal to take a new statement from Con. As I drove alone to Shrewsbury with the slashed tyre in the boot, I reflected grimly on these dramatic developments. It was less than a week since Con had rung me; and ten days since a leading national newspaper had printed my challenge to the State security authorities. Was the slashed tyre a brazen new warning to me to 'get off the grass', and frighten other witnesses such as Otter and Con from speaking to the media? On meeting Furber, he listened impassively as I reported it and handed him a corroborating statement from Don. Furber had no choice but to arrange an appointment for me with DCI Rees four days later.

After discussing the Fron Goch fire, Rees undertook to investigate the damaged tyre and send it to the Home Office Forensic Science Centre in Swansea, South Wales for examination. I warned that if it disappeared, I would publicly conclude the police were colluding in a State crime.

On my next trip to Berriew, mechanic Ray Heath told me the police had taken a statement from him. A few days later, two strange men in casual clothes appeared on his garage forecourt. Claiming to be detectives, they leant on him to water down his statement. He angrily refused.

It was mid-August before a letter arrived from Dyfed-Powys Police:

> The report of the examination of your damaged tyre has been received from the Forensic Science Laboratory. The scientist has concluded that "the damage is the result of a concussion impact with an object or bodywork. The damage is not consistent with that caused by a sharp object such as a knife"…

It took another month for the tyre to be returned to Newtown Police Station. Rees reported he had "drawn a blank on the incident" when I retrieved it. On returning home, I obtained the following assessment of the damage from a tyre expert who knew nothing of the circumstances:

> [A] cut was found in the sidewall, and this cut was the cause of the deflation of the tyre.

On reading the letter from the police, he asked: "What made them say that?"

This was the first hard evidence that the police were not pursuing the case objectively. Instead of trying to support Hilda's next of kin, they appeared to be colluding with the State security apparatus, attempting to intimidate anyone who dared provide information pointing to a political motive and a State crime.

Con's ordeal encouraged her to trust her memory of Hilda's last visit. She felt relieved that her determination to help the police in their enquiries had borne fruit, albeit in an unnerving way. She and I now had no illusions about what we were up against in pursuit of the truth; neither had Don, John Osmond and his HTV film crew, Laurens Otter or Ray Heath.

In my second anniversary paper I wrote that the police were, in a sense, also victims in Hilda's murder. Now I feared some of them were willing accomplices. Furthermore, whoever was interfering with the police investigation was so confident of their power to do so with impunity that they simply did not care what damage it did to their reputation.

Hitherto, I had presumed only MI5 and their private agency thugs were likely to be involved. Now, in addition to the police it seemed MI5 interference extended to British Telecom, the Forensic Science Service, Royal Mail and Fire Service. I could also never forget the hostility towards me by the coroner, Cole and Furber, and Acland's aggressive letter to *The Times*.

I recalled in my paper that, at the time of the inquest, a public trial of State security agents was in progress in communist Poland for the abduction and assassination of a 'turbulent priest', Father Jerzy Popiełuszko. To the 'free' world's amazement, they were convicted. In a totalitarian state, little attempt is made to hide the tools of repression and control. On the other hand, excessive zeal can be counterproductive – especially if directed against a popular priest where Roman Catholicism provided a leading source of alternative political power. Therefore, the State needed to be seen to punish such excessive thuggery.

Back in dear old 'democratic' Britain, however, "that sort of thing just doesn't happen, old boy". So British State security agents have a clear run – particularly if they sub-contract the more risky work to private security agencies for deniability if anything goes wrong...

This meant that, if I was to survive pursuing the truth about Hilda's murder, I had to learn from her experience.

On several occasions thereafter when I stayed with the Burys, Gladys insisted on driving me in her car during my local investigations. It was she who first noticed we were being tailed, sometimes discreetly but often quite overtly to unsettle us. During one memorable drive to visit Don, she decided to test our suspicion.

As I got into her Volvo saloon, she pointed out another ubiquitous red Ford Escort parked not far away, similar to those seen in Sutton Road and Hunkington around the murder. Sure enough, when we set off it followed close behind. She took the usual route until about halfway there – when she abruptly turned, without indicating, down a narrow country road. The other car stuck with us. Gladys, who knew the area intimately, made a succession of diversions until we were travelling along near-cart tracks. Our 'tail' was not shaken off until she darted down the drive into Rhiewport Hall.

We enjoyed regaling Don with our experience. However, the point was not lost on us about such misemployment of the Security Service – for a petty burglary gone tragically wrong?

Around then, I recalled with alarm a letter from Don dated 25 June the previous year. That was the day between the launch of Judith Cook's book, when she broke Otter's story, and the joint West Mercia-Northumbria Police press conference. Don had written:

> It is possible that somebody may have had a go at me... Yesterday I drove down to the village on my motorcycle and became aware of an unusual sound, which subsequently proved to be the chain clunking against the chaincase. On arrival in the village I found that both chain adjusters – there is one on each side of the rear wheel – had apparently worked loose, in spite of locknuts, and were dangling; and that, apparently, the only thing which held the rear wheel axle more or less in position would be the big hexagonal locknut on the chain side.

He explained how he had corrected the fault enough to ride home, where he found that the locknut was only handtight:

> This meant that, on my drive to the village, nothing whatever held the rear wheel in position once the chain adjusters had become dislodged – as they would have done through vibration; and that, had I been going to (say) Welshpool at my customary turn of speed the rear wheel would have worked forward until the chain became dislodged from the rear wheel cog and wrapped itself round the drive wheel cog – with spectacular and conceivably fatal consequences.

Just three weeks before, he had tensioned the chain, taking care to follow the instruction book because of the safety implications. Since then, he had ridden the motorbike many times. He continued:

There are only two ways in which this machine could be
sabotaged (a) quickly, (b) without anything showing and
(c) in such a way that the driver would only become aware
that something was wrong when he was actually riding it.
One is the method described. The other is brakes...

Acknowledging that the incident by itself was not significant, he added
it would only become so in the event of further "unexpected happenings".

On 19 September 1986, I was surprised to receive a phone call from Furber.
Straining to be friendly, he probed my recent activities. Then he got to the
point. "Why don't you come to see me anymore?" I replied that, after Con's
treatment and the outrageous investigation into my slashed tyre, I had lost
any confidence in the police. He told me that the lawyer and former local
Conservative MP Delwyn Williams had been to see him, to ask what the police
had done about the two 'detectives' who had lent on Ray Heath. Furber had
been unaware of all this. He admitted I might have a point.

My relationship with the West Mercia Police had broken down. For the next
sixteen years, I would rely on my growing network of 'ferrets' in the media,
and other trusted friends and contacts. They served me well.

CHAPTER 7

COMPLICATING DEVELOPMENTS

Don and I discussed the psychology behind a State crime. If we were right, then why abduct an elderly woman, driving her unnecessarily through the centre of town? She could have simply disappeared, or been killed quietly in her home. Why leave such a deliberate trail, and make fools of the police?

Several friends confided that many anti-nuclear women were so terrorised by Hilda's murder that they stopped campaigning. The French have an expression for a demonstration of ruthless, selective State control: *Pour encourager les autres*: 'to encourage the others'.

This led to a new suggestion, which brought some plausibility to the oddest part of the crime – and the only one to be witnessed. What if the driver wanted to be seen? Was there some symbolism in driving past the police station? Was this deliberate flaunting of the driver's impunity? Only Hilda's car keys in her coat pocket linked her with it. So, could the car have been used as a decoy?

Such a scenario made sense of evidence from another witness, Jill Finch. A neighbour and retired headmistress, she had been troubled by an experience around lunchtime on the Wednesday.

At about 12.20 pm on 21 March 1984, Jill is collected by a friend, Diana Lampen, from outside her home at 167 Sutton Road. They drive to the by-pass junction intending to turn right. While waiting for traffic, Jill hears the roar of a powerful vehicle approaching fast from behind. She looks round to see a brown Range Rover coming up on the inside. Convinced it is going to hit them, she throws herself across onto Diana. Somehow, the Range Rover misses them and swerves left out onto the by-pass heading for Atcham. Jill sees that the only apparent occupant is the driver, a farmhand type. The vehicle looks scruffy, as if used on a farm.

The Range Rover was heading for the Hunkington area by the quickest route. Jill knew this because she always went that way when exercising her dog on Haughmond Hill. Experiencing a similar gut feeling to my own on learning Hilda was missing, Jill felt strongly that somehow this vehicle was connected with Hilda's murder.

Soon after hearing Jill's story, Laurens Otter arranged for me to meet a former member of the Irish Republican Army, living in a West Midlands housing estate with a new identity. He told me Hilda's abduction echoed snatch squad operations in Northern Ireland. The victim would be taken away for interrogation while someone disguised as the victim was driven in their own car as publicly as possible, to cause confusion and distract attention from the abductors. If the victim's car broke down on a pedestrian crossing just as their best friend stepped onto it, the fit and well-drilled driver and 'victim' would abandon the car and be picked up by a support vehicle.

What if the operation was made to *appear* to have been botched? The cover of a bungling, sexually perverted burglar helped to discredit any State involvement. But if this burglar was so incompetent and panicky, why had he not been caught? The State could not be allowed to have it both ways.

Don and I also agreed about another deduction. Hilda would not have tried to leave papers with Con and then Otter unless she had come across new, damning evidence that nuclear energy problems were being concealed. If such revelations would have seriously damaged the future of the nuclear industry and thus the Government's campaign against the miners, this would have provided the justification for MI5 to move against her. Reluctantly, I had to accept that the *Belgrano* connection with me would have been another major motive.

Andrew Fox was a producer on the regional current affairs programme *Central Lobby* for Central Television (CTV) in Birmingham. His half-hour documentary, filmed in June 1988, presented an overview of our latest findings.

A dramatic reconstruction was staged of Hilda's abduction in a brown Range Rover by the most direct route via Atcham for interrogation in a safe house near Moat Copse, while Hilda's Renault was used as a decoy. Fox interviewed myself, Don, Dalyell and ex-MI5 agent Gary Murray. Fred Holroyd, a former member of military intelligence working in Northern Ireland, confirmed that private investigators were used for 'dirty' work, and Hilda would have been a prime target because of her anti-nuclear campaigning and her connection with me and leaks about the *Belgrano*. The police refused to take part in the programme.

On 7 March 1989, Fox phoned me. The programme had been pulled, although it had been approved for showing on the fifth anniversary. CTV's controller of factual programmes said it "brought nothing new to the story". Fox protested: the decoy/snatch squad scenario was new. He had also interviewed Acland, who revealed for the first time that he did not carry out any toxicology tests on Hilda's body, admitting he "did not think it necessary". The programme director was equally dismayed as it had cost £40,000.

Fox contacted me again in October the following year. He had found footage from the Hilda programme lying on the floor in an editing room. Had someone been sufficiently interested to copy or destroy the film, and left in a hurry when disturbed?

In November 1986, the *Daily Mirror* printed a front page story headlined 'I'VE KILLED 9 WOMEN'. A 32-year-old Scot, David McKenzie, had been arrested and charged with two brutal and frenzied attacks on old women in London. He confessed to these and seven other murders, including Hilda's.

McKenzie withdrew his confession a year later. Declared mentally unfit to stand trial, he was sent to Rampton Secure Psychiatric Hospital. Despite this, he was taken to Shrewsbury for questioning about Hilda – the first of several interviews with DCS Cole. In February 1990, McKenzie was found fit to plead, put on trial for the two London murders, and convicted of manslaughter on the grounds of diminished responsibility. He was recommitted to Rampton.

During his trial, he repeated his confession about killing Hilda. His solicitor, Paul Bacon, told the press it was "highly likely" his client would now be charged with her murder on the basis of the confession, despite his record as a liar and that he did not fit the description of the driver of Hilda's car. This prompted me to meet a key witness.

An Easter weekend in Shrewsbury in April 1990 gave me the opportunity. Rosalind Taylerson, a highly intelligent teacher married to an Army officer, told me what happened at the start of her lunch break on 21 March 1984. She had a clear view of the driver of Hilda's speeding Renault at the Column roundabout as it cut across in front of her. The man was in his late 20s-early 30s, slim, clean shaven with sandy close-cropped hair and pronounced high cheekbones: "Quite refined-looking and neat". She was troubled, therefore, when the police issued a second artist's impression which differed markedly from the detailed description she had given them.

In November 1986, Mrs Taylerson was summoned to yet another identity parade, which this time included McKenzie. The men were almost all overweight and dark-haired like him. She was an excellent witness, with a good memory. Now she was angry.

Alarm bells rang for me. In Westminster, Dalyell was equally fearful of a miscarriage of justice in an attempt to close the case. When I phoned him, he invited me to lunch at the House of Commons. For six years we had exchanged views via the media. When we met for the first time, Dalyell welcomed me warmly. To clear the air after my initial experience over his bombshell, I handed him a letter explaining why I believed he might have been set up in linking the murder only with the *Belgrano*. He carefully digested my argument that he might have been deliberately fed misinformation to distract attention away from the nuclear industry and discredit me.

To my surprise he did not dispute anything. Instead, he asked who I thought had phoned him to suggest he read Judith Cook's *New Statesman* article? At the time he was uneasy, because it was not how his sources had approached him. He did not receive any more information that way. When I suggested it could have been someone from the Security Service, he nodded grimly.

Dalyell explained why he had devoted so much effort to uncovering the truth about the *Belgrano*. "My motive was not so much the sinking. It was the lying." He was strongly supportive of the Armed Forces. We parted having agreed he would table Parliamentary questions about McKenzie.

Dalyell learned he would be given the chance to put a question directly to the Attorney General, Sir Patrick Mayhew, responsible for overseeing the justice system in England and Wales. To try to prevent him from ducking the question, Dalyell suggested I write to Thatcher's top legal adviser.

In my letter I advised Mayhew that I had spoken to a key witness, who was adamant McKenzie bore no resemblance to the driver of Hilda's car. I drew his attention to a TV programme about confessions by psychiatric patients in which McKenzie was interviewed. I had not seen any evidence implicating him in Hilda's murder. A public statement was needed, either to scotch the rumour that the West Mercia Police were about to charge McKenzie, or to stop them hounding the man any further.

Referring to my letter, Dalyell asked Mayhew to clarify the position with regard to McKenzie. Mayhew stonewalled. A report had been sent by the West Mercia Police to the Director of Public Prosecutions, who suggested 'further lines of inquiry'.

In September 1990, Mayhew informed Dalyell that "the available evidence is insufficient to sustain a charge of murder against any person". McKenzie was off the hook – we had rumbled them. Dalyell did not receive the letter until three weeks after it was sent. He was about to leave for the Labour Party Conference in Blackpool, where he broke the story. This was seen on TV by Paul Bacon, who had no idea until then that his client would not be charged.

Dalyell and Bacon agreed I should write again to Mayhew. This time I asked why the police had pursued McKenzie when they knew he could not have killed Hilda. Paul Foot, in his weekly column in the *Daily Mirror*, revealed more evidence ignored by the police. The day before Hilda's abduction, McKenzie was over 300 miles away in Dundee, living in his mother's flat with no money or transport. The police knew this, and that in 1980 McKenzie was convicted of wasting police time after confessing to a murder he could not have committed.

Despite all this, DCS Cole remained convinced he had found Hilda's killer. Awarded the Queen's Police Medal for Distinguished Service in 1985, Cole had retired from the West Mercia Police in the spring of 1990. *Shropshire Star* journalist David Sharp told me he asked him before he left the force if he could prove McKenzie's guilt. All Cole could say was: "He couldn't prove he wasn't guilty."

The Attorney General's Legal Secretariat finally responded to my letter in November 1990. Their reply began with an apology to Bacon for failing to keep him informed, and denial of any attempt to frame McKenzie. However, there was nothing in papers submitted by the police to suggest they had evidence which eliminated McKenzie – echoing Cole's perverse line that he "couldn't prove he wasn't guilty".

In 1992, the Appeal Court cleared McKenzie of killing the two women in London after hearing evidence he was "a serial confessor not a serial killer". Having admitted murdering Hilda Murrell, forensic evidence ruled him out. The small quantity of aspermic semen found on her clothing could not have been his because he was fertile – Bacon had got McKenzie's semen tested, which eliminated him. The police knew this too.

Years later, I watched a police video of interviews with McKenzie. Cole and Furber, obviously determined to try to incriminate him, took him through some of the most sensitive details in the case with endless blatantly leading questions, to which McKenzie simply agreed. However, when he occasionally had to provide information he was all over the place. I was outraged.

<hr>

I first met Gary Murray in 1988, at one of no less than five different, successful production runs of Chris Martin's documentary play *Who Killed Hilda Murrell?*, inspired by Judith Cook's book. We warily exchanged views on the case. He suspected I had something to hide about the Falklands War. I tried to probe his alleged former MI5 career, suspecting he might be a plant. He was writing a book which would include Hilda's case. In May 1993, *Enemies of the State* appeared, attracting considerable media interest.

With only two chapters devoted to Hilda, I was astonished and touched that Murray dedicated the book to her. He portrayed her character well, but was irritatingly erratic about other aspects of her work and my background. Hilda's research had not 'uncovered a number of flaws in the design of PWRs': Don Arnott had found one fundamental flaw in the Sizewell design. Hilda had no 'well-documented files' on nuclear weapon construction. More damagingly, I knew nothing about any 'Prime Minister's message to *HMS Conqueror*'. I had not 'resigned because of the Falklands War'; nor had I been disaffected.

The most sensational revelation was a five-page affidavit by Trina Guthrie. She had first visited Hilda as a child with her mother, the widely respected anthropologist Ursula Graham-Bower, who became firm friends with Hilda after meeting her on holiday in the Highlands of Scotland in the early 1950s. Ursula was renowned for her work helping the Naga tribe in northeastern India, who acclaimed her as their 'White Queen'. Trina maintained her family's ties with the tribe, and was duly named a 'White Princess'.

Trained as a botanist, Trina's other passion was preserving Britain's natural environment. This led to work at a nature reserve near Shrewsbury and more regular contact with Hilda, who treated her as an adopted niece. She took her and her boyfriend Malcolm Leel in her car on holiday in Anglesey in July 1983. After Hilda's murder, Trina moved to Lincoln, but maintained a close interest in the case through me and her Shrewsbury friends.

She had never been inside a prison until she heard about an inmate who had studied the political struggles of the Nagas. After she wrote to him, he allowed her to visit him. On his release they met again, which was when their discussions led to Hilda's murder. He had heard of it during conversations with a fellow inmate, who claimed he knew who had killed Hilda.

Trina gained permission to meet this long-term prisoner. He told her Hilda died at the hands of a team despatched to search for copies of secret signals relating to the *Belgrano* sinking, which I had been suspected of leaving with her for safekeeping. He shared a cell in a prison near York with another inmate serving 15 years for armed robbery, who claimed to have led a team of two other men and a woman hired by a "secret intelligence department" to do freelance work. The team leader allegedly reported to the Cabinet Office via an MI5 liaison officer. He used the codename Ceres – the Roman goddess of agriculture – for the team, and Demeter, the Greek equivalent of Ceres, as his own codename.

The team apparently entered Ravenscroft on Wednesday 21 March 1984, believing Hilda was on her way to her lunch appointment. When she returned home from shopping, one of the men panicked, threatened her with a knife and masturbated over her. Trina's informant knew about the wet sheets found in the kitchen. To my knowledge, no media coverage had mentioned this.

What Trina was told was so sickening that she left it out of her affidavit. She later told Kate that the sheets were used to torture Hilda to make her talk, draped over her head and soaked to make her feel she was slowly drowning. One of the thugs then attempted to perform oral sex on her.

The female team member, wearing Hilda's hat and old coat, was driven in her car by one of the other men through town and out to Hunkington as a decoy. Meanwhile Hilda was taken to a safe house in an area called 'Little America', where she was subjected to further interrogation under torture with a knife. Two nights later she was dumped in Moat Copse and left to die.

Apparently, one of the men had since died; another was in a secure psychiatric hospital. The team leader was insisting he had been 'fitted up' with his armed robbery conviction. The woman had disappeared.

Trina first contacted me with some of this information in 1991. I immediately realised that, if true, it placed her in great danger. Feeling way out of my depth, I put her in touch with Murray.

He found that the nearest former US military base – an airfield for the 31st Fighter Group in 1942 – was now called Atcham Industrial Estate, on the eastern edge of Attingham Park. Known locally as 'Little America', it was less than five miles by discreet back lanes from Moat Copse. He also unearthed the following hearsay information about the team members:

- The leader, Peter Sanderson, had done a deal in exchange for his silence.
- Malcolm Tyerman, serving 16 years for armed robbery, was being treated for depression in Rampton.

- David Gricewith, a violent professional criminal, had died after "accidentally shooting himself" in a police chase after an armed robbery.
- 'Helga', Gricewith's girlfriend, had vanished without trace.
- Their controller, a former police officer, was an MI5 agent.

The only one of these Murray managed to interview was Tyerman – being treated in the same ward at Rampton as David McKenzie. A senior psychiatric nurse was present during the meeting, which went calmly until Murray produced a large photograph of Hilda. The man immediately became agitated and turned away saying: "I've said too much already, that's why I'm in here." He vehemently denied ever being in the Shrewsbury area, adding it was only a matter of time before he would be dead.

My problem was to assess this information. I knew Trina was a highly intelligent woman of great integrity who had been close to Hilda. She had undoubtedly, therefore, written as truthful an account as possible.

One misgiving was that Murray ignored Don Arnott's link with Hilda, because until 1956 he was in the Communist Party – MI5 indoctrination was deep-seated. If Hilda's contact with Don was enough to cause concern, any suspicion that she was being passed other information, and that another nuclear mole was on the loose, would have caused huge alarm and prompted action.

The *Belgrano* connection served two other important purposes. If anything had gone wrong – or one of the team had 'squealed', as now seemed to have transpired – the overriding priority would have been to conceal the nuclear industry's involvement. Also, the team would have been well motivated after being told that Hilda and I were traitors, hell-bent on bringing down Thatcher over the *Belgrano*.

———— ⌘ ————

In late February 1994, Murray and I attended a packed West Mercia Police press conference in Shrewsbury Police Station. Assistant Chief Constable David Thursfield, flanked by DCI Peter Herbert and veteran of the case, DC Partridge, explained that they wanted to report on the outcome of their investigations into allegations in Murray's book. It proved to be another difficult public relations exercise.

Thursfield began with a surprising admission. "Over these ten years, and in more recent enquiries, we have been afforded every facility by the Security Service, military intelligence, and Special Branch of course…" He quickly invited scepticism by adding: "I can say categorically, there has never been any record of Hilda Murrell in any Special Branch file whatsoever." Turning to Trina's allegations, he said they had interviewed all the cited individuals. "We are satisfied beyond any doubt that… they are not the perpetrators of this crime. They do not *now* say that they are responsible. In fact, the key player says that he was prompted by a rather detailed article in the press, and wished by making such allegations to draw attention to his own plight, which is an alleged wrongful conviction." Was this another example of the ease with which vulnerable prisoners could be controlled?

When Thursfield invited questions, they soon became searching and critical. Was his MI5 contact in a senior position? This question was "out of order". Had the police been given unrestricted access to files? No, but they had seen the files that would have contained the relevant information – if there had been any. Scoffs of derision broke out across the room. Thursfield protested it was preposterous to suggest vital information might have been destroyed or removed. Murray pointed out that Hilda must have been on file because of her nephew's security vetting. Thursfield replied: "It would be interesting if Naval Intelligence recorded the details of the aunts of all their staff." No-one laughed.

I was not only Hilda's nephew; I was her next of kin. Also, I had specifically mentioned her name in 1980 during the vetting procedure for my job as Staff Officer (Intelligence) to Commander-in-Chief Fleet. When Murray raised these facts, he was told the police could not say if Hilda's name appeared in anyone else's files.

One journalist recalled the last police press conference on the case, nearly nine years ago in June 1985. "You have had an inquiry, the Northumbria Report – which you in fact refused to publish… This is, as far as you're concerned, an ordinary murder by a walk-in burglar which you still persist in holding to. The problem is that you are not believed… because what you say is incredible."

<hr />

A week before the tenth anniversary, the headline of Paul Foot's *Guardian* column read: 'Jury is still out on the doctor and the detective'. I was stunned to learn Cole and Acland had published a book, *The Detective and the Doctor: A Murder Casebook*, with the first chapter devoted to Hilda's case. Foot panned it as a "pathetic little book about a crack crime-busting partnership, which starts with a case they never solved".

Their account of how they investigated Hilda's murder contained several surprising errors. It was nonetheless useful, as it revealed their thinking and some new information. Acland rashly described his unusual circumstances when asked by Cole to conduct the autopsy. Recently placed on the Home Office list of pathologists, he was ordered by his Professor at Birmingham University not to accept any more criminal cases, as he was being paid purely as a lecturer in pathology. By agreeing to Cole's urgent request when no other Home Office pathologist was available, Acland defied his university superior and was forced to 'freelance' for the police. This explained why he let himself become their spokesman in his unwise letter to *The Times* in January 1985.

Cole described how the funeral directors – a father and son team – needed help to carry Hilda's body out of the copse and across the field to Hunkington Lane. He wrote flippantly:

> Their van could not get nearer than the road some four hundred yards away and they experienced difficulty negotiating the undergrowth and ditch which led out of the copse… Much to the amusement of police officers standing near the road, Acland took over and, although he considered himself still comparatively fit, the shared weight began to tell as they staggered across the field.

Later, when theories emerged and speculation increased about how and when the corpse found its way into the wood, he remembered the difficulties of that walk.

Apart from demonstrating their insensitivity and the police behaviour, Cole and Acland had provided circumstantial evidence supporting Don's and my assessment that it had taken more than a lone petty burglar to get Hilda into the copse.

In a separate media interview, Acland described what he thought was the easiest way into the copse from Funeral Field. "It was a little narrow track leading into the copse, about a foot wide… where we climbed over the wire fence there were shrubbery and bushes either side…" In fact, it was barbed wire across an overgrown gateway. If alone, Hilda would have had to climb over or crawl under it with her broken collar bone to get into the copse. Or, drugged and already half-dead from torture, had she been lifted over by a team?

To mark the tenth anniversary, Marnie and Colin Sweet had done much more than organise, for the seventh time, a memorial walk up to the quartz cairn where we had scattered Hilda's ashes in the Berwyn Mountains. An economist who had advised the National Union of Mineworkers, Colin's name was among those under surveillance by Zeus at the Sizewell Inquiry. He and Marnie had donated a section of steep hillside above their cottage near Llanrhaiadr for a wonderful project: the planting of a birch grove in Hilda's memory. Over twenty volunteers spent a morning planting fifty birch whips, while three photographers and BBC Radio Wales recorded their efforts. After lunch, I joined 25 walkers up to the cairn in calm spring sunshine.

In the evening, I took part in an extraordinary public meeting organised by the indefatigable Laurens Otter. The Right Rev John Davies, Bishop of Shrewsbury, chaired a panel comprising ACC Thursfield, DCI Herbert, Don Arnott and myself to discuss the case. The undiminished interest in the case was reflected in the 350-strong audience packed into the mock-Tudor Morris Hall in Shrewsbury town centre. They included Trina Guthrie, Gladys Bury and John Stalker, the former Deputy Chief Constable of Manchester turned TV sleuth.

Earlier that day, Stalker had made a bizarre announcement. He had opened an office in town from which he was launching his own investigation into the case. He hoped people with new information who had not gone to the police would feel they could come forward to him. Stalker undertook to reveal the findings of his quest for the truth in a documentary produced by Central Television. Of course, CTV had already made a programme five years earlier, which had been pulled because it may have got too close to the truth.

Thursfield, a surprise last-minute panellist, began promisingly. "I have never known or even heard of, in a case of an undetected murder, such an open and involved debate as we propose to have here this evening. This is history in the making for the police in this country." However, he then claimed disingenuously that those who had information were frightened to come forward, because of the wild speculation over political conspiracies. This was why "we have only today negotiated a reward on behalf of Crimestoppers, an organization which arranges for people to receive payments anonymously to achieve the objective of solving the crime". As usual, it was the first I knew of this. Clearly linked to Stalker's intervention, the £10,000 was never claimed.

After Don and I had outlined our concerns about the case, I read out a statement from Gary Murray, who was unable to attend. Regarding MI5's assurance that Hilda was unknown to them before her death,

> I understand that the only evidence of this is a statement of an MI5 official in London; in which case I respectfully suggest that West Mercia Police remember the case of the Deputy Chief Constable of Manchester, John Stalker, whose unpleasant experiences with British Intelligence are well documented.

This point was perfectly timed. Two years before Hilda's murder, Stalker had led an investigation into the deaths of six men in Northern Ireland. He got too close to the truth: that the Royal Ulster Constabulary had a secret but official 'shoot to kill' policy against suspected members of the IRA. He learned that a barn where the men were assassinated had been bugged, and that MI5 had taped the ambush. When he approached them for a copy, he was led on an endless run-around. As Stalker described in his subsequent memoirs, Sir John Hermon, Chief Constable of the RUC, told him the tape had been destroyed and refused to give him a copy of the transcript. He then demanded that Stalker sign a Special Branch gagging order. Stalker refused. He was later hounded out of the police on trumped-up corruption allegations.

An hour and a half of comments and questions from the floor followed. Trina was first. Echoing Con Purser's experience, she said: "Having come forward with information, I feel pretty bruised by the experience… I suggest there should be an opportunity for further discussion on the [police] findings as a result of their investigation into Gary's book." Thursfield retorted coldly: "You came forward in an interesting manner. It wasn't coming forward to the police as a witness to offer information; it came via this unusual source."

Herbert went further and accused her of withholding information about her sources.

Trina stood her ground. "You come into possession of extraordinary information – some very, very heavy stuff. What the hell do you do with it? There's a feeling of concern about the way the police investigation has been carried out in the past. So we don't rush with this information. It was chewed over for two years, because of our fear of things being brushed under the carpet. We wanted to give this information as public a hearing as possible. That's why we didn't come to you to start with."

A local peace campaigner, Pat Dymond, boldly pressed Thursfield about what he would ask MI5 if he did find evidence of involvement. He replied: "Somewhere along the line, you look them in the eye and form a judgement. If things have been destroyed ten years ago, we can go no further. You may say: 'We believe these highly trained James Bond people will run rings around us out here in the sticks, the police are out of their depth'… If we had been hoodwinked and bamboozled from the beginning, I wouldn't want to be up here in front of you talking like I am."

Dymond replied calmly: "It sounds as if you are agreeing with some of the points we have said. You said if the files have gone, there is nothing we can do about it." Thursfield did not respond.

Herbert, pressed about Don's role in the case, declared: "Dr Arnott presented these findings at the Hinkley C Inquiry in 1989. It did not have any mind-blowing repercussions – Dr Arnott is still sitting with us. So I would suggest it was of no real consequence. Indeed, the nuclear electric [sic] industry tell me that is not a fundamental flaw. It is something they are well aware of and it has been debated on many occasions." Don and I were dumbfounded. Herbert had missed the point. The danger for Don, and Hilda by association, had been *before* the reactor control rod problem had become public knowledge, and when Sizewell B had yet to receive planning approval.

Tony Ward of BBC Radio took up the point. "I would like to hear what Ed Radford from America has to say on that – and Don Arnott." Having helped Don raise the control rod problem in 1989 at the second public inquiry into a pressurised water reactor at Hinkley Point in Somerset, I had alerted the Three Mile Island Public Health Scientific Advisory Board about the issue. This US body was established to follow up unresolved health issues arising from the 1979 accident in Harrisburg, Pennsylvania. I had recently discovered that the Board's chairman, an American physician and expert on radiation health effects named Dr Edward Radford, was living in Surrey, married to an Englishwoman. I briefed him on the control rod issue.

Radford consulted his Board colleagues, enclosing a copy of a summary of the Hilda case by me. One of them wrote back to him how "we're all concerned" that this was the first they knew of the control rod alloy's low melting point, and asked: "What do we do now?" On the Hilda case, he commented:

> It's a hell of a story! I could believe it, after my experiences around Rocky Flats.

Rocky Flats was a US laboratory for developing nuclear energy. The Board wrote to the US Nuclear Regulatory Commission endorsing our concerns, but was rebuffed.

Radford's presence in the hall must have been an unpleasant surprise for Herbert. Speaking confidently, this tall, suave, silver-haired American explained how he reacted when I briefed him. "I was appalled. This was a dangerous situation in a PWR of the type that the Sizewell reactor became. I pursued it through the Three Mile Island committee. The reaction from colleagues was disbelief. They said nobody would be fool enough to put a rod like that in a PWR – they didn't believe me." He explained how I had pointed out to him that a description of the control rod alloy was in the official report on the Three Mile Island accident. The NRC's reply was scientifically incoherent, and did not really address the issues. "I conclude that the nuclear industry, as represented by the NRC in the US, which is supposed to be knowledgeable about these things, does have a problem with this."

Thrown onto the defensive, Herbert insisted that, as Don did not discuss the issue with Hilda, it could not have been connected with her murder. To this, Ward retorted: "But who knew that?" "But that's not the point," responded Herbert. Ward replied: "It is very much the point." He was alluding to my suspicion that the nuclear conspiracy motive came from an urgent Government need to neutralise anyone who might have discovered a problem with the Sizewell design, which Thatcher had been personally determined to introduce. MI5 spooks watching Don would have assumed he had told her. Moreover, they would have feared she would use her presentation at Sizewell to bounce the Inquiry with the control rod problem – or some other even more damaging revelation?

Bishop Davies invited Don to respond. He did not disappoint his now fascinated audience. "I didn't discuss control rods with Hilda Murrell... What I did know was that, at the very time that Hilda Murrell was meeting me, I was myself in the hot seat; and there is no doubt whatever that I was put out of the Inquiry. And the only possibility was that if the information about the control rods came out at Sizewell it could be damaging to the Inquiry; and so they wanted me out of the way..."

It was indeed a historic and unique event – but not in the way Thursfield had hoped. The police were powerless to investigate Dalyell's information that the Security Service had been involved. The conspiracy theories had survived, and the nuclear motive had been strengthened.

———— ∞∞ ————

The tenth anniversary prompted Judith Cook to write *Unlawful Killing*, her second book on the murder. In the final couple of pages, she revealed an extraordinary development. She had received her own independent corroboration, 'on the authority of a senior MI5 operative, now retired', of Dalyell's central claim of British intelligence involvement. According to her new source,

> ...accelerating panic over leaks of information to Tam Dalyell culminated on 19 March 1984, when the government was faced with a set of questions proving that he held precise information. As a result a special committee set up to look into leaks activated a series of urgent measures in a last-ditch attempt to track down the source and that every possibility was considered, however remote.

Shortly before she died of a heart attack in 2004, I learned that Cook, while researching Hilda's murder, was sent, unrequested and anonymously, the minutes of an emergency Cabinet meeting called to establish the source of a leak prompted by Dalyell's questions. She subsequently destroyed them.

Apparently, this secret meeting resulted in a number of searches being carried out including at Ravenscroft, where a freelance unit was used. Her source told her that because of the "ensuing mess", the unit's MI5 handler was "severely castigated". Cook's husband Martin Green was present at a social function in London when this man tipped her off. He recognised him as a former National Service colleague whom he knew as 'John'. Later they saw him on TV commenting anonymously about the secret services after a career in intelligence work. 'John' has since died.

CHAPTER 8

STALKER, SMITH AND INTIMIDATION

Liz and I divorced in 1992. Two years before, tennis elbow had forced me to stop thatching. Then I spoke out against nuclear weapons in the run-up to the first Gulf War in January 1991. This was traumatic, as I was the only ex-Royal Navy Commander with nuclear experience to have done so.

I found my niche in the anti-nuclear movement as chair of the British affiliate of an international campaign called the World Court Project. This challenged the legality of nuclear deterrence in the International Court of Justice at The Hague. When I attended the project launch in Geneva in May 1992, I met and was captivated by one of its New Zealand pioneers, Kate Dewes, whose husband had recently separated from her.

A teacher and veteran peace and environmental campaigner, back in the 1970s Kate opposed a failed attempt to build a nuclear power plant in New Zealand. She became involved in the Peace Squadron – flotillas of protest boats which had swarmed around visiting US nuclear armed and powered warships. Three months after Hilda's murder, David Lange was elected prime minister pledging to make New Zealand nuclear-free. Kate was involved in this political struggle. Friends of hers were lucky to escape unharmed when the Greenpeace flagship *Rainbow Warrior* was sunk in Auckland by French secret agents a year later. In 1988, she was a non-governmental adviser on the New Zealand government delegation to the Third United Nations Session on Disarmament. Her pioneering work on the World Court Project grew out of that extraordinary experience for a 35-year-old mother of three young daughters.

When I told her about Hilda, Kate instantly identified with her as a fellow woman campaigner against nuclear energy and weapons during the same period. Miraculously, I had found a soulmate who could cope with my 'baggage'.

Falling on my feet, with a new family and sanctuary, we were married in Christchurch, New Zealand in 1997. However, my anti-nuclear work and the need to care for my 88-year-old father required me to continue to live with him in Twyford, Berkshire for most of the next two years until his death.

Back in 1992, following my divorce I settled into my office bedroom upstairs in his modest home, the central third of a sub-divided former ancient coaching inn. He stoically put up with indications that the State security apparatus wanted to frighten him into discouraging my new work, with interruptions to his telephone and silent calls. Soon after I returned from meeting Kate in Geneva, a retired Wing Commander living in the front apartment took me aside. While he and his wife were going on holiday, "the police will be using our house as a stakeout for an undercover operation". Not long afterwards my new laptop crashed, mail was interfered with and my newly installed phone line started playing up. I assumed a bug had been placed in the wall of my room from the other side.

One night I returned from a meeting in London to find my father asleep in his armchair. On waking him, he enquired: "Did you return earlier? Before I dozed off, I heard footsteps in the corridor upstairs. I thought you'd not wanted to disturb me and gone straight up." Upstairs on the unpatterned fitted carpet I found a trail of bootprints of black grit from a flat roof outside my bedroom window. They began beside my desk, and stopped halfway along the corridor. One window pane beside the latch was shattered. Nothing seemed to be missing. Had my father woken, and cleared his throat noisily as he always did? There was no point in reporting it to the police. I was alarmed but not surprised when Kate reported her mail was being ripped open in her letterbox. With only phone or fax, we resorted to one line coded fax messages to communicate sensitive information.

⌘

John Stalker suddenly became elusive when I asked to meet him after his dramatic appearance at the tenth anniversary public meeting. On tracking him down to a Herefordshire hotel, he and his sidekick, ex-Detective Sergeant Rita Wilkinson, subjected me to an unpleasant grilling on film for almost an hour about my suspicions and unanswered questions. They ridiculed my understanding of the disputed condition of Hilda's telephone, ignored the arson attack on Fron Goch, my slashed tyre incident and Con Purser's experience on trying to make a new statement, and dismissed my hypothesis of an Ulster-style snatch squad and interrogation of Hilda in a safe house. In so doing they made a mockery of Stalker's initial invitation for those with controversial information to go to him.

At the beginning of the *Stalker Investigates* programme, broadcast nationwide in November 1994, the narrator emphasised that "the police gave Stalker and Wilkinson full access to the Murrell files". Later he pointed out they were also able to examine "scene of crime photos never before seen by anyone outside the police force". After Stalker's dismissive response to my information, I was surprised when he admitted I was "at the heart of this", because I had raised the nuclear motive with the police even before DCS Cole arrived at Hunkington.

The programme made several valuable points. The narrator described the first new finding as astonishing: "The body's rectal temperature was taken but with the wrong thermometer, so the estimated time of death is unreliable. Hilda Murrell could have died much nearer the time that she was found. So, how could such a big mistake have gone unnoticed?" Wilkinson explained: "The police surgeon arrives at 11.45 Saturday morning, certifies death at 12, takes a rectal temperature on a thermometer that only reads as low as 70 degrees F. So it's for a living person basically – it's not a chemical thermometer. You need a low reading [thermometer] for dead bodies. The ambient temperature is not taken. Five hours later, the pathologist attends." Stalker concluded the police and pathologist were therefore working with a flawed opinion. He explained the significance: "If the time of death was wrong, it could be that she hadn't actually arrived at the place where she finally died." He added that "this is bloody crucial – it means the difference between whether she was there or whether she wasn't".

This led Stalker to put ex-DCS Cole on the spot about Scott's crucial evidence that Hilda's body was not in the copse twenty-four hours after it should have been according to the police theory. Retired for four years, Cole struggled as he repeated the lame police line that the body was hidden in a dip in the ground and by undergrowth. He almost pleaded with Stalker to "bear in mind that eventually the body was found by gun dogs – it wasn't actually found by a person..." This was immediately undermined by police photographs of the body in situ. The narrator continued: "Could anyone have missed the corpse if it was here; and if it was not, was Stalker dealing after all with a conspiracy?"

What Cole may not have known was that Scott had told both John Osmond, producer of HTV's *Wales This Week* programmes, and his presenter, that his dogs were with him in the copse. Scott must have told the police this crucial fact, but it was omitted from his statement. His solicitor complained to a mutual friend that Scott came under pressure from the police to change his story. Was this why he was not called to testify at the inquest?

Years later I learned that a woman walked her dogs daily across the fields near the copse. On the Friday afternoon after the abduction, unusually her Airedale dog ran into the copse near where the body was found the next morning by the gamekeeper's dogs. Thinking her dog was after a rabbit, she called it back. This strongly suggested Hilda's body was there by then – which, according to pathologist Bernard Knight, would still have allowed time for hypostasis to have formed as found.

Stalker struggled to come up with a new scenario which avoided supporting any conspiracy, but which still fitted his support for Scott. He suggested the burglar made a controlled stop in the gateway leading to the hedge near where the hat, Hilda's spectacles and knife were found. Her assailant then frogmarched Hilda in an arm lock, stabbing her and leaving her for dead. Stalker added one accurate, if verbose, observation: "[Hilda] would have fought, she would have screamed, she would have struggled, this old lady – she didn't do anything she didn't want to do, this old lady, there's no way she would give up." He then speculated wildly that the panicking thief, having left her for dead, returned to the car, drove off, only to crash it 400 yards down the lane, and fled.

What about the car keys in Hilda's coat pocket? Did the attacker, after crashing the car, dash back and return them to Hilda? What about the police and pathologist's admission that the knife found near the hedge had not inflicted her wounds?

According to Stalker's scenario, Hilda then recovered enough to stumble or crawl along the hedge. Because of her confusion – and even that she might have caught sight of Scott in the far distance – she headed in the wrong direction towards the copse rather than the road. She reached the copse 24 hours later despite the cold weather, the heavy clay field, and crawling with a broken collar bone and multiple stab wounds. This ignored Acland's already implausible statement at the inquest that Hilda could have crawled only about a hundred yards.

The programme broadcast police video footage and photographs of the copse entrance they believed Hilda had used. This matched Acland's description as "just a foot wide and overgrown, with barbed wire across the opening". For an experienced detective like Stalker to suggest Hilda had found it and crawled through was outrageous.

Having asked whether Stalker was "dealing after all with a conspiracy", the programme ducked this despite the implausibility of his alternative theory. Yet when Stalker challenged Don Arnott about why Hilda might have been singled out by the nuclear industry, Don replied that "just at the time the heat was on me was the very time I was working with Hilda here. If they were gunning for me then they were gunning for anyone I was associating with… including most definitely her."

The West Mercia Police could take no comfort from Stalker's intervention.

The decision in 1985 not to publish at least an edited version of the Northumbria Report also backfired badly. Instead of dispelling the notion of conspiracy, it had the opposite effect. Pressure to publish was revived in 1994, but again the police stonewalled. They thought they had succeeded in keeping it under permanent wraps. They were wrong.

Two years later, in February 1996 a journalist working for a major national newspaper phoned me. He asked: "Are you expecting any developments in the Hilda Murrell case?" With six weeks to go before the twelfth anniversary, all was quiet. "OK, you'd better come and see me."

When we met discreetly in London, he handed me a large brown envelope. Inside were two original police files from Shrewsbury containing all the major incident reports during the search for Hilda; copies of both autopsy reports and the Northumbria Report; and a set of colour photographs of her body in the copse and the morgue I was briefly shown at the inquest. The person who delivered these to the journalist wished to remain anonymous, but particularly wanted me to see them. When I returned the files having copied them, I told the journalist they contained nothing sensational, and neither of us took further action.

Ten years on, by 2006 Kate and I had gleaned enough information from other sources to analyse the Northumbria Report in depth. We found that its 83 pages did contain some sensitive evidence, but minor censoring could have allowed publication of most of it. It attempted to clarify the known facts and evaluate all the speculation. Yet Assistant Chief Constable Peter Smith failed to address, or dismissed with his catch-cry of 'no shred of evidence', a number of key questions. On several issues he got facts wrong, and drew faulty conclusions.

In the paragraphs devoted to Judith Cook's allegations, Smith focused on the errors in her *New Statesman* article in November 1984. On the interference with her mail and phone, he noted she had not reported her concerns to British Telecom or the police, and she could not produce the damaged letters. In fact, when he and Hall interviewed her, she had not yet received the threatening phone calls specifically mentioning Hilda.

Smith took my concerns about my telephone more seriously. I had experienced many instances of phone interference since Hilda's murder, including bizarre crossed lines, cut-offs and silent calls. Smith reported that my fears "have been dispelled by a high-level inquiry at British Telecom" – yet the interference had, if anything, intensified.

Lieutenant-Commander Peter Hurst had told Smith he suspected the burglary of his flat and phone interference were linked with his Falklands War intelligence work, which had given him greater access to sensitive information than I had. Smith recorded Hurst had become so concerned that he reported the interference to his supervisor in Naval Security. Again, "inquiries at high levels in British Telecom" had found no basis for his fears.

The report claimed I had been "notified by the Shrewsbury Police" that Hilda was missing. This was not so. It also stated I had heard an "engaged", not "out of order", tone on phoning Fron Goch. Smith had obviously not thought through the different consequences. If I had heard an engaged tone, I would have assumed Hilda was there, and contacted a neighbour to check. It was Brian George who first reported the fault after hearing an 'out of order' tone on the Saturday morning, and alerted the police almost an hour before I learned Hilda was missing. The police file I received from the journalist had an extract from their telephone log noting the follow-up action:

> 09.40 Oswestry requested to check Fron Goch Bungalow,
> Penyfoel. Llanymynech 830131 (out of order).

According to Smith, the engineer who investigated the line found a "faulty electrode" in the protection unit at the bottom of the lane leading up to Fron Goch. The fault was "caused by lightning". Smith had checked, not with the

Meteorological Office, but with "an executive engineer employed by British Telecom at their Shrewsbury exchange" who kept "an overall weather picture" to help him explain varying fault rates. His records allegedly showed lightning activity "in Shrewsbury" on 27 March 1984, and "that it was also present in the area over the whole of the preceding week".

The nearest official weather observation site is at RAF Shawbury, 15 miles east of Llanymynech. The Met Office informed me that thunder was reported at Shawbury only on 27 March. So, if Smith had checked the official weather reports instead of relying on a BT executive, he would have found the fault was almost certainly *not* caused by lightning.

The engineer who repaired the faulty phone at Fron Goch agreed. In 2005, two of his colleagues informed me that he had told them only one electrode had failed. Had it been lightning, more would have been affected. The same fault could have been produced by hitting the electrode with a hammer. On 4 March 1985, *World in Action* broadcast the engineer's assessment. Two days later, he succumbed to police pressure and made a new statement agreeing with Smith's version.

The whistleblowing engineers also suspected an unauthorised intruder had been inside the Llanymynech exchange after normal working hours in the weeks before Hilda's death. The engineer who worked there was concerned enough to stretch "access telltales" – cotton threads – across the door which were subsequently disturbed by the mystery visitor several times. My informants had similar concerns at the Shrewsbury exchange. One commented that such behaviour was "very dodgy, because of the risk of unexpected callouts at any time". In those pre-digital days there were two ways of intercepting a telephone conversation: a technician employed by MI5 either broke into the target's property and planted a bug in the phone, or entered the exchange to install intercept equipment on the line.

The Northumbria Report stated there had been a "systematic and tidy search" of the house including purses and handbags, but "nothing is known to have been stolen". Smith concluded this was "indicative of a normal burglar looking for cash". Yet not only were jewellery and silver not touched, but Hilda's cheque book and bank card were left on the kitchen table. Was this really typical of a normal burglar? Smith also ignored the family's insistence that Hilda's current handbag, purse and document satchel were missing.

The report did not address whether any of Hilda's papers might have been taken.

On checking the nuclear papers in her house, I did not find two which she referred to in her diaries for 1983 and 1984. One was called 'Radiation Aspects of a Nuclear War in Europe' by Dr Patricia Lindop, and the other was a draft Sizewell submission by American radiation expert Dr Rosalie Bertell. Both papers discussed the genetic effects of radioactivity, among other sensitive issues. Why did Smith not interview Harry and Gladys Bury about this aspect? Was it because Gladys would have recounted her discovery of two bogus detectives trying to search their house? Smith also failed to mention, let alone comment on, an attempt to prise open with a crowbar the front panel of two kitchen window seats, on one of which Hilda kept most of her nuclear papers. The spaces inside were empty, but would have been obvious places to check in any search for documents, which could then have been removed.

To my amazement, Smith mentioned none of the twenty fingerprints I now know were found in the house. He only referred to the one on the inside of the rear window of Hilda's car. He commented:

> This mark still remains outstanding after a most exhaustive search eliminating 1200 suspects to date.

This was the only fingerprint found in the car. There were not even any prints left by Hilda. Why would Hilda's abductor have touched the inside of the rear window? Presumably, no prints were found in any of the obvious places in the vehicle, like the steering wheel, driver's and front passenger door, or keys? This strongly suggested that either the car had been cleaned of incriminating prints, or the driver and Hilda had worn gloves. Police photographs show that, while the wheels were clogged with mud, surprisingly there was no mud on the bodywork around them.

Later in the report, Smith helpfully listed all the eliminating factors used by the police:

> (a) Time of offence - between 12 noon and 2.30 p.m. Wednesday, 21st March, 1984
> (b) Sole Pattern - Training shoe (Rumanian make)
> (c) Fingerprint impression - inside of car
> (d) A natural aspermic or person having had vasectomy
> (e) Narrow bladed knife
> (f) Smokes Hamlet cigars
> (g) Drinks alcohol

The police examination of the footprint issue was incompetent. The lack of detail about a training shoe print under a chair in the kitchen and in front of the telephone was surprising. Police documents state that photographs "clearly showed the pattern and suggests a size around size nine". Several of Hilda's relations, including myself, and other visitors who had their fingerprints taken were never asked about their shoes – including David Williams and Mrs Latter, whose fingerprints were identified. The last two eliminating factors demonstrated the inadequacy of the investigation. The Hamlet cigar wrapper, found in the car, was inconsequential compared to all the other evidence available to the police, including fingerprints in the house. If they had asked me, I would have volunteered that a family member smoked them. However, they were completely ignoring anyone who, for example, might have returned to Ravenscroft after the abduction to turn on lights, draw curtains and leave the side door open.

On why the car keys had been found in Hilda's coat pocket, Smith speculated this suggested

> ...she was in the car when it left the road. It seems she tried to make good her escape with the keys across the fields in the direction of the coppice whilst the offender was attempting to free the vehicle...

Again, Smith had not thought this through. Witnesses who inspected the car said the driver's door was jammed into the bank. The only way out for the driver was via the passenger door – which would have meant clambering across while pushing Hilda out. The police argued a mudstained guidebook on birds, shoved under the front offside wheel, proved an attempt was made to drive off the verge. Cole told the inquest: "There were obvious signs that an effort had been made to move the vehicle after this minor accident." Both he and Smith failed to deduce that the driver must have got back into the car and restarted it. So was Hilda waiting patiently for the opportunity to steal the keys? Did Smith believe she could have got back into the car, stretched across to the ignition – assuming her right collar bone was not broken at this point – and grabbed them?

Such a farcical scenario points to the far higher probability that the keys were planted in a clumsy attempt to provide some circumstantial evidence that Hilda had been abducted in her own car. Just as nonsensical was Smith's supposition that Hilda would head for the distant copse across the field, instead of making for John Marsh's much nearer farmhouse which was clearly in view ahead of the Renault – or waving down a passing car?

The report confirmed the weapon used on Hilda was "a narrow bladed knife which has not been recovered". So why did Smith not criticise the police for claiming it was probably Hilda's large kitchen knife found near the copse? Smith also missed an important deduction, raising further significant questions: if the murderer already had a narrow bladed knife, then why did he take the kitchen knife? Or did someone else plant it?

Smith assumed Hilda died on the day she was abducted. His 'open mind' was clearly closed to the evidence that the time of death could have been as late as Friday – and Acland's public admission that this was a possibility. Unlike Stalker, Smith agreed with Cole that Scott must have been mistaken. Despite describing Scott as "intelligent and extremely alert for a man of 78 years", Smith decided he must have been looking up at the trees, not where he was walking. After reading Scott's statement, and seeing the police photographs of Hilda's body in the copse, Smith must have known this was specious grasping at straws. As Stalker undoubtedly realised, Scott's evidence was very damaging to the police line. Taken together with the bizarre abduction and changes to Ravenscroft, these strongly suggested not only a far more complicated crime, but professional involvement.

The Northumbria Report also defended the two police officers who failed to visit Hilda's home after inspecting the abandoned car. Yet in Smith's concluding remarks on the overall police response to Marsh's first report of the abandoned car, he contradicted himself by admitting

> ...it delayed the commencement of a murder enquiry for possibly two days, a period which the Police Service would accept from long experience as being the most crucial 48 hours in any Homicide enquiry.

Smith reserved his sharpest criticism for PC Paul Davies, who had visited Ravenscroft on the Friday evening but, despite finding the door open, lights on and knowing her car was crashed five miles outside Shrewsbury at Hunkington, had failed to raise the alarm. Nonetheless, he still relied on the constable's description of the house – kitchen curtains closed and lights left on – and implied this had been the case since the Wednesday. Why did Smith omit the highly significant evidence of the postman, milk lady, friends and neighbours that this was not so?

He failed to mention that the next morning PC Lane had been almost as incompetent. Not only had he not searched the house properly on his first visit at 7 am, but he left the side door open on leaving. At least Davies claimed he closed it. Lane also failed to notice the telephone had been disconnected – he had to have this pointed out to him by Brian George. It took a phone call by Dalyell to Smith to make him interview George.

The telephone controversy was given a great deal of attention in the report. This was hardly surprising. The whistleblowing incident following the refusal by the engineer to change his first statement about his examination of the Ravenscroft phone to agree with the police line that it had been ripped out was almost certainly the trigger for Cozens to instigate the Northumbria review. *So why did neither Smith nor Stalker interview him?* Instead, when Stalker interviewed me he tried to make a fool of me on camera, ridiculing Brian George's concerns and showing me police photographs of the phone I had never seen before.

Smith reported the Scene of Crime Unit had

> ...established that another cable not in use, which had been part of the original installation, had obviously been wound around, folded over and tucked into the junction box.
>
> The live cable was made up of four inner wires each fitted with an open ended spade connector. These two cables, old and live, had been **stapled side by side onto adjacent woodwork** and were both in a convenient position to have been ripped out together in one aggressive action. (my emphasis added)

Twenty-one years later, I was able to show this to Christopher Mileham, the engineer who had carried out a detailed inspection on the Monday following the murder. He said it did not make sense. There were not two 'cables'; there was one cable and one cord. A redundant, cream-coloured cable led from the junction box to an extension which was once installed in another part of the house. A thicker cord connected the junction box to the telephone. Mileham emphasised that at the time he often saw the damage caused by the receiver cord being pulled out of such a junction box, usually by workers tripping over the cord.

Smith was determined to ram his interpretation home:

> It would seem that the most obvious way to quickly disconnect the breakfast room telephone from inside, would be to wrench the two cables away from the junction box severing any connection the operative line may have had. Both were hung close together and could be grasped and pulled out with one hand. This sort of treatment would force away the staples supporting the cables to the window surrounds, which is what happened.

Those final four words are evidence of Smith manufacturing fact from speculation.

Mileham had several concerns about the police photograph of the phone, which Stalker used to discredit Brian George's story and wrong-foot me. When I showed a copy to him, he said: "It wasn't like that when I checked it." In the photo both the cord and cable were lying across the window seat, with the four wires at the end of each clearly visible disconnected from the junction box. Mileham was adamant that when he saw it, the cream cable was still stapled to the wall around the end of the seat – if it had not been, he would have mentioned this in his report. He explained that the dark grey receiver cord "was never stapled" – it was always left loose, otherwise the telephone would have had to stay in the same place.

In light of Mileham's disturbing response, were these photographs taken after he left Ravenscroft having examined the telephone? On reading the typed copy of his police statement I had handed to him, Mileham wanted to check it against his original handwritten report – which was held by the police, or had been destroyed.

The Northumbria Report offered this explanation for Smith's conclusion:

> Such force would have applied pressure to the grommet surrounding the operative cable on its entry to the junction box. In support of this a broken piece from the entry aperture to the box was found on the window seat below. This type of force could well be expected to pull the spade terminals from under the screws without damaging them as was the case. This would leave the four holding screws loose which is what happened, giving rise to speculation that they had been manually turned.

Mileham was stunned to read this. He was certain the junction box was undamaged. Bakelite pieces broken off the box opening were well-known indicators that the cable had been yanked out, so he had specifically looked for them. Had he found any, he would have recorded this. The police had not mentioned this to him: was that because a piece had not yet broken off?

Mileham added: "This was a deliberate unscrewing. The yank from pulling out wires would not cause unscrewing." A loose screw risked a poor connection, causing malfunction and noise on the line. If a phone cord was pulled out, the wires almost invariably broke at their weakest spot, the connection with each spade terminal – which would be left undamaged and still under each screw.

Soon after Derek Woodvine broke the telephone story on TV in March 1985, Mileham came under outrageous police pressure, led by Assistant Chief Constable Drew himself, to agree that the telephone had been "ripped out". After refusing to buckle, he was left with the strong impression that "my view was not one that the police were comfortable with." Was this another reason why the police did not publish the report, and neither Smith nor Stalker interviewed him, in order to avoid Mileham's potentially disastrous complaint of misrepresentation and implied manipulation of evidence? Apparently, a British Telecom colleague told Woodvine that the card for that job had disappeared.

Smith volunteered one other over-confident, unwise observation:

> If the theory of a well trained Government Intelligence officer is considered, then the cutting of telephone wires is the most usual method adopted by professionals in pre-conceived situations.

On the contrary, unless MI5 had decided to telegraph that it was responsible, their agents would have taken enormous care to avoid leaving any evidence that this was their work.

Both Smith and Stalker had access to all the witness statements. It took me until 2009 to discover the full extent of evidence that the appearance of the house had changed between the Wednesday and Friday, and of suspicious activity around Ravenscroft and the copse. Why had two such senior and experienced detectives, let alone their West Mercia colleagues, ignored all this?

Only towards the end of his report did Smith start to ask the right questions:

> The following events are probably the most difficult to understand. Why take her from the house and expose himself to the risk of being identified? Did she know or recognise him? Did she think she was being taken for medical treatment? Who dressed her and considering the circumstances, why was she wearing a hat?

What happened was indeed difficult to understand. What became utterly implausible was trying to make the facts fit the theory that the killer was a lone bungling burglar. That last question, for example, was a good one: it pointed to the likelihood that her car would be recognized as Hilda's, and witnesses would assume it was her – but the hat concealed the wearer's face.

Curiously, Smith's most helpful conclusion in his entire report was his final sentence. It would undoubtedly have been seized on by the media had it been published:

> However, this is only an opinion which in no way should dampen the appetite to follow up speculation.

Here was the first acknowledgement that the police could have been wrong. Publication of his report would merely have fuelled further speculation, and risked exposing his collaboration with West Mercia Police to try to make some of the facts fit their theory. Its errors, omissions, misrepresentations and sweeping assumptions would have reinforced, not repaired, West Mercia's damaged image. Was this why it was shelved?

Nine years later, Stalker used his proven detective skills from Ulster to expose the outrageous refusal by Cole to accept that Scott had been right.

———— ∞ ————

After my father died in 1999, I sold his house and formally emigrated to New Zealand. In due course, a container of belongings arrived in Christchurch, including my archive on the Hilda case. The removal man gave a baffled shrug when I insisted he squeeze a slashed car tyre between the legs of my father's old piano.

Within days of unpacking, I received a letter from the *Shropshire Star*, forwarded by West Mercia Police. Deanna Delamotta, the new Woman's Editor, wanted an update on the case and my situation. Wondering what had prompted this and when her article might appear, I emailed her some notes.

Two months later, Kate and I returned from several weeks working overseas to disturbing news. During our absence a young woman, who had recently started working for us, stayed downstairs in our house with two of Kate's teenage daughters sleeping upstairs. She described what happened:

> One morning early on I woke to find the back door wide open. I had been sure I had locked it the night before, so felt a bit guilty for my apparent oversight. That night I paid special attention to securing the back door before going to bed; yet the following morning it was wide open again. This left me feeling sick…
>
> I didn't want to worry the girls, but needed to check if they had been coming in and out of the back door at all during the night - they assured me they had not. This left me feeling quite anxious at night and a lot more sensitive to movements in the house…
>
> During one night I rose to go to the toilet. There were

> heavy drapes at the end of the hallway that I needed to
> pass through to get to the bathroom... I froze: there was
> breathing and a definite shape in the drapes as I approached.
>
> I scuttled back to the bedroom and convinced myself
> that I was being silly. Despite my vigilance, the back
> door was unlocked again but not wide open.
>
> It was on one of these mornings that, on entering the
> living room, I found Hilda's chair and a table lying on
> its side under the window and everything that was on it
> placed around: very strange...

Hilda's kitchen chair was one of the few antiques I had kept from Ravenscroft. Kate's daughter Lucy also saw the upturned furniture as she walked past the living room that morning. She thought it particularly odd because the table legs were right up against the wall below the window, which could not be opened because of corrosion. Ornaments and plants had been carefully moved onto a nearby couch and the floor. In an adjoining front room, the girls found a window slightly open and newly hung curtains partly pulled off their hooks. An intruder must have tried to make a quick escape, and after failing to open the window in the living room, fled into the front room, swinging on the curtains on his way out.

Kate could immediately tell her office and other rooms had been meticulously searched. Nothing seemed to have been taken. Before we left, we had removed sensitive documents to a safe location. Nevertheless, my stomach churned. I had long feared my new family would not be immune from harassment. It was therefore a huge relief and comfort when Kate, her daughters and our assistant all angrily expressed their determination not to be intimidated. On the contrary, they redoubled their commitment to support me in my pursuit of the truth.

Delamotta's centre-page feature article had appeared on 12 October, complete with a large recent photo of me. Her account was remarkably accurate, broadly covering my latest position on the murder which had not been in print before. The break-ins had begun soon after its appearance in the *Shropshire Star*.

Apart from ongoing interference with our mail, we had no further trouble for a year, when Kate and I had to go overseas again. Lucy was no longer living at home, but decided spontaneously to visit and stay the night before our departure. She was alone in the house after we left at 5 am:

> I heard the lounge sliding doors opening and closing
> downstairs. At first I wasn't alarmed until I checked my
> watch and realised it was 7 am, and it wasn't Mum and Rob
> moving around downstairs. Because I hadn't heard my parents
> leave in the morning I didn't want to worry in case their

flight had been delayed. I went to school and then emailed
my Mum and Rob to ask them: their flight had been on time.

When we returned home we found nothing apparently missing, but drawers in the lounge had been rifled through and our family photograph albums damaged. After these incidents, we assumed our house had been bugged. Slowly we became resigned to the irksome, irritating discipline of never discussing sensitive issues in our home.

CHAPTER 9

COLD CASE REVIEW

Tony Blair's landslide victory in May 1997 had one unexpected outcome: for the first time Shrewsbury elected a Labour MP, Paul Marsden. Unknown to me, he took advantage of the fact that, after eighteen years of Tory rule, Britain had a Labour Home Secretary.

With encouragement from Tam Dalyell, Marsden wrote to Jack Straw asking him what the Home Office knew about the Hilda Murrell case. His frustration and suspicions grew when he was referred back to the West Mercia Chief Constable.

Soon after the 15th anniversary in March 1999, Dalyell – now a veteran backbencher – argued that revolutionary advances in DNA forensic techniques provided grounds for re-opening the moribund case. A year later, Straw agreed to meet a persistent Marsden. In support, Dalyell asked in a Parliamentary question whether evidence had been referred to the DNA Centre in Birmingham. Straw admitted it had.

Marsden reported all this to me at our first meeting in July 2000 in the House of Commons. He also gave me a copy of a five-page Home Office brief on the case, written by officials for Straw. It included the following statements:

- The Government at the time stated categorically that the allegations of Security Service involvement were without foundation.
- The Security Service does not kill people or arrange their assassinations. Not now, not at the time of Mrs [sic] Murrell's death.

The final paragraph of a background note revealed a major development in the police investigation (my emphasis added):

West Mercia advise that the case has remained open, being subject to regular review. In particular the forensic evidence is being reviewed, using the Forensic Science Service's procedure of **"cold case review"**. The exhibits from the case are currently with the Forensic Science Service for further tests. These were previously referred for review in the early 1990s when it was attempted, unsuccessfully, to develop DNA from the samples in the police's possession...

Anger welled up in me on reading this. While I was grateful to both MPs for ferreting it out, yet again West Mercia Police had failed to inform Hilda's family.

⸺ ∞ ⸺

Nearly a year later, on a visit to Britain, I contacted Marsden. It was a serendipitous phone call: the next day he was to meet Detective Superintendent John Cashion, Senior Investigating Officer of the Cold Case Review. Marsden suggested I go instead; and a surprised DS Cashion agreed to see me.

This was my first meeting with the police for eight years; and I had never been to West Mercia's headquarters in Hindlip Hall near Worcester. Cashion explained that an experienced team of detectives and forensic experts was being assembled, and no theory would be excluded. The review would involve much more than re-testing forensic exhibits for DNA. First, all written records of the case would be transferred onto a new computerised investigation system.

In 2002, on the 18th anniversary of Hilda's abduction, Kate and I had a progress meeting at West Mercia HQ with Cashion and DC Partridge. Involved in the investigation since 1985, Partridge was now its 'walking memory'. We were allowed to view police colour photographs of Hilda's house and car, and her body in the copse and mortuary. We read both autopsy reports, and the suppressed 1985 Northumbria Police Report. I did not reveal that I already had copies.

In a long and intensive discussion, Kate emerged as a serious new contributor. She raised searching new questions and perceptive suggestions about the forensic evidence, and made observations totally missed by the police. The meeting again ended amicably. After the years of suspicion and refusal to discuss my findings, I felt we had made a significant breakthrough.

⸺ ∞ ⸺

While we were in the UK, alarming reports appeared posing new questions about the safety of Sizewell B. It was the first, and still only, pressurised water reactor (PWR) built in Britain – on Thatcher's orders despite the narrowly avoided catastrophic failure of this US nuclear power plant design at Three Mile Island in 1979.

In 1988, following the 1986 Chernobyl disaster, I had taken up Hilda's anti-nuclear energy torch when a public planning inquiry was announced into the second British PWR. This was to be built at Hinkley Point, on the Bristol Channel coast some 35 miles upwind of my home in Dorset. Having registered as an independent local objector, I used most of Hilda's modest bequest to me to bring a brilliant former US Navy nuclear engineer, Dr Richard Webb, to be my expert witness. He had been in Admiral Hyman Rickover's elite team who designed the prototype PWR extrapolated from the propulsion system for the first nuclear submarine *USS Nautilus*. Dr Webb challenged the entire safety case. Thereby, he helped extend the Hinkley Point C Inquiry by over a month. It was then overtaken by Thatcher's plan to privatise the electricity industry, which destroyed the economic case for any more PWRs like Sizewell

B. Effectively, we helped stop Hinkley Point C. In 2010 history was repeated when the government announced a major programme of new nuclear power plants, including one at Hinkley Point. Yet little progress had been made to improve their safety or economic efficiency, and there was still no solution to the radioactive waste problem.

On 29 March 2002, the Wolverhampton *Express & Star* made the connection with Hilda in a feature article headed 'Sizewell and a murder puzzle'. Recalling an earlier, award-winning *exposé* in 1993, it reported:

> This week, nine years later, safety at Sizewell has been dramatically called into question. A similar reactor in America has been closed down because of unexpected corrosion in the main pressure chamber.

A routine four-yearly inspection of the Davis-Besse reactor near Toledo, Ohio, revealed leaking boric acid had eroded a hole 'about the size of a brick' through the six-inch thick, heavy carbon steel lid of the container for the reactor core. Only the lid's three eighths of an inch thick stainless steel liner, bulging up into the hole under 2,000 pounds per square inch water pressure, had kept the radioactive coolant from spewing into the reactor building in a potentially catastrophic accident like Chernobyl.

Ironically, the leak was from a tank installed as a result of the Three Mile Island accident. This was designed to inject the neutron-absorbing acid into the core's cooling water in the event of failure of the control rods to shut down the reaction.

Six million Americans lived within a radius of a hundred miles of the Davis-Besse plant. This lucky escape was another warning about the safety problems of nuclear reactors, and particularly of PWRs. The article added that the UK Health and Safety Executive refused to discuss its implications. The British nuclear industry was still determined to hide the dangers from the British public.

It took two years for West Mercia Police to announce that a Cold Case Review was underway. *The Guardian* reported in April 2002 that the police hoped

> ...fresh forensic analysis of material found on Ms Murrell's clothes and a review of other evidence, including unmatched fingerprints and casts of a footprint, might finally lead to her killer.

Soon after, Cashion retired early. The review continued under DCI Jim Tozer, who accepted my challenge to visit us in New Zealand for two weeks to examine my archive.

This forced me to brief Kate fully about it. Fortunately, she relished plunging into my boxes of old files, posing many more fresh questions from the point of view of an experienced woman anti-nuclear campaigner. Her rigorous research techniques, honed while writing her doctorate, and her proficient touch-typing enormously enhanced our preparation. Our list of questions became the agenda for the British detectives' visit, and Kate kept a record of all our meetings.

One of my aims was to achieve some healing and reconciliation with the police after over fifteen years' estrangement. As Hilda's representative, I wanted to help lay her murder to rest. To do this I had to challenge the police negligence and flaws in their theory, and brief them on various attempts to intimidate me, my family, and witnesses who had come forward with inconvenient information. Our intention was to make the review a more worthwhile exercise by pooling information and intellectual resources.

Tozer, who brought DC Partridge with him, was a generation younger than his predecessor. In his early thirties, his easy, urbane manner was pleasantly surprising, and he was clearly high-calibre. Over a dinner in our home to welcome them, Tozer declared a personal ambition to solve the Hilda Murrell case.

For our first formal meeting, we borrowed a local barrister's house. This had the desired effect of raising the awareness of both detectives about the constraints under which we lived, courtesy of the British Security Service. I began by airing my grievances about the handling of the case. I requested, and later received, three written apologies from Tozer on behalf of the West Mercia Police. First, for their failure to act more quickly during the first three days when Hilda was missing. Second, for the sudden release of her body after keeping it for four months for unexplained reasons. And third, for the brusquely hostile response from the coroner during my correspondence with him over the long-delayed inquest.

The first agenda item was to 'introduce sensitive material'. Both detectives looked suitably startled as we produced copies of the Northumbria Report and two Shrewsbury police files. Tozer considered asking us to hand them over, but then acknowledged I had kept quiet since receiving them six years earlier. In return, we gave them copies of some missing documents from their files.

My next exhibit was the slashed car tyre from the 1986 incident outside Don Arnott's home, still sporting a label from the Home Office Forensic Laboratory in Swansea. Partridge helpfully revealed his father had been a tyre specialist. After he and Tozer reluctantly performed passable comparisons with 'doubting' St Thomas as they fingered the cuts, I had the satisfaction of hearing two detectives at last accept the tyre had indeed been slashed.

I reiterated my concerns about the January 1985 arson attack on Hilda's weekend retreat Fron Goch; and the unacceptable behaviour of the police after Con Purser asked to make another statement in 1986. I described how the attempted conviction four years later of David McKenzie sustained and deepened my alienation from the police, and caused me to team up with Dalyell.

For the rest of the detectives' visit, we met each working day at a discreet neutral location. We were treated as ex-officio members of the review team, and made a significant contribution. Together we watched some of the police videotapes of Moat Copse and Hilda's house, discussing them in detail. We showed them my copy of Andrew Fox's 1989 CTV documentary, pulled for spurious reasons and never shown. They agreed it presented a balanced view of the possibilities, and should have been broadcast.

We went through my hypothesis regarding the conspiracy theories, focusing on how the nuclear and *Belgrano* motives overlapped; the political climate at the time; and Don Arnott's concern about the Sizewell reactor control rod design. I explained the significance of Dalyell's 19 March 1984 letter to Heseltine as a trigger for MI5 to be let off the leash against Hilda. We discussed the possibility of false trails from planted evidence, and how the police would inevitably have to follow them; and the disputed condition of the telephones at both of Hilda's homes. Finally, I challenged Tozer to review the evidence of Laurens Otter that Hilda had phoned him from a callbox on the morning of 21 March 1984 asking him to meet to receive sensitive documents from her. The two detectives even confirmed that anonymous tip-offs, some of which I divulged to them, were permissible as evidence in court.

The discussions went smoothly until a wrap-up session. Suddenly, Tozer casually speculated that the damage to my tyre could have been done before I left Dorset on the four-hour drive to Don. Something in me snapped. Outraged, I exploded back at him: "So, that would have been attempted murder! You mean they didn't just kill Hilda – they were out to get me as well?"

Shocked by my outburst, Tozer tried to soothe me, suggesting I was "still suffering from post-traumatic stress". Having never seen me in such a state, Kate demanded that they let me express the full extent of my pent-up anger and sense of betrayal to them as representatives of the British State. My relief at this opportunity to release these deeply held emotions was mixed with amazement that they were still so strong. It was also cathartic that the police were at last having to listen to me.

As this final session drew to a close, I requested a favour. I showed them examples of our mail, especially from Britain, which had obviously been intercepted and opened. We explained that skilled intruders had searched our house on several occasions without apparently taking anything. "Jim, could you ask your New Zealand colleagues to arrange for our house to be swept?" Tozer thought for a moment, then replied smoothly: "Ah, Rob: that could be a problem. If there are bugs and they are state of the art, they won't find them. If they're not, and they do find them, do you want another break-in?"

Eight months later, I could not let go my shock, disappointment and a sense of deep foreboding on hearing from Tozer that Andrew George, the teenage truant, had been arrested. After all I had discovered about the case, the hopes built up and huge resources poured into the Cold Case Review, I found Tozer's attempted assurance that "we can make it fit the facts" difficult to accept, and a sinister portent.

———— ⌘ ————

Slipping back into a well-worn routine, I made my own enquiries. Andrew George had been born in Shrewsbury, the middle of three brothers. Aged two, four and five when their parents had abandoned them, they had grown up in local authority homes or with foster families.

A Shropshire journalist sent me details of all George's court appearances until his last offence in 1997. Involved in a few minor burglaries, drunken fighting after football matches, and possession of drugs or stolen goods, each time he had been quickly caught and admitted his guilt. He had never been imprisoned. Nonetheless, with George's semen found on the underslip on Hilda's body and his fingerprints in her house, his chances of proving his innocence looked poor. Yet his description bore no resemblance to the driver of Hilda's car.

Following George's arrest, Tozer reluctantly handed responsibility for the investigation to the senior West Mercia detective covering operations in the Shrewsbury area, DCI Mick Brunger. Brunger phoned to warn me that all evidence was being reviewed again by a team of 70 detectives. Miscarriages of justice in the 1980s had prompted a requirement to disclose all relevant evidence to the defence, in order to avoid any 'ambushes' during the trial. Accordingly, for three weeks in February 2004, we hosted meetings with two detective sergeants and George's solicitor as they trawled through my archive. The latter showed interest in my conspiracy theories, and even discussed having me as a defence witness.

Two weeks later in Shrewsbury, we mingled with Hilda's friends gathering in the Shropshire Wildlife Trust carpark for the 20th anniversary field trip on 19 March 2004. Suddenly, a maroon car drove up festooned with handwritten posters protesting 'My Brother Is Innocent'. Andrew George's younger brother Adrian wanted to speak to me. Kate intercepted him: "Let's talk in Court on Monday." He relented. Two days before, we had been angered on hearing for the first time at a briefing from Brunger that Andrew George was to appear in Birmingham Crown Court, twenty years to the day after Hilda had been abducted.

On 21 March 2004 in Birmingham Crown Court, Kate and I watched him plead not guilty to abducting and murdering Hilda Murrell. We sat in the public gallery, surrounded by members of his family. When George stood up in the witness box, we were struck by his height: he was still scarcely more than five feet tall – almost five inches shorter than Hilda. Staring up pathetically at us and the parents he hardly knew, I tried to imagine how unthreatening he must have looked as a 16-year-old boy.

Immediately after the hearing, Adrian spoke with Kate for nearly half an hour as the police and I watched anxiously. He was adamant Andrew was innocent, and could prove it: he could not drive in 1984, and still had no licence.

CHAPTER 10

THE TRIAL

In another creepy coincidence, on the 21st anniversary of Hilda's abduction, and exactly a year after Andrew George pleaded not guilty in a court in Birmingham, Kate and I sat in the main court in Stafford's modern Combined Court Centre for a preliminary murder trial hearing before Justice Sir Richard Wakerley. Staffordshire's county capital, some thirty miles east of Shrewsbury, was chosen so that a jury would be less likely to have been influenced by media coverage of the crime.

As representatives of Hilda's family, we were seated in the well of the court looking across the barristers to the jury. The detectives responsible for assembling the prosecution evidence were literally breathing down our necks behind us. Andrew George would sit behind a bullet-proof glass screen only five yards to our left, beneath the public gallery.

Richard Latham QC, leading the prosecution team, had arranged for slim computer monitors to be installed. Tall, suavely handsome and confident, he was a barrister in his prime. He had established an English electronic precedent in his previous case, a high-profile trial where a Cambridgeshire school caretaker, Ian Huntley, had been convicted for murdering two girl pupils.

Kate apparently also made a little English juridical history by being granted permission to transcribe proceedings on her laptop. I had written to the Judge requesting this after discovering only audiotapes were now kept of trials, and a transcript would cost us around £10,000. Besides, I needed to be free to observe proceedings. Justice Wakerley, an archetypical Judge looking ten years older than his 63 years, noted with amusement that Kate was already quietly chronicling his words. Then he cleared her request with Latham and Andrew George's barrister, Anthony Barker QC.

———⌘———

Before proceedings resumed on Wednesday 6 April 2005, there was a traditional ceremony to mark the opening of the Spring Term of the High Court in Stafford.

Her Majesty's High Court Judge, Sir Richard Wakerley, resplendent in long wig, red robes, black breeches and silk stockings, led a procession into the handsomely mediaeval Collegiate Church of St Mary. An organ introit by Elgar was followed by a hymn, confessional prayers and then an Old Testament reading by Lord Francis Stafford, the High Sheriff of Staffordshire.

His Chaplain read the Gospel and delivered the sermon, before the main prayers. I found three of them relevant for their irony:

"We pray for the High Court of Parliament and all who hold positions of power and authority in this land: for the upholding of freedom and truth and all who work for the common good.

"We pray for all the Judges and Magistrates, Barristers and Solicitors, the Police and the Probation and Prison services and all who administer the law, that they may be people of wisdom, courage and compassion.

"We remember before God all who have suffered injustice; those whom our society and our institutions have failed; all who are vulnerable, in need or in trouble in our communities and to whom we have a duty of compassion and care."

After another hymn and blessing, the service ended with the National Anthem. The congregation remained standing while the procession of civic dignitaries, church leaders and senior police officers emerged into the spring sunshine and followed Wakerley along a path lined by soldiers of the Staffordshire Regiment to the Court Centre. Eerily timed, this pageant flaunted the power of the British State. In light of what we had uncovered about Hilda's case – let alone what was to come – it exposed the deep, cynical hypocrisy of its representatives and their faithful servants.

❦

An 'abuse of process' hearing requested by the defence began on 6 April with a statement by Barker. He argued that a fair trial was not possible because of the length of time since the crime. Also, in 1984 the police eliminated Andrew George as a suspect because the fingerprints did not match, and they were looking for a much bigger, older man as the car driver. Footprints found in Hilda's kitchen were about size 9, yet the accused had size 6 feet at the time. A police replica of the footprint had been lost. Barker cited an independent expert's report that, contrary to the police view, it was possible to match George's fingerprints in 1984; and Latham did not challenge this.

While summing up, Wakerley read out a startling, brief new defence case statement by Andrew George which had just been handed to him. George now admitted burgling Hilda's house on 21 March 1984. His new defence was that he followed his older brother Stephen to the house with a view to stealing money, and found him in the kitchen attacking Hilda. Stephen dragged her upstairs to a bedroom and tried to rape her. Meanwhile, the defendant went into another bedroom to burgle it, before joining Stephen who also tried masturbating an unwilling and shocked Andrew. Stephen then forcibly abducted Hilda in her car. Andrew took no part in the abduction or killing, remaining in Ravenscroft. Later he returned to the local authority home, Besford House, where he was living.

We were shocked. Until then we had expected his defence team to run with some of the conspiracy theories. Why had Andrew changed his story at the last moment? The prosecution objected to the new defence case statement, but Wakerley ruled that justice could still be done. Andrew George would stand trial for Hilda's abduction and murder.

Now, all the defence had to establish beyond doubt was that Andrew George was not the driver of Hilda's car, so he could not have abducted and then murdered her. However, most of the prosecution's problems had fallen away. Latham could stick doggedly to the original police line, and attempt to discredit witnesses who argued the driver looked nothing like Andrew or Stephen because both were small and scrawny teenagers.

Over the next five weeks, we became increasingly frustrated by both sides as the list lengthened of key questions that were not being raised. The trial was a harsh demonstration that the adversarial English criminal system is about winning or losing a case, not uncovering the truth.

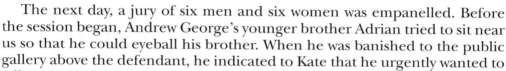

The next day, a jury of six men and six women was empanelled. Before the session began, Andrew George's younger brother Adrian tried to sit near us so that he could eyeball his brother. When he was banished to the public gallery above the defendant, he indicated to Kate that he urgently wanted to talk again. Over a late lunch in the empty Court Centre cafe, he apologised for his behaviour the year before – because now he believed Andrew was guilty.

Not long before their father Harold died, Adrian took him to visit Andrew in prison. When Harold demanded the truth, Andrew confirmed he had been in the house. He said he had disturbed two men who held guns to his head and threatened to kill him. They told him that if he kept his mouth shut he would be paid £60,000. The money never came – so Adrian did not believe this account. At their previous meeting, Adrian told Kate his brother could not drive. Now, after being challenged by the police on this, he had changed his mind. Apparently, his older brother Stephen was unaware that Andrew was trying to frame him until the *Shropshire Star* man phoned him the previous night about what was said in court. As the trial unfolded, we noticed Adrian was often smoking outside with a leading detective from the investigation team.

The start of the trial coincided with the funeral of the Pope, and Prince Charles marrying Camilla. We were relieved when celebrity media coverage almost forced the trial off the front page of the *Shropshire Star*.

As the opening presentation for the prosecution began, the screens filled with an attractive colour photograph of Hilda I had not seen before. Latham turned to the jury and told them: "The victim in this crime was Hilda Murrell, who was murdered on 21 March 1984." I glanced at Kate, who also realised he was restricting her time of death to the first day. He described how Hilda was a well-known native of Shrewsbury who "studied French history at Oxford University in 1927". We grimaced at each other at this flawed attempt to flaunt his knowledge of Hilda's academic background. Her Cambridge degree was in English, modern and mediaeval languages, and French. Our reactions prompted a reprimand from the Judge to us via the police for showing body language in front of the jury! No doubt he was aware we probably knew too much about the case. We responded by respectfully asking that Wakerley and the QCs pronounce Murrell correctly, with emphasis on the first syllable. He duly apologised, and directed the court to comply. Such simple errors of fact undermined our confidence that the truth would emerge. As further inaccuracies followed, we resorted to squeezing each other's knees or scribbling notes. Everyone else seemed free to express their emotions, including the Judge, barristers and defendant! Also, we learned to shield our notes after a young police officer brazenly tried to correct Kate's spelling on her laptop.

Hilda's photo was replaced by an aerial shot of Shrewsbury followed by one of Ravenscroft. The court heard about her trip to the bank and supermarket, and then the police theory on how the defendant attacked and abducted her, leaving her to die in Moat Copse. Without warning, she was on the large screens again – as a corpse sprawled in the copse. As Latham described Hilda's clothing, a police officer held up each item, including her slip, bearing a watery brown stain, the lingering residue of blood, and a hole where a sample had been cut off for DNA analysis. Then Hilda's naked cadaver was shown on the mortuary slab. Sickened, I turned away while a detailed, illustrated lecture proceeded about her stab wounds and bruises. The jurors were told they needed to see the images, which according to Latham were "sad and unpleasant – not horrid".

At every opportunity he dwelt on the sexual angle. "There was no physical sexual damage – that doesn't mean to say there was no sexual activity… She was wearing no skirt, no knickers, no suspender belt…". He was relentlessly building a picture of a brutal and perverted killer. However, he claimed that:

- Hilda apparently died five to ten hours after her abduction – despite the fact that it may have been as much as 36 hours.
- She crawled around Moat Copse – although she had a broken clavicle and hyoid bone as well as multiple stab wounds.
- The car driver was only seen fleetingly – when in fact several witnesses had a clear view of him, some twice.
- The defendant attacked Hilda in her home, where she was "seriously injured" – yet no blood was found there or even in the car.
- "Without her glasses, Hilda could not see more than a metre in front of her" – not so: she only needed them for reading and driving.
- The telephone cable was "torn away" from the junction box.

Latham stated the police went into Ravenscroft on the Saturday morning, omitting to mention PC Davies' visit the previous evening. He warned the jury to "put conspiracy theories to the back of your minds. Don't allow yourself to be contaminated by them; they are speculative, and merely tell you more about those putting them forward". However, Latham revealed that, among several contradictory claims, Andrew George had told his partner of six years during an early prison visit in 2003: "This is bigger than the Shrewsbury police".

The first evidence concerned the abduction. The prosecution described how George Lowe met Hilda shopping and later saw her turning into Sutton Road. However, no-one pointed out she had clearly been somewhere else. Four statements were read out from women who saw Hilda wearing a wide-brimmed floppy hat. The fact that the Totes rain hat found in the hedge was quite different, and not recognised by close friends and family as Hilda's, was not mentioned.

The witnesses who were called all testified that the man they saw driving Hilda's car bore no resemblance to a 16-year-old Andrew George. The prosecution's response was to try to show that these witnesses may have been confused. Rosalind Taylerson, who had two of the best views of the driver, was the only witness to be shown a picture of Andrew George aged 16, under cross-examination by Barker. To George's visible relief, she was adamant he was not the driver.

Retired PC Robert Eades recounted his response to reports of an abandoned car in Hunkington Lane with his colleague, PC Davies. Eades described how he discovered the body in the copse the following Saturday. He admitted he also saw Hilda's clothing on the ground. Nothing was said about the crucial issue that Ian Scott had apparently missed both this and her body.

The trial turned to medical and forensic evidence with Dr Peter Acland first to take the stand. Latham prefaced his cross-examination by declaring: "There is no dispute about what is in the findings". By this he meant the defence was not challenging anything in the pathologist's autopsy report. Barker raised very few of the anomalies in the evidence because he was focusing primarily on what happened in the house.

Acland had grown more cautious over the years. Unlike at the inquest, he now acknowledged the imprecision of his science. Latham shrewdly built on this, to the point where he obtained his agreement that the ability to pin down time of death from examination of rigor mortis and hypostasis was a myth, especially in cold weather. Acland asserted it was very cold on the first day of the crime – when in fact it was well above freezing, sunny and calm.

Yet in an earlier interview he claimed it was "below freezing in the daytime".

The consensus between Acland and another pathologist, Dr Nathaniel Carey, was that Hilda's kitchen knife found near the copse was too wide to have caused all the stab wounds. According to veteran pathologist Professor Knight back in 1985, another narrow-bladed knife which was never found must have been used. Carey, who had re-examined the medical evidence for the Cold Case Review, agreed with the police line that Hilda's neck injuries indicated she had been held in an arm lock and frogmarched while a knife was stabbed into her stomach. He was asked to explain why the wounds were so close together and did not go any deeper. He answered that the attacker was probably keeping control of the knife, determined not to cause very threatening injuries. The wounds were "almost deliberately superficial".

Barker cross-examined both pathologists further about this. "If an individual is stabbing another, once the knife goes in surely there is very little resistance? So if the intent was to kill, why not go in up to the hilt?" His inference was that, even if the defendant was Hilda's attacker, the charge should be downgraded to manslaughter.

Carey admitted Hilda would have had very limited movement in her right arm because of her broken clavicle and the knife wound right through it. Several other questions were not asked. Why did a panicking teenager want to inflict "deliberately superficial" wounds when he was about to leave his victim to die? Did this not seem more like torture, perhaps to extract information? Just as baffling, how did the attacker keep such control of this knife (or two knives?) while restraining his victim and struggling across a heavy, muddy field in broad daylight? This was even more difficult to imagine if the attacker was nearly five inches shorter than the victim.

⁓⁓⁓

The next expert testimony concerned Hilda's coat. We realised the importance of what we were about to hear after an earnest discussion between the Judge and the two opposing barristers without the jury in court. Latham told Wakerley: "It doesn't look like the knife has gone through the coat." A few minutes later he added: "The coat can't have been covering the body at the time the knife went into the body." This made nonsense of the police line that Hilda had been stabbed while being frogmarched. It also raised other more likely scenarios for when and where she had been stabbed, which were not mentioned. The discussion concerned whether Carey should be required to comment on this information, which was in the testimony of the next witness, Mark Webster. Another forensic scientist, he had worked on the original investigation, but had recently reviewed his findings.

With the jury back, Webster was called. As the coat was held up, he explained it had been deliberately cut down the back during the post mortem. We presumed this was to avoid touching the buttons. If so, who did them up?

Were they checked for fingerprints? No such questions were asked. Initially he found six holes in the fabric: one on the right sleeve and five at the front around the bottom button in the right number and area to match the stab wounds. However, closer examination more recently showed three of the cuts did not even go through the inner lining of the coat. To complicate things further, he also found about half a dozen small cuts in the lining which did not touch the coat fabric, for which he had no explanation.

Webster said the coat could have been lying open or hitched up when the injuries were inflicted, or it had not been worn at all during the attack. This made the prosecution case absurd. It inferred that the panicking teenager, after carrying out the stabbing, had bothered to button it up. Could one explanation be that the cuts in the main coat fabric which did not even go through the inner lining had been done in a hurry afterwards as part of the cover-up?

Webster found cuts in Hilda's rainbow-striped cardigan, aubergine jumper, vest and slip which corresponded with the stab wounds on the body. He also discovered cuts in the skirt but, significantly, did not mention whether these matched the knife wounds.

He was asked why he thought the skirt was not on the body. He said it could have been taken off by someone or by Hilda due to hypothermia, which in its advanced stages dilates blood vessels in the body's extremities, making the body feel hot. And the suspender belt? He replied that, as it was designed to stay on, it must have been removed deliberately, although it may have come off during dragging. Thus expert opinion had finally discredited the idea of Hilda losing her clothing while crawling around. Webster clearly realised it would be unlikely for the skirt – and impossible for the suspender belt, supposedly attached to the stockings – to have come off by crawling or been removed by Hilda.

When the court adjourned, Kate asked for a closer look at the clothing before it was taken away. The suspender belt, which looked home-made, was frayed and torn, and the clasps were fastened. The exhibits officer said that was how it was found in the copse. He also confirmed the skirt was found zipped up and inside out. This ruled out the possibility that it had been pulled off by the attacker or taken off by Hilda – unless either of them had then zipped it up again. None of these deductions, or their implications, was raised by either side.

Webster told the court he found only two traces of semen, both aspermic. An extremely small amount was on the front of the slip on the body. Though rain could have washed some of it away, there was still nowhere near enough semen for a full ejaculation. The other positive result came from a handkerchief stained with Hilda's blood found in the back spare bedroom, but it could not be matched with anyone's DNA. Again the quantity was negligible. No sperm was present, for which Webster gave no explanation.

For the next two days the trial covered the evidence found at Ravenscroft. Retired PC Edmond Lane recalled his visits, which confirmed he noticed very little and had no sense of urgency.

The jurors saw the inside of the house as excerpts from the police video were shown. More evidence about its condition came from people who first went inside on the Saturday morning. Latham read statement excerpts from housekeeper Mrs Latter and gardener David Williams – but not those of either Brian George or his wife, who insisted the telephone had been carefully disconnected. Both could have been called as witnesses. Latham did not mention Mrs Latter was unable to positively identify the handbags on the table, and was sure Hilda's current bag was missing. Nor did Mrs Latter recognise the Totes rain hat found in the hedge.

Regarding the state of the telephone in the kitchen, Latham pointed out in the police video how "the white cables have been cut. The white telephone wire was originally stapled along the edge of the timber work. Plastic staples have moved onto the floor in front of the chest of drawers". This was why he read out only short extracts from the two statements made by Christopher Mileham, the telephone engineer. As with Brian George, Mileham could have been cross-examined over the disturbing anomalies about the telephone; but the defence chose not to challenge this. Was this because Andrew George would later claim he pulled out the phone when he heard it ring – despite the fact that Mileham confirmed the bell circuit was disabled, so would not have rung?

The prosecution failed to find any convincing evidence that Andrew George could drive. Successive witnesses were called who knew him at Besford House in Shrewsbury in March 1984. Only one of them said he could – although, under cross examination, he had trouble distinguishing between Andrew and Adrian. None of the others ever saw him driving. Latham did not ask Andrew's former partner.

Having established George lived with her for six years from 1997-2003, Barker asked her: "When you got together you had to get a person to drive you because neither of you could drive?" "Yes." She confirmed George bought a very old Metro car for £200 for her to learn to drive. She eventually passed the test, whereas he did not even have lessons.

Later I found further corroboration of George's lack of driving ability from another Besford House boy. A few months after Hilda's murder, Andrew and Adrian George went with him and two others in a stolen car to Torquay. When the driver became angry and left the car, Andrew tried to move it. He failed because he could not work the clutch and accelerator together.

More problems arose for the prosecution from witness descriptions of the defendant as a 16-year-old. Most agreed he was strong, but he was also "small but wiry", and "there was not much of him". Another former worker at Besford House recalled he was short, slim and looked very young for his age.

———— ⨯⨯⨯ ————

Nevertheless, when Michael Appleby presented the DNA evidence matching Andrew George from seminal fluid on Hilda's slip, it seemed compelling. The chance of it being from anyone else was a billion to one.

Appleby said he also examined a knotted, torn and threadbare ironing board cover found on the bed in the small back bedroom. DNA analysis came up with genetic material from more than three people, including an extremely rare sample which appeared in only one in 12,000 of the population. This particular DNA was found in Andrew George as well as his mother, Dorothy, and Adrian – but not his older brother Stephen.

The court listened to several hours of discussion between Latham, Appleby and Roger Ide, an expert on knots. The prosecution tried to establish that George used the cover to restrain Hilda, perhaps tying her wrists to the broken baluster – but they were not tight enough. No straightforward explanation for the knot and loops emerged; and no-one raised the fact that Mrs Latter told the police she did not recognise the cover. She suspected it came from a drawer where old bandages and rags were kept.

———— ⨯⨯⨯ ————

The next prosecution witness was retired Detective Sergeant John Ingham. On 28 March 1984, while working on Hilda's case, he interviewed George, who had just been arrested for a shotgun burglary in Shrewsbury.

Ingham confirmed George immediately admitted the burglary, whereupon the detective quizzed the teenager about Hilda's murder. Latham read out George's statement about what he did that day, and what he wore, including Doc Martens boots. Ingham followed this up at Besford House, and established that George did not then possess any trainers. Moreover, the rest of his clothing did not match that of the driver of Hilda's car or the running man. Barker then cross-examined Ingham, who agreed George had not fitted the description of the suspect in the Hilda case. "Yes, his general demeanour, his fingerprints were negative, his shoes were negative...".

During Ingham's testimony, it emerged via a question from the jury that Latham had been reading from a typed copy of the relevant handwritten statements. Ingham's cross-examination unwittingly revealed that in Latham's copy George's age had been changed from 16 to "over 18"; he had grown from 5 feet 2½ inches to 5 feet 3 inches; and his hair colour had changed from dark brown to black. A juror had alerted the Judge to these discrepancies, because the jury had been reading the original handwritten statements. After scrutinizing both versions, Wakerley himself pointed out the age change, adding that there were "many differences" between the original and the copy. He queried how this had happened. Latham replied that the typist might have created these "minor differences" when transcribing the original statements onto computer.

Our suspicions deepened after the following extraordinary exchange. Barker asked Ingham: "You had a desk diary and a notebook, and you handed them in when complete?"

Ingham: "They were retained for a period of time because it was a murder investigation… My diaries were placed in a safe, tied with the name Hilda Murrell on top… expecting today to be able to stand before you. However, they have been weeded and destroyed, after the Northumbria Report came out" – which had been in May 1985.

Wakerley interjected sharply: "You said 'weeded'?"

"Yes, my Lord."

A fingerprint expert said twenty sets of prints were found in the house. Advances in analysis left no doubt that two came from Andrew George. A partial palm print was discovered on the underside of the downstairs toilet seat. His fingerprint was found on a box for buttons in the large guest bedroom. No categoric forensic evidence linked him to the small back bedroom where the sexual assault was alleged to have occurred.

Why did Barker not use this opportunity to cross-examine his independent fingerprint expert following his unopposed challenge in the abuse of process hearing? He could have asked why the fingerprints were not used to identify Andrew George in 1984, as they were sufficiently detailed for this. What if the police had done this a week after Hilda's murder? The implications for me and the case were huge.

The court heard that of all the other prints, only six could be traced to people who were known to Hilda. So, with two identified as George's, where did the other 12 prints come from? Again, the question was not asked.

Keith Barnett took the stand as a footprint specialist who examined shoe marks found in Ravenscroft. Although the sole impressions were incomplete, matching trainer prints were discovered on the tiled floor of the kitchen, two of them close to the phone and one under a chair – which would have had to be moved first. Another partial print was found in the doorway of Hilda's bedroom.

Barker reminded Barnett that in 1984 the police were confident the prints came from a size 8 or 9 Romanian-made Gola trainer, with a distinctive sole pattern. Yet the defendant's feet were size 6, and he had no trainers. Now no-one was sure about anything on this issue. Casts of a trainer footprint, mentioned in the 2002 police press release announcing the Cold Case Review, had since "gone missing".

Barnett said he could no longer specify the size. However, when questioned about a photograph of the footprint under the kitchen chair, he admitted: "What you are seeing there is a series of U shapes typical of Doc Martens boots, fairly often worn by police officers at the time – or anyone…"

Although the issue of the running man was covered cursorily, both sides seemed keen to dismiss him. Originally central to the investigation, had the runner lost his importance because he bore no resemblance to Andrew or Stephen George? At the time Stephen was also small, shorter and even younger-looking than Andrew.

The most controversial witness could only be referred to in court as 'Mr A'. His identity had to be protected because he had been an informer for Staffordshire Police. Despite his sharp suit, West Mercia Police knew he was an unreliable witness with previous convictions for arson, criminal damage, assault and theft. However, they badly needed his help.

Mr A was in Blakenhurst Prison in 2003 when he met Andrew George on remand. They were in separate cells in the same wing where Mr A was a cleaner and also claimed to be a "listener" trained by the Samaritans. This proved to be a lie. Was he sent in to get George to talk? Were the police now relying on cell block confessions, after rejecting Trina Guthrie's inconvenient information from at least two prisoners about Hilda's murder?

Mr A gained some trust with George. He claimed George initially told him the murder was linked to MI5, the *Belgrano*, and Greenpeace. Three agents were involved who had been watching the house for some time because the owner was suspected of possessing papers about the *Belgrano*. For this, he was dubbed 'George the Spy'.

George then allegedly started giving a different version of events. He had been taking amphetamines and inhaling gas when he went into the house to search for drug money and was confronted by an elderly woman. He tied her up with a scarf or scarves, using a technique he had seen in a film about the SAS. He apparently gave Mr A details about taking a can of lager, using the toilet and finding between £30-50 in a handbag. In another conversation, a struggle was mentioned which resulted in the baluster being broken.

According to Mr A, George left the house to get help from one of his "brothers" who turned up later with a car. He put the woman in her own car which he found difficult to drive. He tried to reach a place which he called "the death slide", a spot on Haughmond Hill where he used to play games with others from Besford House. He was followed by the other car driven by someone referred to as "brother", which could have been either a friend or one of his brothers. After crashing the car, George walked the woman through fields into a wood where he and his brother stabbed her. They left in the second car and returned to the house and searched it more thoroughly.

Despite these wildly fluctuating and extremely far-fetched stories, Mr A consistently talked about more than Andrew George being involved. Mr A came up with the names of two accomplices nicknamed 'Cock-eye' and 'Laney', who were known to be friends of Andrew. However, both were short and scrawny youths too, nothing like the witnessed driver.

Barker's cross-examination of Mr A brought a surprising revelation. He told the court that a set of witness statements, which had been given to Andrew George, had been stolen from his cell. According to Barker, details of the case were "common knowledge" within the prison. It was also suggested Mr A had books about the case, obtained from the prison library after asking another prisoner to order them for him. Barker accused him of providing information based only on his research and lies.

The defence devoted most of a day to demolishing the character and reliability of Mr A. Three Staffordshire police officers, who had used him in other investigations, were called to give their opinions. None of them now trusted the man. Inconsistencies made one detective increasingly suspicious that Mr A was "running with the hare and the hounds" and deliberately passing on false information. He wrote a report, based on five years' involvement with the informant, warning West Mercia Police: "Mr A was extremely unreliable and dangerous". Another officer described Mr A as violent, untrustworthy, and "lies at any opportunity".

Latham admitted in court he was relying on Mr A's evidence. This demonstrated the weakness of the case against George. The prosecution could only prove he was in Ravenscroft, not what he did there or why. There was no evidence to place him in the car or the copse, apart from the seminal fluid on Hilda's slip which allegedly got there in the house. The prosecution relied on the testimony of a hardened, violent criminal known to be a liar, who was being investigated for perverting the course of justice.

Barker's first witness was Andrew George, who outlined his upbringing in local authority care. He remembered being placed with foster parents, but he was mostly "being shoved from home to home". He only had one brief childhood memory of his mother.

On 21 March 1984, George recalled a chance meeting with his older brother Stephen in Shrewsbury. "Mooching around", they found a footpath which took them into Sutton Road past Ravenscroft, where they spotted an open door.

George said he was probably first to enter the house. He started searching for money when he heard a woman shouting: "What are you doing in my house?" He went to investigate and found Stephen with his arm around the woman's neck and demanding money. He said his brother dragged the woman, still shouting and struggling, upstairs.

When asked how he reacted, he said he did not know what to think and carried on his search of the downstairs rooms. A couple of minutes later he looked up towards the landing and saw Stephen and Hilda: she was putting up a fight. He thought Stephen kicked and broke the baluster.

The defendant said Hilda was then forced into the bedroom at the top of stairs. When he went into the room, Hilda was lying on the bed. Stephen was on top of her "doing unsavoury things", trying to rape her. He said Hilda was not tied up and he did not remember seeing an ironing board cover.

According to George, his brother tried to make him have sex with his victim. "He started playing with me – getting the thing out and wanking me off." Asked if he ejaculated, he replied: "I wouldn't like to say, sir." He said Stephen tried to masturbate him on previous occasions when they were with foster parents and later when his brother had his own flat.

Apparently, Stephen dragged Hilda out of the room, down the stairs and out of the house. Left alone, Andrew resumed his search and found between £30 and £40, at some point taking a can of lager, and went to the toilet. He claimed both he and his brother were wearing gloves. When asked how he had left fingerprints inside the house, he thought there may have been holes in them.

Questioned about the telephone, he said: "I heard it ring, so I ripped the wires out of the junction box." This was the most blatant example of the defendant trying to make the alleged facts fit his story. Obviously he could not blame his brother for this because, according to his version of events, Stephen was busy either attacking or abducting Hilda.

George said he did not discover Hilda had died until he was arrested the following week for the shotgun burglary. News of the murder scared him, he said. "I tried to blank it out of my head."

His evidence then turned to his recent experiences in custody. He explained that he knew he would be targeted by other prisoners, so he spread the story that the murder was connected with the "secret services". He found a book called *Unsolved Murders* which included a chapter about Hilda and MI5. When anyone asked him about the case he fed them information from the book. If word got out why he was in custody, "someone was going to stick pool balls into me... I'd have had my throat cut if I'd have told the truth". By this George meant that, on remand charged with murdering an old woman, such punishments were meted out by inmates. He said Mr A was just a liar: "Half of what he came out with yesterday was just not true." He did not say which half.

On Thursday 21 April, two weeks into the trial, the prosecution counsel stood up, stared intently at the accused, and invited him to tell the truth. "This has got nothing to do with Stephen, has it?" was Latham's icily delivered opening gambit. "Yes, it has," replied George. It was the first exchange of an intense cross-examination lasting a day and a half.

With a sneering "Let's look at your lies together", Latham began by asking him about the stories he had told to cover his movements on 21 March. George told the court he had lied because he was frightened. Latham was incredulous. If he was so scared and concerned, why did he carry out another burglary, and fire off a shotgun, at the house in Castlefields? "I don't deny that, sir. I pinched it, sir," came the reply with a plucky politeness that often characterised his responses under pressure. "I let off a couple of rounds in the house, sir – does that make me a bad person?" Latham snarled back: "It doesn't make you a shy and retiring little person" – unwittingly acknowledging how small George was.

George insisted he knew nothing of the murder until he was interviewed by the police, despite the widespread news coverage. Latham reminded him that he soon started talking in prison after he was charged in 2003, where he claimed the murder was somehow linked with the Security Service. It was not only other prisoners but also members of his family who were given the line about MI5. George explained why he lied to his own mother. "I was put in a children's home when I was about five. I have this woman claiming to be my mother – I didn't recognise her – she could have been a police officer asking me personal questions."

Latham told the court one person George was anxious to see was his former partner; yet when she visited him in prison he also lied to her. George replied that he loved her, but the relationship was over. "I didn't know whether to trust her – she was just finished with me. I wasn't going to tell her the truth. What if I told her the truth and she went off to the police?" Latham then goaded him with a sustained onslaught of questions aimed at tripping him up. George stood up to him surprisingly strongly. The Crown QC said his story about Stephen's involvement was fiction. The defendant was in the house alone, which was why he needed to tie up his victim using the ironing board cover. Yet the knot expert had established that the loops in the cover were too big to tie anyone up.

Latham pressed harder: "If Stephen was present in the house and carried out the assault, then where were his fingerprints and DNA?" "I was not in that house on my own," George retorted defiantly. This was a line he repeated several times; and it was an interesting choice of words. It would have been more natural for him to have asserted "I was with my brother," or "Stephen was there." How, Latham wondered, did the informer get hold of the names

... the fact that a big finger-stone which had stood on the pass to guide travellers from time immemorial, and which fell down about the end of my walking time up there about thirty years ago, had been set up again. It is a splendid stone, 8-9 feet high and slender, I greeted it like an old friend. It was warm to the touch. It was a miracle day. I had seriously thought I might never get up there again. What luck to have the time and the energy just on that marvellous day.

Best love + best wishes

Hilda

The photocopier has run off the bottom of p. 12; the rest of the sentence is on the back. The word-processing is nice, isn't it?

<u>Monday</u>. I am now seriously thinking of going to London on Sat. Just <u>in case</u> of "anything happening", as they say, could you see that the paper (just as it is) goes to Gerard Morgan-Grenville, Henbant Fach, Llanbedr, Crickhowell, Dyfed some time in Nov? I don't want to be melodramatic, but I have put in a lot of work on this thing + I want it to get to the target.

Hilda's postscript in her last letter to Robert Green.

Pilgrimage to Hilda's cairn for 20th anniversary in 2004. (Photo: Jane Gilmore).

From top: Billboard, Shrewsbury, March 1984. (*Shropshire Star*)

DCS David Cole at the place where Hilda's body was found. (*Shropshire Star*)

Artist impressions of suspect. (West Mercia Police)

Romanian Gola trainer print pattern. (WMP)

Andrew George aged 16. (*Shropshire Star*)

Andrew George during the trial. (*Shropshire Star*)

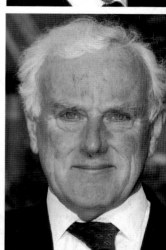

From top left: DCI Jim Tozer shows Robert Green the Shrewsbury Police files on the case, 2002. (WMP)

Richard Latham QC.

Kate Dewes and Robert Green attend the trial in Stafford Crown Court. (*Shropshire Star*)

Anthony Barker QC, Defence Barrister. (*Shropshire Star*)

Adrian George, brother of Andrew. (*Shropshire Star*)

L to R: DI Rik Klair, Detective Superintendent Mick Brunger and DCI Chris Knight at Press conference outside Stafford Crown Court. (*Shropshire Star*)

DCI Jim Tozer, DC Nick Partridge and Robert Green during Cold Case Review in Christchurch, New Zealand.

From top left:

Postcard to Lady Dora Russell, 12 April 1985.

Ian and Thalia Campbell with Robert Green. (Photo: Kate Dewes)

Laurens Otter. (Photo: Kate Dewes)

Don Arnott and Robert Green, 1989. (Photo: David Hurn, Magnum)

Gordon Dale, Kate Dewes, Teresa Leggett (Patsy's 84 year old mother), Robert Green, Stephen Davis, Patsy Dale in Ennis, 1998. (Photo: Eoin Dinan)

Philip Griffith.

Dr Warren Tucker, Director New Zealand Security Intelligence Service and Robert Green, 6 July 2009.

Laney and Cock-eye? "I don't know where he got those names," countered George. "He may have been given them from Shrewsbury police – not me."

The defence called more witnesses who had seen Hilda's car. During the investigation each was asked to examine a photograph album of possible suspects. Not one identified Andrew George.

The only witness called who saw the car outside Shrewsbury was David Lewis, who had been riding his Honda 90 motorcycle along the road towards Haughmond Hill. Stopping at temporary traffic lights, he was joined by a car, its engine revving noisily. As soon as the lights turned green, the car sped past him, but had to stop again at a second set of lights. Lewis said he studied the car and its occupants because he suspected something was wrong. The driver was in his late thirties, broad and above average in height with light brown hair. A woman passenger was slumped forward, as if unconscious or asleep. She was wearing a dark hat.

Lewis's evidence had previously been carefully considered by police, who had requested his help over 150 times in three years to identify possible suspects. They had even issued a TV appeal in 1984, basing their description primarily on Lewis's information: 'White man, 30-40 years old, powerfully built, collar length brown hair, long sideboards, blue anorak with a D-ring on the back.' Yet Latham pilloried him about his attempts to identify the driver from police photographs, ridiculing a conscientious witness. Now that his evidence did not suit their line, he was treated with derision.

Compelling evidence about Andrew George's driving ability came from civil engineering contractor Ivor Dorricott. He first met George in 2001 during a foot and mouth disease outbreak when workers were recruited to help dispose of slaughtered cattle. Dorricott employed him again on other projects which required him to drive a dumper truck. George jammed the gears "because he did not know what a clutch was". He was not considered safe even driving an automatic truck, and was only allowed behind the wheel in big open fields.

Latham asked Dorricott if he would be surprised if George lost control and drove off the road – an obvious allusion to Hilda's car crashing. Dorricott replied: "I would be surprised – because he would not have been able to get it on the road in the first place."

As the trial drew to a close, the prosecution was given the go-ahead to re-open their case and call Stephen George as a "rebuttal witness" to refute the allegations made against him by his brother. Stephen admitted a number of offences when he was young including theft, criminal damage and breaking into shops. He had last appeared in court in 1986, charged with gross indecency after masturbating over a three-year-old child. He denied ever sexually abusing his brother. He, too, said he could not drive a car.

On Thursday 28 April, the presentation of evidence ended and the summing up began. Latham told the jury the case came down to a stark choice: the murder was either committed by Andrew or Stephen George.

Barker belatedly posed some obvious unanswered questions. Why would someone who knew the area take his victim in her own car through the town? Why could none of the witnesses identify the driver as Andrew George? The evidence was overwhelming that he still could barely drive.

No-one had raised the issues which undermined the police line that the crime was committed by a lone, petty burglar – not least the careful disconnection of the telephone, the changes to Ravenscroft by the Friday, and the evidence of Ian Scott.

<hr />

Friday 6 May 2005 dawned with Tony Blair having secured an unprecedented third consecutive term as a Labour Prime Minister. Fortunately, this overshadowed Day 20 of the trial. Two days had passed since Justice Wakerley sent the jury out to deliberate. I used the time to brief selected waiting journalists on our concerns. The consensus was that the longer the jury stayed out, the greater the chance they would dismiss the abduction charge for lack of evidence. At least the murder charge could be reduced to manslaughter.

Pulse rates jumped soon after noon, when the jury returned for clarification of the definitions of murder and kidnapping. The Judge complied, taking the opportunity to rebrief them on the definition of manslaughter: "[W]hat if you are not sure that the intention was to kill her or cause her serious injury – it may have been just to leave her there?... if he didn't intend her to die, that would be manslaughter – the only distinction between them [murder and manslaughter] is the question of intent...

"On the definition of kidnapping... the real issue is whether you are sure that it was this defendant who drove her away, as opposed to being in the house and continuing with the burglary... the question is, are you sure that he drove her away or took her away by force?" He gave the jury until 3 pm. A Bank Holiday weekend loomed, with all the complications of extending into a further week.

There was no need. At 2.45 pm the jury returned, and announced to the packed court that the defendant was guilty on both counts. Andrew George seemed to faint, then became very agitated. Barker asked the Judge to consider redemption/mitigation arguments before sentencing, "bearing in mind this was a one-off offence, and that Andrew George has been in custody for 700 days".

Wakerley then addressed George severely: "You should receive life imprisonment with no release ever." However, as he was a teenager at the time he would get a minimum of 12 years. "You were a burglar. You did horrible, unspeakable acts to that old lady in her house, not killing her, but using a knife for the next hour or more. You could have paused and stopped, but you didn't. These were aggravating features. However, because of the lapse of time, I recommend that you serve a minimum of 15 years before being considered for parole." Deducting just under two years for his time on remand, he sentenced him to 13 years and thirty days. With the public gallery in uproar, George shouted: "F...ing lying bastards – it's a set-up!" as he was led away. The Judge then thanked the jury, adding: "I hope that you have seen justice at work, and the English Bar at its best..."

Kate and I sat dumbfounded and sickened. We slipped out of the courtroom and prepared to face the media downstairs. In my statement before TV cameras outside on the forecourt, I thanked the police for their efforts to solve the crime over 21 years. Then I added: "However, the full story of what happened to Hilda has not emerged. There are many unanswered questions. The jury had to reach a judgement without being asked to take into account some key evidence which was known to both sides." I finally asked: "If this was just a bungled burglary by Andrew George, why have I and others pursuing the truth continued to be intimidated? And if only a bungled burglary, why do people continue to come forward to me with information which they did not wish to give to the police?"

As we turned to go back inside, Brunger and his assistant DCI Chris Knight emerged triumphantly to the media. We waited in the foyer. Standing alone only a few yards from us was Andrew George's mother. Throughout the trial, I had taken care to avoid her, though Kate had spoken briefly with her at a chance meeting in the toilets. Now, we suddenly felt the need to reach out to another victim's family. We asked her to tell Andrew we did not believe he abducted or murdered Hilda. When we met George's solicitor soon afterwards, he said: "I've just been with him. He's in deep shock. What he's heard from you via his mother is the one thing that'll keep him going."

Three hours later, on Radio Shropshire I repeated my concern that George's conviction was unsafe in a twenty-minute feature on the case which summarised the conspiracy theories well. Tam Dalyell, who had decided not to stand again for Parliament, was much in demand for his opinion of the verdict. Ironically, it was fitting that he should end his remarkable and controversial political career by talking about Hilda's murder. He had pursued it for nearly half his 43 years as an MP, as part of his wider concern about deception and misuse of power by State authorities.

Dalyell declared: "The prosecution's version of events stretches the imagination to breaking point." He believed the jury had not been told the whole story. He reminded listeners of the paranoid, fevered political atmosphere at the time. "The Thatcher government felt under siege from its opponents, and concealed the facts behind the sinking of the *Belgrano*. It was not a matter of national security, but of political embarrassment." When challenged whether he still believed the abduction and murder had involved MI5, he quickly responded that he had never singled them out: "I stick to exactly what I was told." He was asked about the DNA evidence – surely that blew a hole in his conspiracy theories? His reply was: "I believe the person who told me the security services were involved." As the interview came to a close, he added: "Andrew George alone did not do this"; and he called for a judicial inquiry.

CHAPTER 11

A STITCH-UP

After we thanked our Stafford homestay hosts we drove to friends in the heart of Shropshire to recover and take stock. On the way, we stopped at a filling station displaying a billboard with Hilda's photo above a *Shropshire Star* strapline shouting 'JUSTICE AT LAST'. The newspaper carried a special eight-page supplement on the case.

Dalyell was shocked by the verdict. When I phoned him, he recalled his anguish on re-reading a letter from me the previous year after he confirmed to us his main source had died. In it I expressed my frustration that still he could not name him because of the risk to the source's family's financial security:

> I would ask what evidence you have that any Crown servant has suffered in terms of pension for exposing Government malpractice? Moreover, if such a threat ever eventuated, who is better placed than yourself to call the Government's bluff on this? Where you lead, others could feel emboldened (and sufficiently protected) to follow: I have in mind [name deleted]'s relative, who worked for the Security Services and has told him that he knows it was a State crime; and the ex-CID man whom [name deleted] knows who agrees.
>
> Substantiating what we both have reason to believe happened to Hilda may well require more Crown servants to do what Clive Ponting so courageously and rightly did. If your sources are dead, naming them would not breach your pledge to secrecy while they were alive, and could encourage those still living to come forward.

Now I pleaded with him to reveal his main source's identity as the most effective way to challenge the verdict. We suggested visiting him to discuss the issue, but he was too unwell. Instead, he urged us to meet his old friend Professor Peter Hennessy.

Over the next few days, Dalyell rang me several times in some turmoil. The widow of his main source had now died. He had checked with their family who understandably did not want him to go public. He told me: "As a man of my word, I will carry this man's name to my grave." His concerns for a dead man's family, reinforced by his establishment ancestry and connections, had overridden his best chance to provide crucial evidence confirming the involvement of the British State in a murder, and correct a serious miscarriage of justice. After all he had risked in his tenacious pursuit of the truth about the *Belgrano* sinking, I was deeply disappointed.

We visited Peter (now Lord) Hennessy. The leading expert on the British system of government, he had recently published his book *The Secret State: Whitehall and the Cold War*. He suggested the "quiet, constitutional route" would be for me and/or Dalyell to ask the Parliamentary Intelligence and Security Select Committee to examine the unanswered questions about the trial as part of their duty of oversight of the Security Service. Also, as was my right under the Data Protection Act, I should request my MI5 records and any material from the Positive Vetting Agency.

Without Dalyell as my parliamentary champion, approaching the Select Committee would be a waste of time and energy. However, I did apply to see my MI5 file – and Hilda's. I received the following Kafkaesque reply, with their emphasis:

> We have conducted a search of Security Service records, and have determined the Service does not process [sic] any personal data to which you are entitled to have access under section 7 of the Act. **You should not take this response to imply that the Security Service does or does not hold any personal data about you.** This reflects the policy of successive Governments of applying the principle of 'neither confirm nor deny' with regard to the activities of the security and intelligence agencies in the interests of protecting national security.

As for my request for any records on Hilda, MI5 could not help with this either, (a) because she was a third party, and (b) she was dead.

Immediately after the Radio Shropshire feature about the verdict, a man telephoned to say he had information for me. I was sceptical, but met him at the Shropshire Wildlife Trust in Shrewsbury. He risked contacting me because "I don't like to see injustice done". A business acquaintance had confided in him some five years back that he was contacted by two telephone engineers who came under pressure about the leak to the media in February 1985. This tip-off led us to them.

During this conversation, Kate had been busy. We had noticed a young woman browsing among trays of wild flower plants a few yards away. To our astonishment, it was Andrew George's former partner. Kate introduced herself and told her how impressed she had been by her testimony at the trial. The woman was very upset because she believed Andrew was innocent of abducting and murdering Hilda. Once Kate told her we agreed, she talked freely.

She confirmed that, during an early meeting with George in prison after his arrest, he told her: "This is bigger than the Shrewsbury police", and that

Hilda's side door was open when he went in. Then he said: "Hilda was kept in a stable or hut for two days". This echoed the reference in Trina Guthrie's affidavit to Hilda being interrogated in a safe house in 'Little America', now Atcham Business Park. He was always adamant he had not killed her. When she first met him he could not drive at all – she had to teach him how and when to change gear. Besides, if he could have driven, "he would never have gone through town – he would have gone out through Atcham". The neighbours where she had lived for 15 years would not talk to the media about them. They could not believe George killed Hilda because he had a reputation for helping old people.

The young woman explained that, during the six years they lived together, "Andy came off drugs and committed no crimes. He admitted I always knew when he was lying". After charging him the police pestered her to pretend she wanted to resume their relationship in order to get him to talk. She said she gave him a copy of the book *Unsolved Murders*, despite knowing he could only read comics. She never met Stephen, and only met Adrian once.

We discovered an extraordinary attempt to intimidate us by the Royal Mail Interception Service. Our hostess in Stafford had already experienced harassment during the trial, twice getting silent phone calls in the middle of the night. Now she phoned in an agitated state to report that a letter had arrived from New Zealand with the envelope slit along the bottom and most of the top. If this had been done before it arrived in the Stafford sorting office, the greeting card inside would have fallen out. Kate instructed her to sellotape it up and redirect it to our Shropshire address.

When it arrived, we were stunned to see that this time one of the shorter sides of the envelope had been completely slit open, while the other was slit two-thirds of its length. This happened after I said publicly that Andrew George's conviction was unsafe. Here was rare evidence that our hosts' phones were tapped, and of State security involvement.

The slit envelope became an exhibit at a tense post-trial meeting with West Mercia Police in Stourport on Severn Police Station. DCS Mick Brunger had fended off our questions before the trial by promising a meeting. Now he stonewalled with a new excuse. Andrew George was appealing against his conviction, so the case was still *sub judice*.

To our surprise, the police agreed the letter appeared to have been intercepted and opened with a very sharp blade like a box-cutter. Brunger even offered to have it tested for fingerprints and forensically examined for DNA, before quickly adding that a match would be impossible. He suggested it was probably to do with our work. We retorted that the only work we were currently doing was related to the trial. Besides, if it was a safe conviction why was this happening to us?

When asked if we would like police protection, Kate, my hitherto docile Rottweiler, snarled back: "No thank you. Why don't you just haul off the people who are trying to intimidate us?" She angrily eyeballed an uncomfortable DC Nick Partridge, summoned from retirement as a safe pair of hands. "If anything happens to us, I want *you* to go back to New Zealand and tell my daughters why." He had met two of them during his 2002 visit with Tozer.

We persisted trying to get answers to our list of updated questions, starting with reports of changes at Hilda's house by the Friday. Brunger coolly suggested that, as with Ian Scott, many witnesses familiar with visiting the house could all have been mistaken. It was my turn to feel my blood boil.

Of the twenty fingerprints found at the house, he explained that six belonged to Betty Latter and David Williams; two were from Andrew George; four remained unidentified, while the other eight were considered insufficient in detail. The one on the rear window of Hilda's car was checked against every suspect, including George, with no positive results. Brunger claimed George's fingerprints could not be matched in 1984. We countered that, as mentioned in the pre-trial abuse of process hearing, the defence's independent expert concluded it was possible to obtain a match from the two prints at that time. However, in the prosecution's skeleton argument responding to Barker, Latham conceded George's fingerprints had been identifiable in 1984. The police had no answer to this.

Brunger confirmed there had been a "huge investigation" to identify the one fingerprint in the car. It was from Trina Guthrie's boyfriend Malcolm Leel when he helped pack the car while on holiday with Hilda in July 1983. We reminded Brunger that we had suggested they check this possibility in 2002. His lame reply was that "Leel should have come forward to have his fingerprints checked as a possible suspect."

The police could not explain why George did not match any of the descriptions of the driver of the car. They knew of George's report to his father about the two men putting guns to his head and threatening to kill him, but it gave them "no avenues to explore the conspiracy theories". There was nothing suspicious about the fire at Fron Goch.

Next, I raised the painful issue of returning Hilda's body parts to us for burial. Brunger had warned me in 2004 that some were missing, including her brain. His response now was callously offhand: "Certain parts were held and they were lost. It is the responsibility of the Forensic Science Service. You should write to them."

When challenged as to whether any toxicology tests had been conducted, Brunger turned to Partridge. At first, he claimed the only test done on Hilda's blood in 1984 was for alcohol. After pressing him – we had seen a forensic report referred to in the trial – he admitted a test was done for sodium penthanole, but they could not find the report. When it was re-tested in 2003 there was no evidence of other stupefying drugs, and the coffee grain type substances found in her stomach were a feature of hypothermia, not of a drug overdose.

During the trial, reference was made to a forensic report written by Ian Humphreys in September 2003. This was in response to our request during Tozer and Partridge's New Zealand visit to analyse Hilda's blood for the presence of a range of common drugs. Tozer had specifically wanted thiopentone tested because it is used in the induction of anaesthesia of short duration. Humphreys reported:

> A positive result was obtained to indicate the possible presence of amphetamine or a closely related substance.

However, because further tests showed the presence of "putrefactive compounds which have a similar chemical structure to amphetamine and can give rise to false positive reactions", he concluded that "no amphetamine related drug or any other drugs listed above were detected". He could find no trace of any sedatives. Attempts to determine whether or not thiopentone was present in the blood specimen were unsuccessful. He therefore considered it "highly unlikely that any thiopentone had been used by, or administered to, Hilda in the hours prior to her death".

When we asked to see Hilda's clothing, we were only allowed a cursory glance at the Totes rain hat, moccasin boots, green skirt and stockings. Partridge admitted that, despite a considerable effort, they "never got to the bottom" of what happened to Hilda's missing regular handbag and her document satchel. Brunger promised to show us all exhibits at a final meeting if George's appeal failed and the case was closed. The Northumbria Report could probably be released then too.

As we were ushered out of the police station, I felt that my relationship with the police had reverted to the moment in 1986 when I broke off contact. Their 'open mind' had slammed shut, as they resorted to stonewalling, denial, obfuscation and fob-offs. After all my efforts to re-engage with them through the Cold Case Review, the old hostility and mistrust were back. However, though feeling disempowered, we left with some satisfaction that their triumphalism had taken a private knock.

⁂

We met the telephone engineers. The first one told us he had spoken out in 1985 on behalf of two colleagues who feared for their jobs. One still worked for British Telecom; but the one whose statement was selectively used in the trial, Christopher Mileham, was now freelance. He was prepared to talk.

When shown what Latham quoted from his 1984 statement, he exclaimed: "But my main finding wasn't mentioned! I'm surprised the defence didn't challenge this. I thought I was more likely to be useful as a defence witness."

Mileham vividly recalled the large team of police around him in February 1985 when he was summoned back to Shrewsbury police station after the telephone controversy in the TV programmes. Assistant Chief Constable Bernard Drew personally tried to persuade him to make a new statement. "They seemed desperate to make me say it was pulled out." He held firm, using his forced supplementary statement merely to clarify the condition of the bedroom phone and confirm his original findings. BT management admitted they were under pressure from the police to sack him. Another BT engineer whose job was also on the line suggested they should get advice from their union secretary.

Mileham's former colleague, who was still working for BT, told us that in 1984 they were viewed as the senior local engineers. Mileham was the authority on what happened at Ravenscroft and he had total confidence in him. "His statement would have been solid and correct." This third engineer's memory of the case was clear, because at one point he was also a suspect. He was a tall, big man with large feet.

In a succession of unfortunate coincidences, he repaired faults on both Hilda's phones, at Fron Goch and Ravenscroft, during the previous year or so. On the day of her abduction he worked on an unrelated fault in the green junction box in Sutton Road where Hilda's phone was connected. He was then seen that afternoon several miles north of Hunkington on another repair job. The police took his worksheets off him to see whether he had time to drive Hilda's car out there. Also, he was wearing trainers.

The hapless engineer made five statements to explain his alibis, and was able to show he and Mileham did a joint job in the Army's headquarters in Shrewsbury at the time of the abduction. Nevertheless, the police made him show them his trainers. Exasperated, he volunteered that he knew they were looking for large ones with an unusual sole pattern, because he had seen a big photograph of them on a wall in Shrewsbury police station – where he had put in ten new phone lines! He added that, if he had killed Hilda, he would have burned his trainers. The police never checked Mileham's footwear, despite him standing where the footprints were found. Unlike his colleague, who matched descriptions of the quite big man – over six feet tall and heavily built – driving Hilda's car, Mileham was short and slim, more like Andrew George.

At our suggestion, Mileham met Brian George. They established that the phone condition changed between when Brian saw it before the Scene of Crime Unit had taken over the house on the Saturday and when Mileham examined it on the Monday. The police told Mileham the telephone condition was as they had found it. However, as I learned from the Northumbria Report, the junction box lid had been removed for forensic examination; and neither Brian nor Mileham saw any damage to the box opening, or broken piece of Bakelite.

Brian felt vindicated that the lid was present when he saw it, lying not screwed down over the spade connectors at the end of the receiver cord. They were all inside the box with one of them still loosely positioned around its connection. By the time Mileham saw it however, all the cord wires with spade connectors intact were clear of the box. Furthermore, I discovered the lid was not re-examined for DNA in the Cold Case Review, because it was assumed it would not have been touched by the man who "pulled out" the phone. Was this a spin-off benefit from police insistence on this scenario?

At the trial the prosecution showed a police video taken inside Ravenscroft, allegedly on the Sunday afternoon – the day before Mileham examined the phone. The narrator, Detective Sergeant Perriton, described the kitchen extension: "White cables have been cut. The white telephone wire was originally stapled along the edge of the timber work. The plastic staples have moved onto the floor in front of the chest of drawers." In Hilda's bedroom he commented that "the telephone by the bed is working – we are yet to determine where the line enters the house, in light of the condition of the downstairs phone." According to Mileham's second statement, made under duress almost a year later, the police were not able to make a connection from this phone on the Monday. Yet his first statement confirmed that "the bedroom extension was in full working order", except it would not ring.

In the police photograph of the kitchen phone, shown in the trial and reproduced in the *Shropshire Star*, the junction box cover was in place as Brian George had seen it. Both Brian and Mileham were certain the redundant cream extension cable was in place stapled to the wall around the end of the window seat when they saw it on the Saturday and Monday respectively. We subsequently saw a police statement confirming that extra photos of the phone were taken at 4.30 pm on the Monday after Mileham had done his inspection. This was also when the footprints were photographed. We found differences between some police photographs and video footage, including curtains, furniture and handbags moved, windows open then shut, and a cummerbund over the post at the foot of the stairs but not there in the video. With no date and time on the photographs, it is therefore sometimes difficult to establish what was the original situation.

Perriton made a written statement that on 12 April 1984 he obtained from 52 Sutton Road the "cream coloured telephone wire which had been wrenched from its securing clips in the breakfast room". Three weeks after the Scene of Crime Unit had finished, and Ravenscroft had been cleared, why was it necessary to return and remove this?

—— ∞∞ ——

When we were finally able to view copies of the complete statements referred to and quoted from in the trial, we were shocked to make some explosive discoveries which were not put to the jury.

Forensic expert Michael Appleby stated on 11 December 2003 that 1mm of each of Hilda's fingernails from each hand were sampled for DNA. Partial, mixed DNA profiles were found which matched each other. These were his conclusions, with my emphasis added:

> DNA possibly originating from a single male individual was detected on the tips of the fingernails taken from Hilda Murrell, items PA/22, and 23. This DNA – if it is assumed that it originated from a single male individual – **could not have originated from Messrs Harold, Steven** [sic], **Andrew or Adrian George**.

This was a forensic bombshell. Until then I had no idea that pathologist Peter Acland had kept all Hilda's fingernails. In a list of body parts provided by the police, no mention was made of them. Such powerful evidence almost certainly would have acquitted Andrew George, and proved Hilda had fought another man. For obvious reasons this had been ignored by the police and prosecution. Apparently the defence team did not raise it because it undermined George's defence that his brother was the culprit. Why on earth did he persist with it when this counter-evidence would have trumped George's semen DNA? Perhaps he hoped the abduction charge would be thrown out, whereupon the prosecution case would collapse. Or was his most mortal fear that proof of another unknown man attacking Hilda would lead to overwhelming pressure to explain what really happened – to which he had been a key witness?

On our return to New Zealand, I wrote to the Forensic Science Service in Birmingham asking them to locate and return Hilda's body parts for burial. They included her brain, liver and fingernails, plus samples of her blood, urine and bile.

Two months later David Parry emailed warning that 'it is taking longer than anticipated to obtain the necessary information about retained material'. No further communication about the case was received for ten months, when I was informed that George's appeal would be heard in early June 2006. I faxed and emailed another letter. Almost immediately Parry replied apologising for the delay and listed which body parts were retained. Then I was horrified to read:

> The following items have not been found, despite exhaustive searches at the National Archive, Priory House and Chorley FSS locations:-
>
> PA3 – The body sheet; PA24 – Urine; PA27 – Stomach Contents; PA28 – Bile; PA29 – Liver; PA30 – Brain.

I demanded to know when and where they were last held, and why it was necessary for the pathologist to remove and retain Hilda's brain. I refused to accept that the missing body parts had been disposed of, but must have been mislaid. I insisted the search for them be continued, so that one day I could complete Hilda's burial and achieve closure in this respect. Parry replied that another search was underway; however, while I should direct my second question to the pathologist, he confirmed that in his experience it was common practice 'to remove the liver and brain in case they were subsequently required for toxicological analysis'. He then launched into a tortuous explanation to try to justify such incompetence, ending with an apology on behalf of the Forensic Science Service 'for our inability to locate, or inform you of the fate of the missing samples at this time and for any distress that this is causing you'. I wrote twice to Acland, but received no reply.

When I asked a leading New Zealand pathologist who had worked in Britain if there was any significance about the group of missing body parts and body sheet, he said simply: "Toxicology test for drugs". He was very surprised even one part had been lost, let alone this whole group, in such a high profile case. Challenging Humphreys' 2003 forensic report on testing for amphetamine and thiopentone, the New Zealand pathologist was adamant there would have been no putrefaction, because all blood samples were always frozen.

On 8 June 2006, we arrived at the Royal Courts of Justice in London for George's Appeal.

⁂

Lord Justice Moses was irritated. The three Judges began the Appeal Court hearing, only to discover Anthony Barker QC was in another court, having double-booked. His client Andrew George was not in the dock, held up in traffic on his way from the top security prison in Parkhurst on the Isle of Wight. Barker turned up after five minutes, whereupon Moses angrily adjourned the hearing for an hour.

I seized the opportunity and confronted Barker about the fingernail DNA counter-evidence. Expressing ignorance, he went back into the court and challenged Brunger about it who, switching to damage control mode, undertook to email him details. After conferring with prosecution counsel and the Crown Prosecution Service, we overheard the police tell Barker the DNA was "only partial" and "probably contaminated".

When George arrived, the hearing resumed. Barker introduced his skeleton argument for the Appeal. Suddenly, he departed from his text and raised the fingernail DNA, on the grounds that "members of the victim's family have just brought it to my attention". Wanting it put on the public record, he repeated the police line: "There was DNA under her fingernails which proved it was not from his brother or him – but it was only 11 of 20 alleles, and a mixed specimen. In those days, the mortuary attendants used devices which weren't sterile, and on the deceased's fingernails there was DNA of unknown origin…" Moses looked sharply at Barker, nodded but made no comment; whereupon Barker resumed his prepared argument. It was a bizarre moment. This was probably the most important single statement in the entire proceedings. None of the few media present seemed to notice, let alone realise its significance.

The basis of the Appeal was that Justice Wakerley – who had recently died – misdirected the jury in his summing up regarding George's bad character, and too much weight was given to the police informant Mr A's evidence. Moses commented wearily: "When the Crown calls this sort of person there are problems... It rebounds... No police force can resist calling them. One day they'll stop." After Latham had given his counter-arguments, Moses announced he would give judgement at 10 am the next morning. When he did so, his concluding words were: "We refuse leave to pursue the renewed grounds of appeal. In relation to the substantive grounds, we dismiss them. We are not persuaded that the verdicts were unsafe. This appeal is dismissed." He directed that a transcript of the judgement be sent to the victim's family. In it I was not surprised to find no mention of the fingernail DNA. On enquiring with George's solicitor, I was told it was dismissed because it was not part of the defence's grounds for appeal.

The police were jubilant. We had to stop them telling the media how relieved Hilda's family were that the case was formally closed. As Barker hurried to a taxi, Kate asked him for his view on the outcome. "It's a stitch-up" was all he said before making a quick getaway.

One unexpected email had arrived before the Appeal, in April 2006:

Mr Green,
I apologise for contacting you like this and would like to have spoken with you in court but i was not allowed. I was Mr A at stafford crown court. If you have any questions you would like to put to me i would be more than happy to talk to you.
Glyn (Mr A)

I was intrigued, particularly by his claim that the police had forbidden him from speaking to me. In my careful reply I suggested he leave a message with our Shropshire friends, warning him that our mail had been interfered with and email and phone were insecure. Mr A responded: "Forwarded brand new unregistered mobile to your friends." On arriving to stay with them after the Appeal, we phoned him. Once he was satisfied who we were, he texted a rendezvous. We proposed another closer to Shrewsbury. He accepted this – then stood us up.

Subsequently, a BBC TV reporter tipped me off that Mr A had been to see him, and he had seriously considered making a programme about what he told him. Apparently, the police did not want me to know George had indicated that at least three others were involved, and that a white van followed Hilda's car as back-up. I recalled that one witness, driving a truck along Telford Way when the car overtook him, said his view was obscured by a white van tailing it. This threatened the police line that George had acted alone, and corroborated the fingernail DNA evidence.

Determined to get answers to questions on which the police had stonewalled at our post-trial meeting in May 2005, I demanded a final meeting. On 20 June 2006, we returned to Stourport on Severn Police Station where we spent three hours with newly promoted Detective Superintendent Brunger, DI Rik Klair and retired DC Partridge. Once again, Kate took detailed notes.

Brunger assured us that, although the case was finally closed, the police would retain the 600 boxes of material and all the exhibits forever. In response to my allegation of a potential miscarriage of justice, he declared: "This is about the search for the truth. If you thought there was some form of injustice, how could I and all the other officers sleep at night? There were over sixty officers on this case. If you ask each one of them if they have any doubts that Andrew George was the sole person, there will not be any. We all agree we've done the right thing – don't we Rik? Nick?" Vigorous nods; after all, careers, reputations and pensions were on the line.

I presented them with copies of the Forensic Science Service replies to my letters about Hilda's missing body parts and body sheet. Again Brunger was offhand. "I'm not surprised they're missing – not surprised at all; if some items deteriorate, they get rid of them." Kate challenged him that there must be records available which showed where body parts had been stored, which ones had been destroyed, and why. The records seemed to have gone missing too. His excuses were unbelievable: "In those days there were lots of missing body parts"; "It was complete chaos"; "There was room for human error"; "No request was made for them to keep anything"; and "Forensics are dealing with lots of murders."

After the fingernail DNA evidence episode at the Appeal, I demanded a detailed explanation. Brunger explained that tests on nail clippings from both Hilda's hands had resulted in a partial, mixed response of 11 alleles for someone other than Hilda. "Therefore you could not identify it to a specific person, but you could eliminate suspects." Partridge had identified over a hundred suspects, collecting their DNA and eliminating them.

A Besford House inmate in 1984, who was eleven years old at the time, later told us the police admitted to him in 2003 they did not believe George committed the crime alone. Evidence for this was that, after he was charged with Hilda's murder, all staff and inmates – including him – were fingerprinted, photographed and DNA samples taken! Using this procedure, they also cleared 'Cock-eye' and 'Laney', mentioned by Mr A as George's accomplices, and the rest of his family.

Brunger tried unsuccessfully to convince us that the fingernail DNA was contaminated. He claimed the mortuary procedures were not sterile; the pliers used to extract the whole fingernails on each hand could have been used in previous post mortems and not properly cleaned. DNA "could have come off the top of the fingernails, or off someone touching the body – it could have even come off her hands, or even have got under her nails from another body which had previously been on the slab."

We were incredulous. Suddenly all-conquering DNA was no better than a fingerprint. Did they think the cadaver had somehow "scratched" DNA off the mortuary table? Surely the mortuary staff would have been wearing gloves when handling the body and would have cleaned down the table after each autopsy? We understood fingernails were only removed in a murder case, so the pliers would not have been in regular use. DNA from under Hilda's fingernails or from her hands would most likely be from her male assailant. If it was sufficiently uncontaminated to eliminate over a hundred suspects, surely it should have been good enough to eliminate George?

To our surprise, Brunger suddenly agreed the fingernail DNA was not Andrew George's. An intense exchange ensued between him and my enraged Rottweiler, while furiously touch-typing on her laptop.

Kate: "Matching male DNA from under fingernails from both hands is highly significant evidence." This proved Hilda put up a fight. "Hilda would have done that – she was a feisty person. She said she would fight to protect her papers. Remember how I sent you extracts from her diaries recounting how she threatened boys stealing her fruit?"

Brunger blustered: "Hilda may not have put up a fight – I know a lot of women in rape cases who didn't fight back. Some people are petrified in a frightening situation. They don't always act to personality. Police officers who are big men can suddenly panic, whereas small men can sometimes become aggressive. It's not an exact science. Some people can become petrified by a knife."

Kate: "Hilda may have been petrified, but she had defensive wounds when she put her hands up to stop the knife – surely she would have tried to stop a rape as well? Anyway, how can you hold a knife and try to rape someone at the same time?" She pressed harder: "Was Dr Acland's DNA checked against the fingernail DNA and eliminated?"

Brunger seemed well-briefed for this question. "Yes, but his two assistants have since died and their families would not want their bodies exhumed in order to eliminate them." This was off the wall.

Kate: "Was there a report about how hygienic the mortuary and instruments were at the time? When had the previous post mortem taken place?"

Brunger ducked for cover. "You can write to Acland directly for answers to these questions." I did, but received no reply. We subsequently learned that two other autopsies were performed on Friday 23 March, and Hilda's was the only one done over the weekend. Moreover, it was standard practice to sterilise all tables, floor and equipment after autopsies on a Friday.

Finally, we asked to view the exhibits. Kate, determined to shield me from the stress of examining Hilda's bloodstained clothing, took the lead, while

I gratefully made notes. As she interrogated the police from a woman's viewpoint, they became increasingly uncomfortable.

The Totes rain hat was nothing like the wide-brimmed, brown felt hat many witnesses saw Hilda wearing. We were not allowed to see the car keys found in the coat pocket. When asked if they had done a fingerprint test on them, Klair seemed surprised and asked why they should have. Kate: "The driver would have touched them." He looked embarrassed: "They were probably the spare set, and you have to have special sorts of surfaces to have fingerprints taken off." This was farcical nonsense. Caught out, now the police were dismissing the one piece of evidence suggesting Hilda had been abducted in her own car.

The suspender belt was found 24 yards from the body towards the overgrown former gateway through which Hilda was supposed to have crawled. Probably made by her, it was very worn and frayed. There were three tears, not cuts, in the front, and the right rear clip was missing a rubber grommet. It was done up and there was no obvious blood or mud. Kate remembered a grommet was found on the bed in the small back bedroom where the sexual attack was purported to have happened.

Kate's request to view the stockings produced a perverse response: "No, you might put your DNA on them." She retorted that she could prove she was living in New Zealand in 1984 looking after three daughters under five; and she would relish having her DNA eliminated. The stockings were held up – but she was not to touch them. They were extraordinary. The one found on Hilda's left leg was caked in mud and bloodstained around the ankle area; but the other one found nearby was not. Both were darned with brown wool in various places, and one had a big hole near the top.

Kate's mind raced. Hilda would not have worn such old, holed stockings for shopping, let alone to go out to lunch. If her suspender belt came off where it was found, surely both stockings would have come off at the same time still attached to the grommets? So why was the missing grommet not found in the copse? As it was found in the bedroom, then perhaps its suspender belt was with it awaiting repair, along with the stockings? How could Hilda have pulled the belt off if it was still done up as it was found? Her hands were too arthritic and painful from the knife cuts, and she had a broken right collar bone and was right-handed. Had she done so, there would have been more blood on it from her injuries. If Andrew George had pulled both belt and stockings off her in some form of frenzied sexual activity in the copse, as insinuated by Latham, would he have first unclipped both stockings, leaving one on the body, before doing up the belt again and throwing it away nearby? During the trial, forensic expert Mark Webster observed correctly that a suspender belt is not designed to come off the body easily. With all these unanswered questions, our suspicions grew that it, too, had been planted.

Hilda's boots, made of beige coloured soft quilted cotton, were like slippers with rubber soles. The left one had slight bloodstaining on the outside near the ankle, but otherwise was surprisingly clean – which tallied with the bloodstained stocking found on Hilda's left leg. The right one had more blood on the back flaps and was caked in mud right up the heel to the ankle; yet the right stocking had no blood or mud on it. The boots were found 185 yards from Moat Copse, thirty feet apart lying in the furrows of unplanted ground skirting the field. If she had crawled all the way to the copse, why did the stocking ostensibly from Hilda's right leg have hardly any mud on it?

Her spectacles were found broken in half five feet apart. The lenses were intact, but there were about eight broken pieces of the rims in the forensic bag. They were found 20 feet from the other side of the hedge from Funeral Field, and 23 feet from the rain hat and knife in the ditch on the road side of the hedge. Did this indicate her assailant took her along the far side? If so, how did she get through the hedge? Or did her assailant throw them over? Or were they planted by the sinister man in a suit seen following the far side of the hedge by tractor driver Bryan Salter on the Thursday afternoon?

It was unlikely Hilda was wearing spectacles when she returned to Ravenscroft after visiting Mary O'Connor. Neither Mary nor any other witness commented that she was. No-one seemed to have asked why she would have worn them during the car journey. She did not need them for walking, and most witnesses said she looked unconscious in her car. Another pair was found smashed in the back bedroom where she was supposed to have been sexually assaulted. So was this more planted evidence to suggest a struggle upstairs, and then by the hedge – when probably she had been quickly overpowered, drugged and abducted to a safe house?

Next, Klair and Partridge held up Hilda's multi-coloured cardigan made of thick, loosely knitted white wool, with rainbow stripes of pink, blue-green and yellow. The large brown wooden buttons down the front were all done up. There were cuts and extensive bloodstaining around where her arm had been stabbed, and slightly above and to the right of where her navel would have been.

Kate could not resist the temptation. Looking directly at both detectives, she asked if all pieces of clothing had been tested for semen. Klair replied they had, but nothing was found other than on the slip and hanky. Partridge, clearly rattled by her question, took some time before contradicting his colleague. "Yes, there was a weak positive for semen on the cardigan, but we couldn't tell if it was aspermic." When asked if it had been DNA tested to eliminate the George family like the fingernail evidence had, he said "No". He would have been unaware that by then we knew **the forensic expert had concluded the semen on the cardigan, as well as the fingernail DNA, could not have originated from any male member of the George family**. Despite the weak samples, *here was enough corroboration of the fingernail DNA to prove other men were involved, and to acquit Andrew George.*

The aubergine mohair jumper Hilda was wearing under the cardigan had little buttons down the V neck. Like the cardigan, the cuts and bloodstains matched the body wounds. Her vest was cream, long, very old and worn, with its left shoulder strap broken at the back. It was soaked in blood around the cuts near the liver, and there was diffuse bloodstaining down the right hand side.

The very thick old brown coat was slightly muddy down the front where four large buttons were done up. A 2 cm knife cut in the right sleeve clearly matched the wound in Hilda's arm. There was no mud on the underside of the sleeves: we had expected to see some because of the police theory, backed by Acland, that she had crawled across the field.

In the trial, Webster noted several small cuts in the lining which had not penetrated the outside of the coat, and which did not correspond with the wounds to the body. Latham made the obvious point that if there were knife wounds with no matching holes in the coat, "the knife can't have gone through the coat to the body." However, cuts in the coat which did not match the wounds raised the possibility that *the coat cuts had been made afterwards.*

The inside of the coat, on the right-hand side, was heavily bloodstained. If she was stabbed standing up, being frogmarched as the police suggested, we would have expected blood dripping down her body to have stained her skirt and suspender belt.

The light green skirt, found zipped up and inside out near Hilda's body, had no obvious mud or bloodstaining on it. It had a silk lining, elastic waistband, a brand name tag at the back, and would have been above the knee on Hilda. There were three holes close together at the *back* of the skirt near the tag, and another half inch cut in the front above the hem.

When Kate checked her trial transcript she was surprised by Webster's detailed account of the cuts to the skirt. Crucially, he did not state these were in the back. Later we discovered the police were aware of some of these very significant anomalies. An extract from the transcript of the interrogation of George by two police officers at Shrewsbury Police Station in June 2003 follows:

> ...Because there's some cuts in her skirt you see that coincide with the cuts on her body but if they were to coincide, match up, she would have to have been wearing it the wrong way round.

Kate also spotted that the cuts on the skirt bore no relation to Hilda's wounds, even if she had worn it back to front. The wounds were too high on her body. A more plausible, but sinister, explanation is that *the skirt cuts had been made after it had been taken off Hilda* – if she was ever wearing it during her abduction.

At the trial, Webster confirmed there was no trace of semen on the skirt or suspender belt. However, it was never established whether the staining was on the underside or skirt side of the slip. He could not determine whether the semen staining was deposited when the skirt and suspender belt were being worn or after they had been removed. This brings into question whether both garments were even being worn by Hilda in her house during the alleged attack? This becomes more plausible when Webster stated the staining could have been produced by contact with a semen-wet object, for instance another garment or a hand bearing wet semen.

According to Mrs Latter, the skirt's matching jacket had been lying on the bed in the back bedroom for some time; and one old suspender belt had been waiting to be repaired in the large guest bedroom for weeks before the murder. Hilda would never have changed into such old clothes for a lunch date, or even to go shopping.

So why had the police ignored the obvious deduction: who forced her to change? Was it because this effectively ruled out a lone, petty burglar, and raised the inconvenient likelihood that more than one intruder must have been involved? In sum, did all these anomalies, questions and suspicions point to a deliberate decision to demonstrate the State security system's power to finally control and humiliate Hilda?

After his failed appeal, Andrew George gave me permission to visit him in HM Prison, Parkhurst on the Isle of Wight. He could have refused to see me. I knew that at any point he could end the meeting, but we were together for over an hour. I did not know if he was speaking the truth, and some of his answers contradicted what he said in the trial. However, throughout George remained alert, respectful, held eye contact and showed no sign of stress.

I asked him directly: "Was Hilda's car there?"

"No. I saw the door open facing the road. I never tried burgling a place if anyone was there – it was too much grief."

This led me to go through his shotgun burglary a week after Hilda was abducted. George confirmed he knew the teacher who owned the gun, where he lived and that he was teaching. "I did it because I felt extremely frustrated and angry about things."

"Did you fire it to get arrested and be taken away from Shrewsbury?"
He nodded.

"Is it true you told the police that when you went into Hilda's house, two men held guns to your head, warned you not to talk about what you saw, and promised you £60,000 if you kept your mouth shut?" Another nod. I added: "There were a lot of valuables to steal, like silver. I know, because I cleared the house." Nod and chuckle. "I also know about your burglary a week before, where you stole just a little cash and shared it out to friends in Besford House."

He grinned: "Yeah, I was a bit stupid."

When I described my theory about the abduction route, he nodded again, and said: "She never was in the field – they took her somewhere else."

How did he know that? I told him about Ian Scott's story that the body was not in the copse on the day after Hilda was abducted – and how this meant the crime was much more complicated than the police theory.

He agreed: "It was much bigger than the Shrewsbury police."

"So in your trial you had to say things which were not true to try to blame your brother?"

He nodded, replying: "If I had murdered Miss Murrell, I would have topped myself. I had lots of opportunity, especially when I was taking drugs."

I told him about our mail interference, which the police agreed was professionally done.

He said: "Why was this happening to you if it's just about me? You take care, Mr Green."

I described how I met a woman in Shrewsbury who taught him. "She said you were naughty – but only a rascal, not a murderer."

He replied: "Though I was always getting into trouble, I've never served time before. I always got caught and admitted it. The police let me go because they thought I hadn't done it. I wouldn't have stayed in Shrewsbury if I'd committed such a terrible crime." Pause. "Perhaps it was my fate."

CHAPTER 12

OTHER RELATED VICTIMS

During my pursuit of the truth about Hilda's death, I came across others who had experienced surveillance, harassment, death threats, assaults or worse when trying to give the police information pointing to a more sinister motive than a petty burglary gone wrong. I have described what happened to Don Arnott, Con Purser, Judith Cook, Dora Russell, and the telephone engineer.

The stories that follow about Ian and Thalia Campbell, Laurens Otter, Avraham Sasa, Philip Griffith, Karen Silkwood, Dr Rosalie Bertell, Dr Patricia Sheehan, Patsy Dale, Willie McRae and Dr David Kelly also help to answer a question often put to me: why was Hilda singled out for such horrific treatment? My answer is that her experience was part of a widespread pattern. In five of these latter cases, we met the victims and/or their family representatives, who gave permission and indeed asked us to publish their edited stories – and to tell the police about them. Four of them relate to witnesses with dangerous or inconvenient information about Hilda; and the remainder had information threatening the nuclear industry. My final case study about Kelly has several parallels with Hilda's case, with which it has been linked by the British media.

───────── ⊗⊗⊗ ─────────

Ian and Thalia Campbell are well known anti-nuclear campaigners. Thalia helped found the Greenham Common women's peace camp in 1981 against US cruise missiles. From the moment they offered inconvenient information to the police about Hilda, they experienced intimidation.

Early in 1984, Ian Campbell was running for election to the European Parliament as the Labour Party candidate for North West Wales. After speaking at a campaign meeting shortly before Hilda was found, two women who knew Hilda told him she feared for her life – hence her consequent daily contact with trusted friends by telephone. They were concerned Hilda had not been in touch recently and, when they had phoned her, there had been no answer. Late on Saturday 24 March, the Campbells returned home to hear of Hilda's murder on the midnight news. Shocked, Thalia phoned Shrewsbury Police at 1.30 am on the Sunday morning. The duty sergeant took a keen interest when she explained Hilda's friends' concerns. Two days later two men came to their door. One introduced himself as a senior detective and the other as his 'driver'. Both treated the Campbells with contempt, telling them it was an opportunist burglary, they had a suspect, and not to take it any further. Thalia told me: "We felt they were there to find out what we knew, and to bully us and head us off." Ian was so concerned he phoned his media contacts – but they all accepted the police line.

Ian was driving out of Llangollen alone late one night a few weeks later when a car with no lights followed him. At the end of street lights, it drove gently into his car from behind. He tried to slow down, but it pushed him along the road. He steered towards a phone box in a lay-by, jumped out and dialled 999. As his pursuer drove close up against the door to prevent him opening it, he saw it was a marked police car with two men inside. On the phone he demanded that the police call off their patrol car – whereupon it put on its lights, reversed and drove slowly away. Campbell told the operator he would make an official complaint.

The following morning, he did so with a local Labour MP at the police area headquarters near Ruabon. Later he was told "both officers had accepted early retirement on health grounds, so his complaint could not be pursued". Undeterred, the Campbells spoke to reporters and at peace rallies and meetings about their concerns about Hilda's murder, despite more harassment.

Some years afterwards, they met a retired police officer in Wales and became friends. "He said he had been in the West Mercia CID at the time of the Hilda Murrell case." Apparently, he had been taken off the case after expressing misgivings about it to the Chief Constable. "He told us he was compulsorily sectioned and detained under the Mental Health Act for two years in a mental institution. He was released on condition that he never spoke to anybody about this, otherwise his pension would be stopped. He accepted early retirement on health grounds." About ten years later, he confided to them that "it was a State murder". When we interviewed a sympathetic retired West Mercia detective, we asked him to check this out. He confirmed it – but warned us not to try to meet the poor man, who had lost his memory.

⸻ ✤ ⸻

Early in 1988 Laurens Otter wrote asking if I had received a letter from his long-standing friend, Avraham Sasa, in Bath. I had not. Sasa's sister had just told him he had died in September 1987. Apparently, one wet evening Sasa was walking into town for a CND meeting when a car stopped on the other side of the road. The driver called him over asking for directions – whereupon another car knocked him down and drove off.

Otter realised with a shock that Sasa's last letter had arrived about ten days after his death. It took two weeks to be delivered, and was obviously opened. Sasa had unwisely asked him for my address, because he had "learned some information relevant to the Murrell case too sensitive to put in a letter". Aware that I lived nearby, he intended to brief me and tell Otter about it when he visited him before Christmas – but of course he had not appeared.

Castle Frome, where Sasa was involved in organic farming, was a training ground for the Special Air Service. Having been involved in military intelligence in World War Two and done military service in Israel, Sasa could well have been confided in but overheard, or had heard a pub conversation there.

Also, Otter told me that on 4 September 1987 he had received an anonymous phone call from a man who said: "Why don't you top yourself? Because people like you poke your nose in where it's not wanted, we killed the Murrell woman; and now we've killed your other friend."

"Which other friend?"

"You don't know about that?"

What was more, twice within the previous week while Sasa's letter was in the post to him two cars had narrowly missed Otter when he was out walking. On the first occasion, when he heard a car mount the pavement behind him, he threw himself behind a brick pillar in a gateway. A couple of days later, a car sitting in a lay-by suddenly started off and drove rapidly towards him; again if he had not jumped out of the way he would have been knocked down.

On 3 May 1986, I met Eileen Griffith, an anti-nuclear campaigner and rose grower friend of Hilda's who lived near Fron Goch. When I introduced myself to this 68- year-old little hunch-backed woman, she gasped: "This is amazing. A year ago today, my son Philip was found murdered in Brighton – because he had found out something important about Hilda's murder. Come and see where he is." She led me across her beautiful garden beside a disused chapel. On his grave she had planted a Hilda Murrell rose. She said he knew Hilda and had visited her a couple of times.

Over mugs of tea, she told me that on 3 May 1985 her 31-year-old adopted son Philip had phoned her from a public callbox in Brighton sounding upset and scared. He warned Eileen against making any more enquiries about Hilda. "Please don't – I know what you're like. And keep quiet about this: I've just come from a pub where I overheard three men bragging about how they had killed her. I know a lot of what happened." When she told him to go the police he told her not to be so naïve: "The police are up to their necks in it." He wanted to stay the weekend with her because "it is all so dangerous here". Philip then phoned his younger brother Jerry "in a terrible state – he feared for his life", before phoning his older sister twice. The first time, he said he had a ticket for France departing the next day to pick fruit and stay with friends as he had done for many years. She was surprised when he phoned again at about 6.30 pm, sounding "strange: as though he had been drinking, but not drunk – and very frightened". He kept repeating: "Please listen to me, I will telephone you when I get to France." A man called 'Sime' took over the phone and reassured her Philip was OK. This call was made 90 minutes before the alleged official time of death at 8 pm.

However, David Thomas was walking his dog in Queen's Park when he found Philip 'still alive' propped up against a tree at 6.02 am on 4 May. He recognised him immediately because he was his bricklayer foreman on a building site. He had tried to revive him and went to phone an ambulance. The police surgeon was unable to give a cause of death. A used hypodermic syringe was found on the body.

Eileen assumed Philip's failure to contact her meant he had gone to France. It took two weeks before her local policeman gave her the terrible news. When she and her daughter formally identified him they saw a severe wound on his forehead: "It was a big, round bloody mess. He had been hit with something like a hammer." Yet when Thomas left him, he was adamant there had been no head wound. So someone had finished him off. When his family challenged the police, they said it had happened when his body was being carried into the ambulance. This convinced the family that Philip had been murdered, and they suspected the police were not investigating it objectively because of the link with Hilda's case. Mindful of Philip's warning, Eileen did not tell the police the contents of his last desperate phone call to her.

His flat had been emptied by someone. Except for his watch, an expired 12-month British Visitor's passport, £3 cash and an empty wage packet, all his possessions – including a ticket to France and a new suit bought specially for the trip – were missing. The police initially treated the death as a potential murder, but later suspected suicide. He had three injection punctures above his right elbow. A Home Office forensic pathologist, Dr Basil Purdue, told the inquest Philip had "morphine in the blood but not enough for a lethal overdose". He was a "well-nourished, muscular young man", with no evidence of other drug-taking. The autopsy report stated that 'a very large amount of alcohol in the body would have contributed to his death, but would not on its own have proved fatal in the absence of postural asphyxia or inhalation of vomit, evidence of neither of which was present'.

In a letter from the police to Eileen, they stated that Purdue also reported:

    ...the presence of numerous superficial bruises and
    directional abrasions about the body, especially on the
    limbs and trunk suggest that the body was manhandled into
    the place and position in which it was found at about the
    time of death or very shortly before or after. There is
    no evidence of a fight or struggle, and the injuries would
    in no way have contributed to death.

He made no mention of the severe head wound; nor did he comment that no-one could have injected himself three times above the right elbow, and then placed the syringe somewhere on his body.

Philip was quite a heavy man. If he was drugged, then dragged from a house and driven in a car to the park, it would have taken at least two men to do it. Who were they, and what was their motive? To the credit of East Sussex Coroner Edward Grace, he said: "Because Philip had drunk so much, it was possible that he was not able to resist someone else injecting him with the drug. Perhaps he did take too much drink to be good for him; but what happened after that I am sure was not his fault. I am sure he would not have deliberately injected himself or allowed himself to be injected if he were sober. Something happened which we can only guess at to cause his death." He recorded an open verdict.

Eileen had few doubts about what happened. Philip's abrupt exit from the pub alerted the thugs to the probability that he had overheard them. He had to be silenced; so they followed him, to find him emerging from a public phone box.

Frustrated by the lack of information from the police and unsatisfactory outcome of the inquest, the Griffith family demanded a meeting with senior police. Among many other unanswered questions, they asked why Philip's flat was not searched until two weeks after his death. Eileen then employed a solicitor to follow these up. When he challenged the police that Philip had been murdered, Assistant Chief Constable Dibley wrote back:

> There is no evidence of corruption, murder, assault, of any other offence and no evidence of any injustice. The person or persons who placed a body in the park have not been traced in spite of substantial effort by police... At no time was it ever assumed by Police that this was a case of suicide... there is certainly a strong possibility, that having consumed excessive alcohol [Philip] took a voluntary or accidental drug overdose.

He reassured the family that the case was not closed and they "would be contacted in the event of any further developments".

The family was outraged by the police suggestion either that he might have been suicidal or on drugs. Morphine was found in the used syringe. This is used for only two purposes: as a painkiller, or to kill. However, as it is derived from heroin, it was far more likely that his killers had confused the trail with both alcohol and morphine.

I promised Eileen to do what I could, and persuaded John Osmond of HTV to send researchers to Brighton. On 18 September 1986, *Wales This Week* featured a programme about Philip's mysterious death. No direct link with Hilda's murder was established; but there had undoubtedly been some form of cover-up.

Things went quiet until, following the tenth anniversary of Hilda's death, Kate and I visited Eileen. Soon afterwards, I received confirmation from a reliable source that Philip had been followed out of the pub. When the thugs had seen him go into a phone box, "they got some of their mates onto him. He was drugged in the flat and pulled down the stairs, and placed in a sleeping bag. The names of two of the guys who beat him were Peter and Simon…".

At the end of July 1994 I visited Philip's sister, a solo mother with two young children. Nevertheless, after I had briefed her, she resumed investigating her beloved brother's murder. She then experienced phone harassment, including silent calls, and was watched for 4-5 days by two men parked in a strange car in her *cul de sac*. When a male friend challenged them, they drove off "like the clappers" and never returned. Understandably, she abandoned her enquiries. Since then, the family has heard nothing. Eileen died in 2005 without even receiving a copy of Philip's death certificate.

Hilda has been labelled by some media as the 'British Karen Silkwood'. In 1974 Silkwood, a 27-year-old American union activist at an Oklahoma plutonium processing plant, had compiled a damning dossier of violations of safety regulations involving workers exposed to dangerous levels of radiation and denied protective clothing. She arranged to hand over her evidence to a *New York Times* journalist, but the meeting never took place. She was found dead at the wheel of her car, which had left the road and crashed into a concrete culvert. Tyre tracks indicated she had been forced off by another vehicle; the dossier was missing; and her home was found to have been deliberately contaminated with plutonium.

Although Hilda never spoke to me about Silkwood's death, she had kept the issue of the *Ecologist* magazine featuring her case.

Shortly before her murder, Hilda sent a donation to support the work of American Catholic nun and researcher for the National Cancer Institute, Dr Rosalie Bertell. Like some other whistleblowers against the nuclear industry, there were attempts on Bertell's life.

In 1977 Bertell discovered that radiation in the atmosphere, even at low levels accepted as safe, was responsible for increased incidence of leukaemia – and also diabetes, hardening of the arteries, cataracts and coronary disease. This had serious implications not only for people working in military and civil nuclear plants but also for anyone living in neighbouring communities.

When we first met in 1994, Bertell told me: "The retaliation began. It was a surprise – mail opened; a nasty article in the local paper; a fuss at work led by a man whose research was funded by the Defence Department." As she became more widely known as a speaker, she found herself being met at airports by strangers who addressed her by name and offered to take her to her hotel. On one occasion she allowed a man, posing as an airport official, to lead her to her flight: she missed it and her speaking engagement. She also suffered mysterious cases of sudden and severe illnesses at gatherings where no-one else got sick.

In 1978 Bertell was openly threatened after she performed better in a TV debate than a physicist from a local nuclear power plant. Afterwards an executive from the power company angrily warned her: "Stay out of the Rochester area or we'll get you". Ten months later she returned, a week after the power plant had malfunctioned attracting major publicity. Having given a presentation in the local hospital, she set off home along a three-lane expressway to Buffalo.

Suddenly, a car following her came up on her left side and tried to force her to crash into a car in the slow right-hand lane. As she braked to avoid a collision, the lone male driver accelerated ahead of her and dropped a metal object out of his window. It landed directly in front of her car and was sharp enough to puncture a brand-new, steel-belted radial tyre, and heavy enough to bend the wheel rim. Bertell's car veered left across the fast lane. By some miracle, the cars following avoided her. She regained enough control to come to rest on the median strip.

As she was inspecting the damage, a brown car with 'Sheriff' written on the side and two blue lights on the roof stopped. The two male occupants were not wearing uniforms, and did not get out. They were only interested in whether she had noted the licence number of the car which caused the damage, and whether she retrieved the object. When she said no, they told her the Rochester police would come, and took off. The police never came. On reporting the incident, the sheriff's department confirmed there were no brown cars in the department fleet, and regulations required officers to stay with a disabled vehicle until help arrived. They also failed to investigate the incident. Later she learned her assailant was probably an employee of the security agency at the nuclear power plant.

Bertell moved to Toronto in Canada, where she later founded the International Institute of Concern for Public Health. On 19 November 1981, as she and three fellow nuns were going to bed, four shots were fired through the fourth floor bedroom windows at the back of their convent. No bullets were recovered; however, from the bullet holes in the windows, the police believed the shots were fired from over 50 yards away – so the bullets were from at least a .22 calibre rifle. The harassment stopped after that incident. According to Bertell, "the Jesuits talked with the Secret Service and put a stop to it".

In 1983, she accepted an invitation from Gerard Morgan-Grenville to speak at the Sizewell Inquiry. Soon after I presented Hilda's paper, she presented her latest research into the deaths of low-weight babies, born downwind of nuclear reactors in Wisconsin. This provided further evidence that low-level radiation caused other illnesses apart from cancers and genetic disorders. Hilda had donated £50 towards Bertell's costs to attend Sizewell and another

£50 towards getting her book *No Immediate Danger* published. Morgan-Grenville then sent Hilda Bertell's draft submission. This, and another paper on the genetic and other effects of radiation by British Professor Patricia Lindop, were two documents I never found when clearing Hilda's house. In her early fifties, Lindop suffered a stroke at around the same time Don Arnott had his heart attack.

Bertell told me that only a fraction of the attacks on anti-nuclear campaigners were ever made public. In some cases activists were successfully intimidated into silence; in others, they were effectively eliminated in 'accidents'.

———∞∞∞———

In the early 1990s Sellafield, on the Cumbrian coast, was causing increasing concern on the other side of the Irish Sea. The massive Thermal Oxide Reprocessing Plant (THORP) was due to open in the face of opposition from campaign groups and the Irish Labour Party. It was feared more radioactive waste would be blown or washed across the sea. Meanwhile, new evidence was emerging about the impact of the world's first serious radioactive fire in 1957 at Windscale, which subsequently was renamed Sellafield because of this.

Back in the 1980s, Irish scientist Dr Patricia Sheehan had discovered a cluster of children born with Down's syndrome whose mothers had been at a boarding school together in the Irish coastal town of Dundalk in the 1950s. Her study of 157 mothers showed they had eight Down's syndrome babies, twelve with other birth defects, two stillbirths and one death within six weeks of birth.

A few months before her suspicious death in a car crash in 1994, the Irish papers reported Dr Sheehan's results of a recent study amongst 319 women who had been at another boarding school on the coast at the same time. She had found that five gave birth to Down's syndrome babies, and 33 were born with other serious conditions including spina bifida, heart defects and deafness. Five mothers had stillbirths, seven babies died within weeks and six more died in childhood. Among the 1,086 pregnancies there were also 161 miscarriages and 23 premature births.

British Nuclear Fuels dismissed the Irish concerns about fallout – but someone tampered with the weather records. Dr Chris Busby, an independent expert on the health effects of low-level radiation, tracked down records for Windscale from the Meteorological Office Archives. Pages covering the day of the fire had been removed and replaced with new sheets, in a slightly different colour, which simply stated "No record". However, the Air Ministry meteorological records clearly showed the wind would have blown the cloud of radioactivity towards Ireland.

In June 1994, a few weeks before she was due to present her controversial evidence to an inquiry investigating the birth defects and alleged link with Windscale/Sellafield, Dr Sheehan was killed when driving alone. The Karen

Silkwood parallels are striking. Adi Roche, Chair of Irish CND, reported to me initially that another car had been involved. Colleagues said research papers she would have been carrying were not found in the car. She had told friends her mail had been opened and she had received death threats to "back off" from her research. The crash was never fully investigated.

The Stop THORP Alliance Dundalk group continued the struggle and was given £350,000 by the Irish Government to pay for 'technical assistance', but had to raise funds to take their case to court. In 2004 the Irish High Court ruled it did not have jurisdiction against British Nuclear Fuels. A judgement in favour of the children would have unleashed millions in compensation claims, creating a greater impact on the nuclear industry than any protest by environmentalists or foreign government.

Patsy Dale (formerly Davis) suffered 27 years of abuse and violence because she became a threat to the Royal Navy's nuclear establishment. Most people cannot believe a law-abiding British citizen could be subjected to such an horrific campaign of intimidation and torture in two 'democratic' countries. With police, media, lawyers, MPs and MEPs aware of the ongoing intimidation; death threats to Patsy and me; rapes and many attempts to murder her, it is astounding that it continued until her death in August 2011. Her story deserves a book in its own right – this is a summary.

In March 1990 I was asked to meet Chris Bangert, a British Telecom employee and Quaker giving Patsy support. He explained that, when two men attacked her in her home near Staines in 1987, only notes for her draft book were taken. Her assailants left behind two photocopied pages depicting the police sketches of Hilda's murderer from *Death of a Rose-Grower*, with 'DEATH' scrawled between them. The message was clear: "Shut up or you will end up like Hilda". Patsy wondered if the thugs were connected to Hilda's murder.

Bangert and I met her in June 1990 just before she fled in desperation to her 84-year-old mother in Ennis in western Ireland to escape her tormentors. She had been married to a sonar operator serving in *HMS Resolution*, the Royal Navy's first submarine armed with Polaris nuclear-tipped ballistic missiles. In 1968 their first son was born perfectly healthy. Five years later Stephen was born with a harelip and a cleft palate, damage to the front temporal lobe of his brain and a defect in his right eye. She had suffered four miscarriages and a daughter, Rosanne, was prematurely stillborn.

Her research, done without her husband's support, uncovered another five deformed children born within 26 months whose fathers were junior ratings in *HMS Resolution*, four of them with harelip and cleft palate – an incidence rate of one in 28. Some children had hydrocephalus and spina bifida.

Patsy's ordeal began when she agreed to be interviewed in a 1985 Yorkshire Television documentary called 'Inside Britain's Bomb' about radiation leaks in

Polaris submarines. Other affected parents were frightened off by threats over jobs, pensions and the Official Secrets Act. In October 1985 Patsy received four calls warning she would be killed if she persisted with the interview. Threats followed from a suited man with short, fair, curly hair and a pock-marked face in a black VW Scirocco as she walked to work with a friend. Other malicious callers listed personal details of her elder son and his friends and their daily schedule, confirming they were all under surveillance.

Yorkshire Television contracted former MI5 agent Gary Murray to investigate. When he met Staines Police on Patsy's behalf, they said the Navy had told them Patsy was trying to extract compensation from the Ministry of Defence. Murray advised her to make a sworn affidavit in case she was killed, and later published it in his book *Enemies of the State*. He experienced sabotage to his car while investigating another case about civilian workers on nuclear submarines. Confirming Patsy's phone was bugged, he showed her how to record all incoming conversations. He then received threatening calls from the same people who had threatened her. Her interview was subsequently broadcast on Yorkshire TV in December 1985. Soon after she found her front and back doors wide open, footprints in the snow, the tape recorder whirring and conversations erased.

In February 1987, two men introducing themselves as police officers knocked on her door at 11.30 pm. One was tall and broad wearing a trench coat and tortoise-shell spectacles; the shorter one had long greasy hair and was wearing jeans and a donkey jacket. She quickly recognised the pockmarks and voice of the taller man as the Scirocco driver whom she nicknamed 'Crater Face'. They burst in and slammed her back into a door. As she screamed, Crater Face tried to throttle her, warned her to stay quiet, and kicked the dog while the other man ransacked a nearby room. They stole her draft chapters, tapes recording phone calls and the phone numbers of affected families. This was when she found two pages from *Death of a Rose-Grower* with 'DEATH' written across it. On reporting this to the police, they dismissed her as a nuisance.

The death threats continued at home and work, despite changing her ex-directory number four times. In February 1989, Patsy armed herself with a friend's truncheon which she used when an intruder wielding a thin-bladed knife tried to strangle her. Her neighbour made a police statement after another man jumped over the garden fence having cut her Citizens' Band (CB) radio aerial lead.

One CB radio friend was Gordon Dale, a former British soldier who had served in Ulster and been a Vietnam mercenary in support of US Special Forces. When he started taking her phone calls and demanding the caller's name, his London flat was burgled and her papers and tapes stolen. After they married in October 1989 two 'police officers' questioned Gordon's sister, Patsy's papers and notes left with her were stolen, and Gordon's car was nearly forced off a motorway flyover by a black Scirocco.

Early in 1990 Paul Foot published details of Patsy's campaign and persecution in his *Daily Mirror* column. Embarrassed into action, Staines Police Detective Inspector Bruton fingerprinted the house and swept it for bugs, but nothing came of it.

Since 1984, Chris Bangert had lobbied five Labour MPs, including Tam Dalyell, to ask parliamentary questions and stir media interest. He also sought legal and police support, without success. When I first met Patsy with Bangert, she impressed me deeply as an honest, articulate and tenacious woman, and a devoted mother. I promised to try to persuade a lawyer to take up Stephen's case, and do some research through my naval contacts.

Immediately after they arrived in Ireland, the police (Garda) accused them of driving a stolen vehicle. Within weeks Crater Face, in the same VW Scirocco, resumed his harassment. On 11 April 1991, he brutally assaulted Patsy in an Ennis community centre toilet after a Bingo night. As she entered he grabbed her by the throat, threw her against a wall, kicked and punched her to the ground, and plunged a hypodermic needle into her leg. The security guard Michael Carmody heard her screams, called the police and took her to Ennis Hospital. The doctor, concerned at the seriousness of her injuries, offered to make a police statement. For the next five days she suffered nausea and vomiting twenty times a day – but no toxicology tests were done.

Patsy began sending me copies of her draft chapters, Gordon's daily log of ongoing harassment, and statements from people who witnessed the intimidation in Britain. At a 1991 conference on the health effects of low-level radiation, London solicitor Martyn Day agreed to take up Stephen's case, by trying to sue the Ministry of Defence for damages. I traced and interviewed retired *HMS Resolution* crew, including Patsy's former husband. I found no evidence of a radiation leak accident – but uncovered a potentially more serious cause.

When welders were repairing coolant pipes in the reactor compartment of the submarine during *HMS Resolution*'s first refit in Rosyth in 1971, several of the fathers of deformed children, including Stephen's, had acted as 'welding sentries', standing next to the welders with a fire extinguisher. None of them was ever required to wear even an industrial filter face mask, let alone an anti-gas respirator. They all confirmed this was so they "wouldn't feel nervous".

Alex Falconer, the European MP for Rosyth and former shop steward for dockyard workers during that refit, confirmed sentries wore white protective overalls, hats, gloves and overshoes – but no face masks. By contrast, each welder was protected by a ventilated suit and visor, and a forced-draught system which blew the fumes away from him – but towards the sentry. Don Arnott confirmed the most likely contamination pathway was inhalation of microscopic radioactive particles containing iron, cobalt or manganese isotopes released when welding stainless steel which had been neutron-activated, or from carcinogenic thorium in the welding arc. The particles would have gone directly into their bloodstream, risking damage to their genes and, consequently, defects in their children.

The problem applied to every nuclear submarine refit from the mid-1960s until the early 1990s, when heavy polythene trunking was finally introduced to draw off the welding fumes. Hundreds of families with deformed children could have been entitled to huge compensation. If established, the health and safety record of British nuclear propulsion would be discredited, and would have implications for the rest of the international nuclear industry. In November 1991, when Stephen was denied legal aid on the grounds of 'Crown exemption', Martyn Day reluctantly dropped his case.

My continuing investigations, plus Gordon's frequent phone calls, probably provoked the next outrage. In January 1992, while Patsy was walking home Crater Face drove alongside her repeating "Keep walking Mrs Dale", until they reached an empty building site. He got out, pointed a handgun at her, "pressed the barrel against my chest and said: 'As for you, and your trumped-up solicitor and so-called Commander – this is what you'll all get'." He then drove off. The Garda Detective Chief Superintendent took this seriously, allocating two detectives to tracing him, to no avail.

The media also showed support. I joined Patsy and Alex Falconer on a local radio programme, and a *Sunday Press* article with the headline 'Ennis woman will sue Britain over son's birth defects' re-ignited interest in her research and intimidation. The next day a folded piece of paper featuring Patsy's story from James Cutler's book *Britain's Nuclear Nightmare* with 'DEATH' scrawled on it was dropped in their letterbox.

The intimidation intensified. Their mail, like mine, was intercepted and tampered with. Patsy was home alone on 15 May 1992 when Crater Face again kicked and injected her, and demanded that she tell the Garda she had been lying. In a signed statement, a neighbour described Crater Face as a "white man, approximately 6 feet tall, wearing spectacles and a great ¾ length overcoat. His face was heavily pocked".

I accompanied the Dales in July 1992 to meet Detective Inspector Bruton again at Staines Police Station. He was impressed when the UK registration number of the Scirocco, E644 EOK, was confirmed false through the national computer. A year later, Gordon reported Crater Face's new white Citroen car number as J223 NCA, which Bruton also found to be false. While in Britain, another policeman confided that they had been told to stop their enquiries into the case. Meanwhile, Bangert convinced three Irish politicians to try to get police protection, but none eventuated.

In 1993 the family was often disturbed, especially at night, by intermittent tapping on doors and windows, or whistles. Letters spelling 'DEATH' were found on the doormat eight times in 15 weeks. Even Stephen, now six feet five inches tall and weighing 16 stone, felt scared after Crater Face pointed a semi-automatic pistol at him. Gordon tried to install a video camera above the front window to catch Crater Face; but the first time Patsy switched it on, he ducked out of sight and never approached the house the same way again.

In September 1993 they returned to Gordon's mother's London flat. Telephone death threats persisted for five weeks, and solicitor's letters and photographs of Patsy's injuries were stolen. So Bangert, who had recently found a publisher for Patsy's book, hosted them for a couple of weeks. Phone problems started immediately, followed by visits by 'police officers'. Within three months he died suddenly from a known heart condition, aged forty-eight. Patsy sent all his papers about her case to us in New Zealand.

I encouraged the Dales to write to MI5's new woman Director General, Stella Rimington. Within ten days all intimidation stopped for 16 months. In November 1995 the incessant window tapping resumed. Sometimes Gordon recorded over 200 different taps only minutes apart. After Gordon reported this to the Garda, Crater Face again threatened Patsy with a gun. Gordon wrote twice more to Rimington threatening to initiate a case at the European Court of Justice. A reply enclosed a leaflet advising he apply to the Security Service Tribunal.

Concerned about my safety, Kate kept copies of all documents in New Zealand and established an international support group. Crater Face warned Patsy not to correspond with Kate, and interference with our mail and phone intensified. After the *Irish Star* highlighted their case, Crater Face beat Patsy with an iron bar across her neck and upper arm. Despite leaving the bar for testing with the Garda, and offering to do a lie detector test, nothing happened. Following an interview for a documentary, a copy of Judith Cook's 1994 *Guardian* article 'True Lies' about Hilda was found on Patsy's bed with the words "Your [sic] dead" scrawled across it. Kate began a letter-writing campaign to citizen organizations such as Irish CND and Amnesty International, and leading politicians including Irish Foreign Minister Dick Spring as well as MPs in New Zealand and Australia. Spring's response was that "all complaints/incidents reported by the Dale family have been investigated with negative results".

Gordon's car then became a target. The air pressure in the tyres was deliberately inflated to a dangerous 60 psi; a new tyre was slashed with spikes normally only used by police; the clutch cable, and the steering malfunctioned while overtaking a slow-moving vehicle. A local mechanic who inspected the car offered to speak out publicly about the sabotage if anything happened to the family.

After two Irish women Green MEPs began asking questions about Patsy's case, for five weeks all intimidation stopped. When the window taps resumed they were witnessed by Irish CND's Eoin Dinan and a visiting Maori elder from New Zealand. A few weeks after Kate and I were married in January 1997, I returned to the UK for six months. Patsy was badly beaten about the head with a brick, and Gordon received a phoned death threat saying "As for Murrell and Sheehan – tell Rob Green he's next". Three more calls followed in quick succession: "Tell Mr Green to watch his grasses"; "The grass is greener on the other side" and, bizarrely, "The Green, Green, Grass of Home".

Kate kept up the pressure from New Zealand by sending photographs and affidavits from witnesses to the Irish Justice Minister and others. This prompted another telephoned taunt from Crater Face: "Katie is my darling, my darling". That same month carving knives were found on the back door mat four times, and Crater Face again half-strangled Patsy. He always knew when Patsy was alone, pouncing within minutes – confirming a comprehensive surveillance system was in use.

In October 1997, after pressure from members of the British Patsy Dale Support Group, Garda Detective Superintendent Kelly met the family and assured them he did not believe Gordon or Stephen were the perpetrators. Telephone monitoring equipment was finally installed, whereupon the family had peace for nearly a month.

We kept Superintendent Kelly updated regularly, and in March 1998 we met him in Ennis. He revealed that one night, when he and his wife were driving home from the cinema, they were followed by a car with no lights on. It sped up behind, raced past and then slammed its brakes on in front, causing him to stop suddenly. He felt the incident was linked to the Patsy case. Immediately after we left Ireland, Crater Face tried stabbing Patsy in the chest, but the knife was deflected by some jewellery. The knife was found on the back door mat and given to the Garda. Within hours he taunted: "Aren't I a clever little boy? I can get away with murder – sorry attempted murder – and I'm not that little." When the Garda turned off the telephone monitoring equipment because there had been no offensive calls for seven weeks, the calls resumed.

In June 1999 Patsy gave up her life-threatening struggle. She had endured 14 years of threats, abuse and assault – and had just been beaten again, this time by a younger, tall, dark-haired man. She had already spent much of the year in hospital and was physically and emotionally worn down. Gordon posted copies of all original documents to us and they moved to a country cottage where they lived safely and happily for nearly seven years.

This all changed after we visited them in June 2006 to check a draft of their story for this book. Aged 61, Patsy was on oxygen 16 hours a day – she had been diagnosed with lung cancer. On phoning them from Heathrow airport a week later, we learned they had received two death threats. We feared our visit had revealed their whereabouts and provoked the threats. One day in August, when Patsy was alone in the garden while Gordon and Stephen were out, a young man wearing a black jacket attacked her, injecting her twice in the thigh. Later, while Gordon took Stephen to the doctor, the same assailant broke into Patsy's bedroom, beat her up and cut the phone wire, oxygen tube, and radio power cord. The farmer landlord found her cowering behind the spare bed. We phoned the Garda repeatedly insisting that they take immediate action. They set up a monitor on their phones which prevented abusive calls for a few weeks until it was removed in late November.

The following day, while Gordon and Stephen were briefly in town with Patsy locked inside the house, her young tormentor returned. He tried strangling her with the phone cord, beat her with a baseball bat which he also used in an anal rape, raped her vaginally and orally and left her unconscious. The attack was carefully planned: the landlord was working in fields and his wife was out all day. Tragically, the Garda took three hours to respond to Gordon's emergency call. If they had sent an ambulance immediately, DNA from the blood and semen could have been retrieved before Gordon showered her and washed her clothes. Amazingly, Patsy recovered slowly with rape counselling and daily calls from us.

Six months later, just before they moved to Kilrush, Patsy was sitting alone in the locked car in the supermarket car park for a few minutes. Her assailant brazenly walked over and bragged to her through the window: "I've got away with rapes in Scotland; I've got away with rapes in Ireland, and now I've got a six-month posting in Wales."

Over the next year things were reasonably quiet apart from a couple more serious assaults. We believe this final, utterly incredible phase of Patsy's suffering was used to try to stop us publishing her story. So, to take pressure off them we told the family over the phone that we were not going to include it in this book. Since then they have largely been left in peace. However, Patsy did not live to read this, nor to see some justice for Stephen and herself. After weeks in intensive care with chronic breathing and other problems, she died in Limerick Hospital on 17 August 2011.

Although there were many attempts to murder her, Patsy probably survived them because, unlike other victims such as Dr Patricia Sheehan and Hilda Murrell, she lived in a house with two large, fearless, supportive men who have witnessed the consequences of attacks by her highly skilled, well-resourced and informed assailants. With an indomitable spirit, Patsy also had a group of supporters and politicians who know about the case, and a media profile that would turn her into a martyr.

Nonetheless, the fact that her tormentors were never apprehended leads to a disturbing suspicion of pressure on the police in both England and Ireland. Only the Security Services associated with the British government and nuclear industry were capable of this. Was their primary objective to break her psychologically as an example of what can be done to those who dare to oppose the British State?

Another suspicious death was that of a leading radical Scottish Nationalist Party (SNP) lawyer and anti-nuclear campaigner, Willie McRae. He was openly critical of the investigation into Hilda's case. On 5 April 1985, a week after the first anniversary of her murder, McRae left for his holiday home in the Western Highlands. He never arrived. The next morning, tourists found him unconscious and covered in blood at the wheel of his car, crashed off the road in an isolated spot. It was treated as an accident until a gunshot wound was found behind his right ear when he was examined in the hospital. He died 36 hours later without regaining consciousness. No formal inquest was held, and cause of death was officially recorded as suicide. However, papers and his smashed wristwatch were found about 20 yards from his car; and the gun, with no fingerprints on it, was in a stream even further away.

His close friend, Mary Johnston, said on an investigative TV programme, *Scottish Eye*, on 5 April 2011: "He wouldn't have done it [suicide]. Everything was going well for Willie: he had so many plans". She outlined several parallels with Hilda's case. Like her, McRae was preparing to give evidence at an inquiry into the nuclear industry, in Scotland. Apparently he told Mary that "now he had something they couldn't wriggle out of... Also, his holiday home was broken into – but nothing vital was taken. He was quite gleeful: they didn't get what they were looking for." Because of this, he told friends he knew he was under surveillance by Special Branch, his phone was tapped and mail opened, and was on a "hit list". One car, registration number XSJ4 32T, followed him to his home a few days before his death. On 6 April 1985, a group of walkers near where McRae's car crashed reported that, during the afternoon, a man drove up the road, parked, got out and fired some shots in their direction as if to warn them not to approach. His car was a red Ford Escort. Two years after McRae's death, Hamish Watt, a former SNP MP and Councillor in Grampian, told the *Aberdeen Press & Journal* that a nurse working at Aberdeen Royal Infirmary, where McRae was taken, told him that *two* bullet wounds were found in his brain – which clearly ruled out suicide.

Like Hilda, McRae was fearlessly opposed to the deep geological disposal of nuclear waste; and Don Arnott advised him at the Mullwharchar Inquiry in 1980 which overturned plans for such disposal in the Ayrshire Hills in southern Scotland. Gary Murray, in his book *Enemies of the State*, described McRae as "probably the nuclear industry's most formidable opponent in Scotland". Murray also wrote that, during World War Two, McRae served in the Royal Indian Navy in Naval Intelligence. While there, he joined the Indian Congress Party, at the time an illegal organization opposed to British occupation. This first brought him to the attention of the British Security Services who, Murray claimed, kept him under surveillance for the rest of his life.

On 7 December 2010, *The Scotsman* reported that, 25 years on, new evidence had emerged about McRae's mysterious death. Former policeman John Finnie, now the SNP group leader on the Highland Council, called for his case to be re-opened after receiving new information from several different sources pointing to a more sinister motive. Apparently, police removed the car from the scene, only to return it when it became known that aspects of McRae's death were suspicious. Another former police officer turned private investigator claimed he was asked by an anonymous client to place McRae under surveillance three weeks before he died; and days before his death his office was broken into.

∞∞∞

On 23 October 2007, a prominent article appeared in *The Times* headlined 'A weapons expert, a rose grower and a fantasist'. In it David Aaronovitch rubbished a sensational new book by Liberal Democrat MP Norman Baker, *The Strange Death of David Kelly*. Over the previous few days, the right-wing *Daily Mail* surprisingly had serialised extensive highlights. Baker exposed anomalies in the police investigation of the apparent suicide on 18 July 2003 of the chemical weapons expert and member of the United Nations inspection team in Iraq since 1991, who had fallen foul of the Blair government over the 'sexed up', 'dodgy' dossier justifying the 2003 invasion.

Parliament had just adjourned for the long summer recess when Dr Kelly's body was discovered. In extraordinary haste, within hours Blair commissioned a non-statutory inquiry by Lord Brian Hutton – a former Chief Justice for Northern Ireland, presiding over many juryless terrorist trials – instead of allowing the Oxfordshire coroner's inquest to continue. This was the first time Section 17A of the Coroner's Act had been invoked for a single death. It meant that, unlike at an inquest, evidence was not under oath, witnesses could not be compelled to attend, and could only be cross-examined with Hutton's permission. The excuse given was to allow witnesses to be examined 'in a neutral way'.

After an unusually quick inquiry lasting 24 days, with just half a day spent considering the cause of Dr Kelly's death, Hutton delivered his report which was published the same day on 28 January 2004. Kelly apparently died of haemorrhage from incised wounds to the left wrist, coproxamol ingestion and coronary artery atherosclerosis, after walking from his home in the Oxfordshire village of Southmoor to Harrowdown Hill. Astonishingly, Hutton recommended that all Kelly's medical records and photographs of his body *in situ* be kept secret for 70 years "for the sake of the family".

Evidence conflicting with the official cause of death raised many disturbing questions with echoes of Hilda's case:

- Two days after appearing before the Parliamentary Foreign Affairs Select Committee, Kelly emailed a US journalist about "many dark actors playing games".
- He left no suicide note. He had arranged to go with his daughter, who was getting married soon, to see a foal that evening. He had booked

a flight to Iraq and emailed that "it will all blow over by the end of the week and I can travel to Baghdad and get on with the real work". He had left an upbeat phone message for a friend looking forward to playing cards on 23 July. Also he was a member of the Baha'i faith, which strongly condemns suicide. The sole witness to an early part of his fatal walk reported he said: "See you again then, Ruth" – and the route he was taking was not to the lonely wood where he was found.

- Shortly before his death he told Mai Pederson, a close US colleague in the UN inspection team, that he "expected to be found dead in the woods" near his Oxfordshire home.

- The Thames Valley Police investigation reportedly began at 2.30 pm on 17 July, about half an hour before Kelly left home and nine hours before he was reported missing.

- According to Mrs Kelly, "a vehicle arrived with a large communications mast on it... then during the early hours another... 45-foot mast was put up in our garden". Were these needed to keep the Prime Minister informed?

- The 'police' sent the family out of the house while they stripped the wallpaper before Kelly's body was found. Were they removing listening devices? He had access to the highest levels of the Security Services and, like me, was cleared to see the most highly classified intelligence.

- The paramedic's Patient Report Form, and a scanned copy, disappeared. Also Kelly's dental records were inexplicably mislaid and then reappeared.

- Pederson claimed an injury to his right arm left Kelly unable to cut even steak with it – he had to do this clumsily with his left hand. Yet he supposedly cut his left wrist with his blunt pruning knife.

- There was not enough blood loss from the cut ulnar artery, which is buried deep in the wrist and can only be reached by an extremely painful process of cutting through nerves and tendons. Neither radial artery was cut, the normal ones in a suicide.

- As with the surprising lack of fingerprints on and in Hilda's car, no fingerprints were found on Kelly's knife, water bottle, coproxamol painkiller pill packs, glasses, mobile phone or watch. He was not wearing gloves.

Regarding motives for State security involvement in assassinating Dr David Kelly, he was one of only a few people involved in drafting the 'dodgy dossier' with its spurious claim not just that Iraq had chemical and biological weapons, but that some of them were "deployable within 45 minutes of an order to use them". Moreover, as probably the most authoritative source on this aspect, he objected to this distortion of intelligence for political purposes. When Alastair Campbell, Blair's senior aide and 'spin doctor', refused to correct it, Kelly briefed Andrew Gilligan, a reporter on BBC national radio's *Today* programme, who went public about it, severely embarrassing the Blair government. For this, Kelly's name and role were leaked, whereupon he was subjected to a humiliating televised pillorying before the Foreign Affairs Committee.

Baker speculated in his book whether Kelly was assassinated by hitmen hired by British, American or Iraqi State security agencies, and his death made to look like suicide. Baker's information pointing to foul play included mugging of informants too frightened to give their names. One had apparently been tipped off by a fellow former MI5 colleague that Kelly's death had been a "wet operation, a wet disposal" – slang for a covert intelligence operation involving assassination, alluding to bloodshed. Three weeks later, in a mysterious burglary, the informant's computer with all the Kelly material on it was stolen. Also, sensitive files about Kelly disappeared from Baker's computer in his constituency office in Lewes, East Sussex.

Aaronovitch used Hilda's case in his 2007 *Times* article to ridicule Baker's hypothesis. Having underplayed the nuclear motive and emphasised that Dalyell's sources were, like Baker's, anonymous, he continued:

> There the accusation lay for more than 20 years – with many playwrights and journalists believing that the Thatcherite State was quite capable of such murderousness – until new DNA evidence and a cold-case review established who the Murrell murderer was. He turned out to have been, at the time of the killing, a 16-year-old petty criminal called Andrew George, who lived in a local care home. In 2005 he was imprisoned for life.
>
> The Dalyell idea of a Murrell conspiracy mirrors in almost every important detail the Baker idea of the Kelly murder, with the dismissal of the "official version" as somehow deficient…

Was this why the State security system was so determined to convict Andrew George and close Hilda's case?

Aaronovitch's 2009 book, *Voodoo Histories: The Role of the Conspiracy Theory in Shaping Modern History*, featured Hilda's case prominently. She was in illustrious company as he also briskly debunked conspiracies surrounding the deaths of John F Kennedy, Marilyn Monroe, Princess Diana and Kelly.

Yet the Kelly case refused to go away. In a dramatic development, on 5 July 2009 the *Daily Express* revealed he was writing a book exposing highly damaging government secrets. Not only had he warned Blair there were no chemical weapons in Iraq. Apparently, he had also decided to reveal that, as one of the world's experts on anthrax, he secretly helped the apartheid regime in South Africa develop germ warfare agents. He had several discussions with an Oxford publisher, and was seeking advice on how far he could go without breaking the Official Secrets Act. Following his death, his computers were seized and it is not known what happened to the information on them or if any draft was discovered by investigators. British author Gordon Thomas said: "I knew David Kelly very well and he called me because he was working on a book. I gained the impression that he was prepared to take the flak as he wanted his story to come out."

On 5 December 2009, six senior doctors began legal action to force a proper inquest into Kelly's death, because they had no confidence in the Hutton Inquiry. Their spokesman, David Halpin, revealed that emails relating to the case had disappeared from his computer, and correspondence was missing. On 9 June 2011, despite intense media coverage and public support built by evidence uncovered by Baker and the doctors, the new Attorney General, Dominic Grieve, ruled out an inquest.

In response, Halpin announced in late August that he and three other doctors were seeking funds for a judicial review. He said: "Britain has great potential for good, but many people know it is now mired in mendacity. They must help the doctors get light into the dark corner of the Dr Kelly cover-up. Truth must out."

CHAPTER 13

CASE CLOSED?

The official closing of the case after Andrew George's failed Appeal in 2006 provoked further releases of information to me. For years I knew the police had ignored reliable reports of changes in the state of curtains, lights and the side door of Hilda's house between the Thursday and Friday. Now, we were able to piece together an extraordinary jigsaw of suspicious activities around Ravenscroft, and Hunkington where Hilda's car was found during the week of the crime. All these were reported to the police at the time – yet they appeared to ignore them, and none was put before the jury at George's trial. Failure by Cole, Smith, Stalker, Tozer and Brunger to connect these dots of inconvenient evidence and accept the implications, deepened my suspicion about their motives.

Two days before Hilda's abduction, at 1 pm on **Monday 19 March 1984**, *a man wearing a heavy, ankle-length coat with distinctive small brown and grey checks is seen standing outside Hilda's house by two men driving past. Aged 35-40, he is short and stockily built with tidy ginger-blond hair, a high forehead, and is smoking nervously. It is too warm to be wearing such a coat, which is too big for him.*

An hour later, the same witnesses see the same man walking along a road near Haughmond Hill. He walks over to where they are working in a field and requests a cigarette. He asks how far the next village is. They tell him – then challenge him that they have just seen him in Sutton Road. Shaken, the man replies: "You couldn't have done", before walking off towards Uffington. An hour or so afterwards, the witnesses spot two other tramp-like men walking along the same country road. One is 30-35 years old, medium height and build, with greasy swept-back brown hair and wearing a dark coat, while the other is younger, slimmer and shorter.

Two days later, between noon and 12.30 pm on the Wednesday Hilda was abducted, the same witnesses see the ginger-blond man a third time, still wearing the distinctive coat. He is standing stroking horses over a wall near the Uffington junction on the road where, less than half an hour later, Hilda's car passes on its way to Hunkington.

Around 7.45 am on either the Monday or Tuesday morning, a woman is cycling past Ravenscroft, where she knows Hilda lives alone, when she sees a white Ford Fiesta parked across her driveway. This is a dangerous and disruptive place to stop, where Sutton Road narrows and bends slightly; so there must be an overriding reason for a car to stop there. The driver is a clean-shaven, well-built 30-40 year-old man with tidy collar-length dark brown hair, pronounced sideburns and is wearing an unusual dark green, peaked cap. The woman cyclist notices he is looking at Hilda's house.

I already knew that on the **Tuesday**, in the morning, Mary O'Connor, Hilda's elderly neighbour living almost opposite, had been concerned about a strange young man outside her home. She found him sitting on the pavement leaning against her low garden wall, smoking an ornate pipe. Having to step round his legs to enter her property, she was concerned enough to fetch a garden fork and go back to her front garden to show him she was watching. He got up, sauntered off across the road and disappeared down the alleyway between Hilda's house and Millmead Flats.

A local woman is walking past Mary O'Connor's house, when she sees the same strange man coming out of the alleyway onto Sutton Road. He sits on a low wooden fence in front of Millmead Flats. The woman meets Mary, and they discuss this suspicious behaviour and his appearance. Aged about 20, he is of medium height and build with dirty collar-length ginger hair, a chubby face, and wearing a black leather motorcycle jacket, blue jeans, a stained waistcoat with badges on it, and black motorcycle boots. Looking around, he walks off past Ravenscroft.

Soon afterwards, a man living in Millmead Flats strolls over and starts chatting with Mary outside her house. They notice another strange man walking towards them from town. He passes them, crosses the road and walks back past Ravenscroft, looking around. They watch him until he is some 300 yards away, near Stonehurst Flats, where he loiters for a while. He is clean-shaven, 35-40 years old, medium height and build, with tidy brown collar length hair brushed forward. He is wearing a khaki coloured mackintosh.

At 2 pm, another neighbour sees a stranger standing outside Stonehurst Flats. He is about 50 years old, medium height and build, with short straight hair but untidily dressed; and he is looking around warily.

At 3.30 pm in Cross Houses, a village five miles southeast of Ravenscroft, a stranger with an Irish accent asks the way to Atcham, the location of 'Little America'. He is clean-shaven, aged about 40, medium height, with well-trimmed collar length mousy hair. He is wearing a heavy fawn mackintosh which almost reaches his ankles.

At about 5 pm the following afternoon, four hours after Hilda's abduction, the same witness is surprised to see the same man in the same long coat walking about 400 yards from Hilda's house.

Wednesday 21 March 1984, the day of Hilda's abduction

Going to work early that morning, Brian George was concerned about an odd-looking man and woman in long coats walking fast and furtively a short distance apart in the same area.

At about 9.20 am, a woman driving along Sutton Road has to stop for oncoming traffic because two cars are parked close together outside Hilda's house. The first one is a white Renault. A wider car ahead of it is a distinctive metallic turquoise blue with a thick white rear bumper. No-one is in or near either car. Ten minutes later, another neighbour notices only a metallic blue Talbot car, now parked on the verge opposite Ravenscroft.

About an hour afterwards, around 10.30 am, a nurseryman who once worked for Hilda is driving past her house when he has to stop suddenly because a red Ford Escort, with no-one in or near it, is parked partly on the pavement. Half an hour later, a similar red car is seen parked about a hundred yards further along the road.

Ursula Penny told me that, around 11.10 am, she was standing on the pavement opposite her house chatting with a woman friend when they saw Hilda drive past into town. Moments later a strange man jumped over a low wall in front of Stonehurst Flats and walked rapidly towards Ravenscroft. He was about 40 years old, medium height, athletic build, with a clean-shaven weathered face, fairish short-cropped hair, and wearing a grey lapel-less windcheater zipped up and grey slacks.

A woman is visiting her daughter who lives opposite Hilda. At about 11.30 am, she glances out of the front window expecting a washing machine repair man. Instead, she sees a stranger standing on the pavement outside Hilda's house. In his late 20s, fairly short and slim, he has a sallow, Pakistani complexion with thick black wavy hair parted in the middle and a small moustache. He is watching the traffic, and fiddling nervously with his coat. It is military style with a belt, full-length and too big for him, dark navy or black with a collar pulled over what he is wearing underneath. The witness is distracted by the repair man arriving. When she looks out again, the suspicious man has disappeared.

Ten minutes later, two plasterers working outside a house near Stonehurst Flats notice a scruffy man in his late 20s walking towards Ravenscroft, looking furtive. As he passes them ten yards away, he turns back to face them, then walks on. Stocky and medium height, he is unshaven with untidy, collar-length wavy dark brown hair parted in the middle and hanging over his face. He is wearing a red and black check lumber jacket and faded jeans with a tear in the right knee. The witnesses keep an eye on him until he disappears from view at the bend by Hilda's house.

Within minutes of Hilda driving into town, three suspicious men had converged on her house, one of whom matched Rosalind Taylerson's description of the driver of Hilda's car. High walls along the front of Ravenscroft, and around a complex of outbuildings with an outside toilet and cover to enter the house through the conservatory, provided plenty of options to lie in wait. The overgrown alleyway down the side of the garden offered discreet and easy access over a fence. Hilda had often chased young boys stealing fruit back over it.

Hilda came home at about 11.40 am, and left her shopping basket in the kitchen before visiting Mary O'Connor. A woman cleaning the front room of another house opposite watched her walk slowly out of her drive leaving the kitchen door open, and returning about ten minutes later entering Ravenscroft through that door. The woman did not see Hilda's car in the drive, so assumed she had parked it in the garage, because its door was shut. Did Hilda put her car away to keep her driveway clear for 'Inspector Davies' coming to question her at midday, as Laurens Otter claimed she told him?

At about noon, a neighbour has to drive around a white transit van parked on the pavement beside Hilda's front wall. Ten minutes later, another man walking past her gateway sees an unmarked white van parked well back in Hilda's drive opposite the front door with its rear to the road – but no white Renault. The van, similar to a Toyota Hiace, has no windows in the rear doors. He sees no people.

So, here was corroboration that her car was in the garage. Hilda had not yet been abducted. What was a van doing there at that crucial moment?

As a young woman leaves her parents' house off London Road a few blocks from Sutton Road to walk into town around midday, she sees a strange man walking towards her. Seeing her, he quickly turns and walks back to the main road, where he stands as she passes. He follows her, dropping back until she loses sight of him. He is about 50 years old, six feet tall, well built, clean-shaven with a pockmarked face and broad nose. He has grey, bushy collar-length hair under a checked cloth cap, and is wearing a stone-coloured full length mackintosh and dark brown trousers.

From London Road there is a pedestrian shortcut through back streets to Sutton Grove, which joins Sutton Road almost opposite Ravenscroft. Was this fourth stranger the same older man outside Stonehurst Flats the previous afternoon?

At 12.20 pm, a woman riding a moped past Hilda's house towards the by-pass has to brake suddenly as a vehicle – 'not a lorry or a van' – pulls out of the Ravenscroft gateway to her right, and drives off ahead of her at speed.

Was this the Range Rover which roared past Jill Finch in her friend's car at the junction of Sutton Road with the by-pass at this time? Was this how 'Inspector Davies' arrived for his 'meeting' with Hilda? According to police, the first confirmed sighting of Hilda's car on its 'abduction run' was some 25 minutes later, at the junction between Sutton Road and Wenlock Road.

At about 12.45 pm, a woman driving along Sutton Road sees a vehicle emerge from Hilda's gateway, and turn left towards town.

When the man who saw the white van in Hilda's drive at 12.10 pm returns at 1.20 pm, it is still there.

This extraordinary weight of evidence, from neighbours who were reliable witnesses, demolished the police theory and hugely complicated the case. While that van was there, witnesses had seen two other vehicles drive out of Ravenscroft. Could the first one around 12.20 pm have been heading by the shortest and safest route to Hunkington with a drugged Hilda hidden in the Range Rover? Here was evidence of the Ulster snatch squad scenario, with the driver of Hilda's Renault and her female impersonator able to get into it unobserved via the side door of the garage. Was she the woman seen walking suspiciously early that morning by Brian George? None of the many witnesses who saw Hilda's car driven through the town recognised the slumped woman passenger as Hilda, because her face was obscured by a large floppy hat. Did the driver and passenger wait for about 25 minutes before setting off on the decoy run, until they knew Hilda was in the safe house in 'Little America', now

Atcham Business Park – as former MI5 agent Gary Murray had postulated?

Did the van then come into its own, removing a terrified 16-year-old petty thief found upstairs after the abduction team held guns to his head, and he had defecated in the downstairs toilet? None of the many sightings of strangers near Hilda's house that week was of a small, scrawny 16-year-old boy and his brother. At his trial Andrew George claimed he was walking through the alleyway beside the house, and saw no car and the side door open. This could have been in the 5-10 minutes while Hilda was visiting Mary O'Connor. The white van was parked outside, invisible behind the wall to George when he took a disastrous snap decision to hop over the fence and burgle Ravenscroft, unobserved by a team waiting in the van to abduct Hilda and search her house after she returned? This would also explain Mr A's claim that George told him at least three others and a white van were involved.

Later that afternoon, there are two sightings by neighbours of another scruffy man near Hilda's house. In his late 20s, medium height and thin, he has greased-back, straggly collar length black hair, and is wearing a light-coloured mackintosh. At 3.50 pm a local woman on an errand to a neighbour notices the man standing just inside Hilda's gateway. On her way back about ten minutes later, he is on the pavement but still in the gateway. As she tries to see his face, he deliberately turns away. However, she notes it is thin, and under the mac he is wearing jeans and a dirty pair of trainers.

About half an hour after this, another woman walking along the alleyway notices a light on in an upstairs room in Hilda's house, on a fine afternoon.

From late that afternoon until at least 11.30 pm, a blue Hillman Hunter saloon is seen parked about 40 yards from the entrance to Ravenscroft.

That evening around 6.30 pm, a neighbour sees a red Cavalier estate stop outside Ravenscroft, reverse to get a better look at the house, then drive on.

Some fifteen minutes later, another neighbour living in Laundry Lane behind Ravenscroft returns home and finds the white gate into his property jammed shut. This gate has been difficult to open, so he always left it ajar. He struggles to pull it open. Concerned, looking around he glances at the unoccupied bungalow next door. A shed door at the back is open, which has never been like that. Entering his house, he finds no other evidence of an intruder.

Was that shed another hiding place for members of the team involved in Hilda's abduction? They only needed to walk down the lane, then a hundred yards along another back street to gain access to Ravenscroft through the secluded bottom of the garden, surrounded by a warren of houses with access lanes and pedestrian walkways between them.

At about 8 pm, a student at the Technical College and his girlfriend walk past Hilda's house into town. They see an unoccupied red saloon car parked on the grass verge almost opposite, facing Ravenscroft. When they return at about 11pm, it is still there.

Around 8.10 pm, a man who knows Hilda by sight approaches Ravenscroft driving into town from the by-pass when he sees ahead two white lights on his side of the road. They are the reversing lights of an otherwise unlit white hatchback starting to turn into Hilda's gateway with its rear door up. The car pauses to let him pass. He notes a black stripe down the side, and a man standing on the pavement close to it, as if directing the driver. The pedestrian is 30-35 years old, medium height, slim build with scruffy shoulder length dark hair, wearing a dirty, light-coloured mackintosh.

This description broadly matches the older stranger seen by Mary O'Connor outside Ravenscroft on the Tuesday morning, and two more sightings on the Wednesday afternoon. Was he also one of the two 'tramps' seen together near Haughmond Hill on the Monday afternoon?

At about 11 pm, a resident of Stonehurst Flats observes a strange Pakistani-looking man with a dark moustache standing beneath a tree near the flats. He pulls back into shadow. In his 30s, he has thick, wavy collar length hair, is of slight build, and wearing a dark coat well below his knees.

Was this the man seen acting suspiciously outside Ravenscroft shortly before Hilda returned from shopping? If so, could he and the driver of Hilda's car have been using one of the flats as a base?

Thursday 22 March

Half an hour after midnight, the matron of the Hollies old people's home opposite Stonehurst Flats is driving back there with her husband. As they approach Ravenscroft, a car is reversing out with no lights on. She switches to full beam to warn the driver. Red brake lights come on, but it has no reversing lights. It is a small grey or pale blue saloon, not Hilda's white Renault. After they pass, it resumes reversing out, still without lights on.

Was this the old blue Hillman Hunter – which had no reversing lights – seen parked near Hilda's house all evening?

Behind Millmead Flats at about 11 am on Thursday, a woman neighbour sees a strange man standing at the end of the alleyway alongside Hilda's garden. When spotted, he walks off quickly down a lane past the bottom of Hilda's garden. In his late 20s, he is short, thin and pale looking, with frizzy shoulder length hair and a black beard. He is wearing a black beret, navy blue sports jacket, blue jeans and dark glasses. The woman last saw him a few weeks before, walking up the alleyway, looking as if he was crudely disguised.

If he was a member of the lookout team, he would have seen Hilda's friends Hana Bandler and Lucy Lunt arrive, check the house and leave.

—— ∞ ——

Meanwhile, local people **around Hunkington** reported equally suspicious strangers and vehicles. Some matched descriptions of those seen near Hilda's house.

*At about 8 pm on **Monday 19 March**, an unattended light blue Vauxhall estate car is seen reversed into the wide field access a hundred yards from where Hilda's* *broken spectacles, knife and hat are later found. It is still there at 7.30 pm the next night, but has gone by Wednesday morning – the day of Hilda's abduction. Then a different witness spots it at 8 am on the Thursday morning, on the concrete pad opposite Hilda's crashed car.*

Around 11 am on the **Wednesday**, *a woman who keeps a horse in a field behind the copse where Hilda's body is later found drives past a stranger walking along Drury Lane. He is about 50 years old, six feet tall, medium build, wearing a cap and a grey mackintosh, with his neck hunched into the collar on a calm, sunny morning.*

The description matched that of the man seen behaving suspiciously in London Road near Ravenscroft an hour later.

Around 11.30 am, a man planting potatoes in a field a few miles south of the copse notices an unfamiliar red, two-door Ford Escort drive by heading towards Hunkington. The sole occupant is a 30-40 year-old, clean-shaven man of medium height and build with short brown hair, wearing a brown jacket.

Was this the same car seen parked outside Ravenscroft an hour earlier? Was the driver on his way to pick up the 50 year-old stranger, who had been checking the copse area, and take him to supervise the abduction?

An hour afterwards, as Hilda is about to be abducted, a similar unoccupied red car is seen parked in a gateway in a hollow just over a mile across fields from where her car will shortly crash.

Around the same time, two unattended vehicles are noticed by three different witnesses parked on the roadside in Haughmond Hill wood: a small white car like Hilda's seen outside Ravenscroft the previous morning, and a pale blue estate car.

The estate car matched the Vauxhall seen parked for over 24 hours in the Hunkington field access, and then again on the concrete pad early on the Thursday morning near Hilda's crashed car.

Between 12.50 and 1 pm on the Wednesday, a young mother who has lived in the area for 16 years approaches the Somerwood crossroads from Haughmond Hill. She drives up behind a small white car with two occupants travelling in the same direction about 20 yards from the crossroads. It jerks to a halt angled in towards the left hand verge. As the witness pulls out past it, she tries to give the driver a dirty look, but he turns his head away.

Was the driver of Hilda's car wanting to let her pass before dropping off his woman passenger impersonating Hilda before reaching the 'crash' site?

Minutes before this, a woman is driven by her husband from a cottage beside Hunkington Farm up to the crossroads, then right towards Newport. They see no crashed car.

An engineer who commutes daily along Hunkington Lane passes Hilda's white Renault crashed hard up into the bank shortly before 1 pm – as he approaches it he tries to tune his car radio to the weather forecast before the lunchtime news. He sees no-one in or near it, and does not stop. Subsequently he passes it twice each day until the Saturday, and sees no change.

These two reports established that Hilda's car crashed around 1 pm. Within the next hour, four other witnesses reported finding it, but saw no-one in its vicinity. Surely, if Hilda had been abducted in the car, she and/or her abductor would have been seen by them near it or in the field?

Around 1.10 pm, a woman living on the other side of the copse near Somerwood Farm notices a strange man walking slowly along the road towards her. In his early 40s, he is of medium height and build, with thick fair or grey hair, wearing an anorak with a stripe down each sleeve. She does not see him again.

John Marsh first spotted Hilda's car as he returned to Hunkington Farm soon after 2 pm. He inspected it, then went back to phone Shrewsbury Police Station around 2.30 pm. John Rogers rode past it ten minutes later. A man on a horse would have had a clear view over the hedge across Funeral Field – but he reported seeing no-one. Yet this was where the police and John Stalker speculated that, within the previous hour, Hilda had been frogmarched at knifepoint.

Around that time, a truck driver who travels along Hunkington Lane every three weeks is delivering goods to Withington. As he drives through Haughmond Hill wood he sees two unattended cars in lay-bys: a green Fiat and an unidentifed blue car. Where the lane enters thickets, he has to slow down for a woman walking in front of a man. They are both in their fifties; she is wearing a dark mac and head scarf, he a light-coloured mac and cap; and he is carrying a shepherd's crook stick.

The truck driver stops for his lunch in the wide field access, and notices the roof of a white car across the field. At about 2.30 pm he drives on, and slowly passes Hilda's car. No-one is in or near it; but an unattended white saloon car about the size of a Ford Cortina is parked on the concrete pad on the left. Further along the lane, he notices an unattended tractor in a field on the left. Looking round for the driver, he spots a strange man at the edge of a copse across the field, with long hair and wearing a long coat. Puzzled, he drives on.

If Hilda had been in the field near where her broken spectacles were found, she would have seen and heard that truck. The driver would have seen her – and recognised her, because he used to deliver goods to her. She would also have seen the white car on the pad, the strange shaggy man in a long coat by the copse, heard the tractor, and crawled towards them, calling out. None of these witnesses reported a 'running man', initially given so much police attention, yet dismissed at the trial.

At about 2.40 pm, a woman who lives near the gamekeeper's cottage is walking her dog with a friend near Somerwood crossroads. As they turn down Hunkington Lane towards Hilda's crashed car, a strange jogger trots by. The man, who looks as startled as they do, is in his mid 30s, about six feet tall, well built with a flushed but unstressed face – and wearing a khaki safari hat and muddy green clothing unlike a jogger's.

Were he and the other man seen near the copse more team members keeping a lookout?

The two women walk on a short distance, when a white car races over the crossroads behind and passes them, then stops suddenly in a gateway about a hundred yards ahead. The car is like one seen by one of the women parked in Haughmond Hill wood an hour and a half earlier. As the women return to the crossroads, a large yellow and green van approaches from Haughmond Hill wood, and drives on down Hunkington Lane. Soon afterwards, a regular male jogger they recognise runs past from Upton Magna, wearing a grey tracksuit. They look back across the field and see the white car still parked in the gateway – and Hilda's crashed car askew in the hedge near the concrete pad.

At about 3 pm, a longtime resident returns to his home in Drury Lane behind the copse. He is surprised to see a strange man with a grey whippet dog walking across a field by the crossroads at the southern end of the lane. He is in his early 30s, six feet tall, slim build, wearing a dark cap, sports jacket, grey trousers and wellington boots.

Ian Scott was known to have whippets, but was an old man. Was this a crude attempt to impersonate him while keeping a lookout, at this most risky phase of Hilda's abduction? Marsh had reported her crashed car to the police, and the Symondsons could have been asking neighbours to check if Hilda was at home.

Around 3.40 pm, the driver of a school bus who collects and returns pupils in the Hunkington area is dropping off children in Uffington, when he notices a man he has never seen before walking quickly through the village ahead of the bus. In his 30s, medium height and build, he is clean-shaven with neat ginger-brown hair and sideburns. He is wearing a clean and tidy grey anorak, stone-washed denim trousers and dark trainers. As the bus catches up with him, he turns to look at it several times, but does not thumb a lift.

This man matched the description of the Ford Fiesta driver acting suspiciously in Hilda's gateway early on the Monday or Tuesday. He also resembled one of the police identikit photos of the driver of Hilda's car.

An hour later, at around 4.30 pm, two young tearaways, Charlie Bevan and Chris Watton, visited a local car dealer to swap Watton's Morris 1000 van for a bigger one. The dealer refused because the Morris was not taxed. Returning to Shrewsbury via back roads to avoid the police, they came across Hilda's car. Watton found the passenger door unlocked, and stole the tax disc.

Fifteen minutes after this they drove on – and spotted a red Ford Escort, reversed into the field access on the right. As they approached, Watton had to brake as the car suddenly shot out in front of them, and sped up the lane out of sight. Watton recognised it as a Mk II model, but more powerful than the 1300cc version, with a screw-on CB aerial in the middle of its boot lid. The words 'Escort' above the rear bumper were in different black lettering from the word 'Ford'. He described the driver, who was alone, as 20-30 years old with tidy straight collar-length dark brown hair. The man resembled the driver of the red Ford Escort seen in the vicinity at 11.30 that morning.

Watton and Bevan appeared in court charged with stealing the tax disc on 18 April, during Hilda's thanksgiving service. In the *Shropshire Star* that evening, DCS Cole also appealed for information about the red Ford Escort seen near Ravenscroft on the day Hilda was abducted. What he omitted to add was that John Marsh and Bryan Salter had reported no less than five sightings of such a car in Hunkington Lane between the Thursday and Sunday. To these Cole should have added two sightings in the area on the Wednesday morning, and this one.

Three weeks later, both young men were required by the police to make new statements under caution. The youths now claimed they had fabricated the story about the red Ford Escort, because they feared they would be accused of murdering Hilda. However, would Watton have made up such a detailed description? Were they, like the telephone engineers, landowner, fireman, tyre changer and others pressured to change their stories, or not to speak to me?

Around 4.45 pm, an unattended white Renault 5 car is seen a few yards from the Somerwood crossroads, parked on the offside grass verge facing towards Haughmond Hill wood. The witness has owned a Renault 5, and notes its lower half is muddy. Fifty yards further along the road on the near side, a yellow van is parked with two men in it conferring.

The van was close to where Hilda's driving documents and AA membership card were later found. Was this the same van seen three hours earlier driving down Hunkington Lane? Was the Renault the one seen parked outside Hilda's house on the morning of her abduction; then in Haughmond Hill wood, before racing past the women walking their dogs, and parking in a gateway some two hours earlier? If so, could it have been a backup car in case anything had gone wrong with Hilda's – and to confuse the police and witnesses further?

Around 5.30 pm, a local woman and her husband drive along Drury Lane and notice two strange men, looking like farmers, standing in a field using what appear to be walkie-talkie radios.

Half an hour later, a van passes Hilda's car heading towards Shrewsbury. The driver sees a dark green Ford Cortina parked in a gateway almost opposite Rogers' cottage facing towards Hunkington. Three men in their 20s-30s are standing beside it.

At 6.20 pm, PCs Paul Davies and Robert Eades arrived to follow up Marsh's second phone call an hour earlier to Upton Magna Police Station where Davies was based. They opened and closed the front passenger door, but failed to notice the missing tax disc. They quickly established Hilda was the owner. Why did they not make further urgent enquiries when the car had been left unlocked?

Around 8.15 pm, a young man drives past Hilda's car, and is concerned enough to stop, get out and try to inspect it despite it being dark. He opens the front passenger door, and rubs his hand along the driver's side to check for any damage, but feels none.

A woman driver overtakes two strange men walking in the same direction just beyond the gamekeeper's cottage at about 8.45 pm. They are both in their early twenties, medium height and slim build with shoulder length hair: one fair and wavy, the other mousy coloured. The fair-haired one is wearing a denim jacket and jeans, the other a red pullover. The weather is fine but cold.

At about 9.15 pm in Drury Lane, Nick Waters told me he saw a dim torch in Moat Copse for about five minutes, focused on a small area rather than moving about. A farmer discovered the next morning that the latch and chain on his paddock gate in Drury Lane had been released. Was this where the mysterious torch user gained access to the copse? Was a member of the team checking where Hilda was to be taken to die the following night after interrogation?

Around 9.30 pm, a man and his girlfriend are about to park on the concrete pad when they see Hilda's car. He pulls up in front of it: keeping his headlights on, he gets out and inspects it. On trying the front passenger door, he finds it is locked. The driver's door is too close to the hedge to get at.

Yet an hour and a half earlier, a local man had found the front passenger door unlocked.

On **Thursday 22 March** *at 2.50 pm, a local farmworker and his wife pass Hilda's car, and see two men about 20 yards from it in the field close to the hedge. Both are aged 35-40, clean-shaven with mousy hair cut short. They do not look like farmworkers.*

Ten minutes later, Ian Scott was seen approaching Moat Copse with two dogs. He checked each tree for felling. Then tractor driver Bryan Salter watched a dark car drive slowly past Hilda's car, park opposite the wide field access, and a suspicious man in a suit walk along the hedge to the copse and back.

At about 7 pm, soon after nightfall, a light-coloured Ford Cortina is seen parked on the concrete pad, and a man walking away from Hilda's car. He is in his mid-late 40s, medium build, in casual clothes.

Half an hour later, a stranger is seen walking towards a red car parked on the roadside in Haughmond Hill wood. About 45 years old, he is of medium height and build, with thinning mousy hair, and is wearing a dark suit and white shirt.

Around 8.30 pm, a van is parked in a gateway between the concrete pad and Marsh's farm. Its headlights are directed across the field towards Moat Copse.

Was this when Hilda was being moved into the copse?

Early next morning, **Friday 23 March**, *back at Hilda's house an unfamiliar pale blue saloon car is seen parked in the drive of the two empty houses owned by the police almost opposite. A dark-haired man in a dark coat is sitting in the driver's seat. At the same time, a tramp-like man is observed thumbing a lift while walking towards town: medium height with a beard, he is wearing a long grey mackintosh and a dirty blue scarf wrapped round his head, and carrying three bags.*

Was the blue car the old Hillman Hunter seen reversing out of Ravenscroft soon after midnight on the Wednesday night, having been parked nearby from late that afternoon? With Hilda placed in the copse overnight on Thursday, by early Friday morning had the team planted the Totes rain hat, spectacles, knife, boots and other clothing, thoroughly searched the house for papers, drawn curtains, switched on more lights, and opened Hilda's side door before leaving a tyre scuffmark in the drive?

At about 6.30 pm that Friday evening, according to Judith Cook and Tam Dalyell a professional counsellor in Shrewsbury who helped with sex crime investigations was visited by 'two senior officers from Shrewsbury Police Station'. As mentioned earlier, they wanted leads on anyone who might have a sexual hang-up with old ladies, and might be violent. The following Monday, the counsellor was shocked to discover via the media that some of the details matched the scenario outlined by the two detectives. He contacted Cook and Dalyell because he realised the detectives had visited him the night before Hilda's body was found.

Around 7 pm on Friday, a man who has lived nearby for fifteen years and done decorating work for Hilda sets off on his regular walk along the pavement opposite her house. As he approaches it, two strange men are standing on the opposite pavement next to two cars parked close together bonnet to bonnet. A small white car like a Mini Metro is facing towards the by-pass with its rear almost alongside Hilda's gateway. The other car is larger, like a Ford Granada, and dark buff in colour. In the gathering dusk, the walker notes the bigger man is in his 50s, clean shaven, about six feet tall and heavily built, wearing a collar and tie, cloth cap, and a long dark brown overcoat. He is talking earnestly with a man in his 30s, clean-shaven with dark short hair and smartly dressed in what could be a police uniform. When they notice the walker watching them, the older man hurriedly gets into the larger car and drives off quickly. The younger man jumps into the white car, and reverses into Hilda's drive out of sight opposite the front door.

The older man's description matched that of the one seen in Drury Lane at about 11 am on the Wednesday, and then in London Road soon after midday. Was he 'Inspector Davies'? Was he leading the 'Special Branch murder hunt' on Marsh's land earlier on Friday? Had he just visited the sex counsellor? Was he instructing PC Davies what to do next having finally taken the initiative and gone to Ravenscroft? If so, the policeman must have been under surveillance for the older man to be there. This would explain Davies' extraordinarily incoherent, rambling statement about his fleeting and incompetent search of the house and lack of subsequent action. Was this why Latham stated in George's trial that the police went into Hilda's house only on the Saturday morning?

———— ⌘ ————

Meanwhile, Besford House records regarding the evening movements of Andrew George read as follows:

```
21.3.84 Went swimming.
22.3.84 Stayed in all evening. In a lively mood, but
reasonably well behaved.
23.3.84 Stayed in watched video, generally well behaved.
```

Staff at Besford House would have noted if he had gone missing at any time, or was behaving strangely. If George had succeeded in overpowering

Hilda and placing her in her car, would he have gone back in, locked and bolted the front door, locked the side door leaving the key on the inside (as a policeman reported on Saturday morning), and found his way out through the conservatory doors? Even presuming he could drive, which he could not, how could he have been driving the hatchback reversing into her drive around 8.10 pm – let alone the unlit small saloon car reversing out half an hour after midnight? Whose vehicles were they anyway? And how could he have come back undetected between the Thursday and Friday and closed curtains, turned on lights and unlocked the side door? Why on Earth would he have bothered, with the huge attendant risks? As for the footprint fiasco, at George's trial why were the prints of an unusual Romanian trainer design size 8-9 apparently first found, only for the casts of them to disappear once George was charged? Instead, the Cold Case Review seemed to find Doc Martens bootprints in Hilda's kitchen – a pair of which George owned in March 1984, but which were also standard police footwear. Was it because his foot size was only 6 at the time and he did not have trainers?

Objective analysis of this avalanche of evidence, concealed from me for over twenty years, made a mockery of ACC Smith's feeble explanation in June 1985 for the extraordinary number of coincidences in the case. Most of these reports were made within days of Hilda's murder, by local people who recognised habitual visitors and traffic. Eleven strangers and ten different strange vehicles acted suspiciously at or near Hilda's house between early on the Monday or Tuesday and soon after midnight on the day of her abduction. Most of these were seen by more than one witness, and some seen twice by the same one. On separate occasions two different strange men were seen by the same witnesses near Hilda's house and in the Hunkington area. Finally, what about that incident in the Horseshoes pub near Uckington after the inquest, when one man was overheard by Hilda's neighbour – the Hollies matron who had almost collided with an unlit car reversing out of Hilda's drive around midnight on the Wednesday – remarking: "That car was put there before she was dead". His use of the word "put" was odd; was this because he knew it had been a decoy?

A comparable pattern of suspicious vehicles and strangers was reported around the copse and then Hilda's car after it crashed. *The police never mentioned any of them.* However, they admitted to us at our final meeting that five of the strangers seen in Sutton Road were never traced. No-one saw any suspicious small teenage boys near the house or copse. Despite several witnesses and police touching the car inside and out, the only fingerprint found was on the inside of the rear window – and in police photographs the car's bodywork looked suspiciously clean despite muddy wheels. Who locked the car on the Wednesday evening after the first police visit, before the keys were subsequently found in Hilda's coat pocket?

What had emerged was a circumstantial smoking gun, pointing to a sinister web of vehicles and disguised agents in a carefully coordinated major operation, encircling poor Hilda and where her mutilated body was eventually found. Above all, the police theory of a lone, petty burglar – let alone a teenage truant who could not drive – was demolished. Anger welled up as I realised how the media, Dalyell and I would have confronted Cole had I known then that the police knew all this.

Meanwhile, Acland had been abandoned by the police. On 9 July 2008, the BBC reported that he had failed to get the High Court to override a decision by West Midlands Police to refuse to give him work. He was awaiting disciplinary proceedings for alleged incompetence in two murder cases the previous year; and four police authorities in the Midlands had stopped using him.

After I openly admitted in media interviews and to friends and supporters that I was writing this book, it came as no surprise when our mail experienced renewed interference, and we had indications that surveillance had been stepped up. The British State security apparatus seemed increasingly desperate to impede us, and frighten us into not finishing it. Of course, the effect of such corroboration that it had things to hide was to encourage us to keep going.

A neighbour living opposite our Christchurch home told us that, for a month after we returned from the trial in mid-2005, he saw various cars parked outside our house for several hours during the daytime with the driver reading, alone. It was so persistent that he thought *he* was under surveillance. This was corroborated by a young woman working for us when she went out for lunch. We were advised that the car was probably fitted with special monitoring equipment capable of picking up our conversations through any electronic appliance in our house, and accessing our computers.

In February 2006, Andrew Fox came to help us start writing this book. Shortly before he left, while we were being interviewed for both British and New Zealand TV programmes on the case, we found a large envelope containing a feature article about us slit open in our letterbox. Earlier that morning, a neighbour saw a strange young man run out of our drive. The date, 3 February, was the centenary of Hilda's birth. Soon afterwards, graffiti of our initials appeared on our gatepost. Feeling threatened, we took the precaution of briefing Prime Minister Helen Clark, whom Kate knew, while she was visiting Christchurch. Thereafter we updated her periodically.

Early in 2008, as we were about to go to Britain for three months to research and work on this book, Fox posted us a CD of his latest draft by 'track and trace' airmail so we could review it before we left. He received notification of its safe arrival on 1 February – but it had still not appeared when we departed ten days later. The day after we left, it turned up at the 'safe' address of a barrister's chambers, with a New Zealand Packet Post sticker indicating it had been re-posted.

Over Easter we visited my sister for a family reunion. Unfortunately she emailed that she had booked us into a local pub. At 1.30 am on the last night of our stay, we were woken by an intruder trying to unlock our door. He had gained initial access through a latch key in an outside door at the top of old stone steps leading into a corridor. Luckily the old deadlock on our door was faulty, and we had inserted our key in it. Viewed briefly through the keyhole, a big man in a blue tracksuit who, unlike a drunk, remained silent, failed, and left. Moments later, vehicle hazard lights flashed in the street below. A white rental van with aerials had been parked across the street since we arrived. The pub manager, who had gone home after closing time, later confirmed we were the only occupants that weekend. On returning to Fox's home to resume work on the book, we had five silent phone calls over the next two days.

We returned home to find Kate's computer running. She had switched it off and unplugged it with instructions to her daughter and a friend house-sitting in an upstairs apartment that it should not be used. They, and two of our assistants who called in periodically, agreed it had been off until about two weeks before we returned. One who visited Kate's home office weekly noticed it was off again at one point and then back on, but assumed Kate had changed her instructions.

Yet again our mail was interfered with, despite being delivered to a PO box in our local post shop. A large padded envelope, filled with United Nations books and pamphlets and posted by surface mail from the UK, arrived unusually quickly. It was torn open, but with a single strip of broad sellotape wound longitudinally around it to prevent the contents spilling out. These seemed complete; but they now included a small padded envelope with a UK airmail sticker and unfranked stamps from a Yorkshire address by someone unknown to us. Marked 'Urgent Spares', it was addressed to a stranger in Wellington, New Zealand. The big envelope had a New Zealand Nationwide Parcel Post sticker with a barcode over the Customs declaration, so it had been re-posted. Having photographed it, we handed the small package unopened to our local Post Shop manager for onward delivery. He agreed this looked like intimidation, and briefed his sorting staff.

Another A4 padded envelope posted at the same time from Shropshire arrived slit open and empty of all documents. It was enclosed in a Royal Mail plastic bag marked 'Item Damaged Before Arrival In UK' – yet it was clearly stamped 'SU Royal Mail postage paid UK'. Again, it had been re-posted in New Zealand. During this time one of our staff once found our PO Box unlocked.

This was serious enough to warrant briefing the Prime Minister again. In a letter, hand-delivered by one of her ministers who was a trusted friend, we explained the latest mail interference, surveillance and pub intruder. We requested that, in the event of any 'accident' befalling us during our next UK visit, she would immediately initiate a formal inquiry. We also asked her to investigate whether there was any involvement by the NZ Security Intelligence

Service (SIS), or if they had any knowledge of such operations. When we next met her, she confirmed that, as head of the SIS, she had been assured they were not involved. Meanwhile, visits to our home by MPs, including Ministers, and journalists to discuss our disarmament work and security problems helped protect us.

Before leaving again for Europe in early July 2008, we warned our middle-aged male house-sitter about earlier break-ins. He expressed sceptical amusement. Late that night, as he drove up the drive he saw through the living room window a man silhouetted by torchlight. On our return after two weeks he described how, thoroughly "freaked out", he had left hurriedly without investigating further. Then, determined not to let us down, he nervously returned. As usual there was no sign of forced entry, and nothing seemed to have been taken. Nevertheless, we had to assume fresh bugs had been installed.

There was another disturbing incident. The same house-sitter, now fully alerted, noticed a car parked outside our house several times. Returning late one evening, he found it still there. Pulling up about twenty feet behind it, he could see a man in his 30s-40s in the driver's seat, apparently doing nothing. Having waited about twenty minutes with headlights on, our now intrepid house-sitter was about to get out and challenge him when the car started, executed a violent 180 degree turn, and disappeared down the street with tyres squealing. We reviewed our security procedures, including never discussing book details in our home, keeping copies of draft chapters in safe locations, and minimising discussion of plans by phone or email.

In April 2009, Kate had a remarkable 45-minute meeting with the SIS Director, Dr Warren Tucker. After explaining that the only motive for such persistent harassment could be that we were writing this book, she showed him the damaged envelopes and a photocopy of the small padded package of mysterious 'spares'. Suddenly, he recognised the addressee: it was an acquaintance of his. Repeating Prime Minister Helen Clark's assurance that it was nothing to do with the SIS, he commented with a wry smile: "You wouldn't know we had been there. These guys wanted you to know." He asked who we thought was trying to intimidate us. Kate replied: "MI5 or MI6." She recounted Tozer's response to my request in 2002 for our house to be swept for bugs before he returned to Britain. Tucker undertook to brief the Inspector-General and Police Commissioner about this blatant harassment of two law-abiding New Zealanders, and request intermittent police protection.

Three months later, he honoured his promise to Kate that he would visit me at home. While she was overseas attending a meeting of the United Nations Secretary-General's Advisory Board on Disarmament (which gave us added protection), Tucker listened carefully for over an hour – aware we were probably being bugged – while I briefed him on why I believed the British State security apparatus seemed so determined to try to intimidate us. I could never imagine having a similar meeting with the Director of MI5. Soon after

Kate returned, we decided on impulse to walk to a local restaurant for dinner. We were pleasantly surprised to see a New Zealand policeman sitting in an unmarked vehicle outside our house.

We were now under no illusions as to what we were up against in trying to finish this book. After twenty-seven years of surveillance and harassment, I had become inured to having to discipline myself to be discreet when using my own phone – and despite this enduring the irritation of phone calls disconnected in mid-conversation. Then there were all the silent calls. There was the need to find and then arrange to use safe phones to make sensitive calls, and to organise safe addresses for mail. Because of the ease with which a mobile phone user can be followed and listened to, I do not have one. Kate became expert at removing the simcard and battery from hers before leaving the house for any sensitive discussion; and we had to ask those we met to do the same. Constantly restraining our anger, we endured the slightly fearful frustration of not being free to discuss the book in our home or car – instead we had to go to safe houses, with the associated risk of involving friends. There was the tedious business of backing up computer files, making and hiding copies, and arranging safe storage for my archive. Finally, where possible we always travelled overseas together; while there we never used rental cars; and we decided it was not worth the risk and stress to visit Britain, where I felt like a fugitive in my own country.

CHAPTER 14

WILD CARDS AND FACING FACTS

In any criminal investigation, the police decide what evidence is collected, let alone what is used or disclosed to the victim's family and the public. However, interfering with evidence is liable to be counterproductive. The source, or a dissident within the police, can release it or allege pressure to change it. The police then risk accusations of a cover-up, raising suspicion about their motive. Closely linked to this is whether the conclusions the police are drawing are consistent with the evidence, and if they are ignoring some valid lines of enquiry.

If the crime has political overtones, the police can come under pressure to lose their objectivity. Despite their protestations, they are subserviently linked to the State security apparatus. They hide behind the fact that evidence pointing to political conspiracy is rare, because it is difficult to obtain. Corroboration – usually involving leaking sensitive documents – risks the career, and sometimes the safety, of the source and their dependents. Also, beneath its veneer of democracy the British system of governance is intertwined with all the carrots and sticks associated with membership of the socio-political-military establishment. This age-old, supremely powerful State-controlled institution suppresses all but a few whistleblowers.

It took me about two years to understand the implications of these realities for the West Mercia Police. As a former Royal Navy Commander turned roof-thatcher and anti-nuclear campaigner, I soon found I was one of a dozen 'wild cards', or unpredictable factors outside the control of the State, in the Hilda Murrell case.

First and foremost was Hilda herself. Born into a family 'in trade', Hilda's formidable intellectual calibre, plantswoman and business flair, and passion for preserving the natural and historical heritage of the British Isles gained her access to the establishment on sheer merit. Her financial and social independence, with no partner or children, meant these customary options for controlling dissidents had little traction when her deep patriotism and moral fortitude drove her to take on the nuclear industry. Paradoxically, Hilda's solitary lifestyle and growing frailty would have fuelled her fearlessness and sense of urgency, which must have blunted intimidation attempts. Also, she would have taken care not to involve me because of my vulnerabilities as a recently retired naval officer, still subject to the Official Secrets Act, who had opted out of the military establishment by choosing an insecure, poorly paid new occupation.

Hilda's qualities and unusually independent situation would have encouraged whistleblowers to confide in her – especially if she showed both willingness and an ability to get dangerous information into the public realm. So had she become an intractable obstacle and a thorn in the side of the Thatcher government? If so, the only remaining option would have been for MI5, with assistance and deniability from a private security agency, to interrogate her to retrieve the information, identify its sources and neutralise them. Abduction to a safe house was the least risky way to do this, after which she would have to be silenced and disposed of.

I was the second wild card. Thatching freed me from the establishment's clutches. Also my first wife was strongly supportive of my pursuit of the truth, had no establishment family links, and we had no children. Because my relationship with Hilda was low-key and long distance, the State security authorities would have underestimated its intensity – let alone the radicalising impact her murder had on me.

One paradox was that my financial situation on leaving the Navy was severely constrained. Within six months of her murder, her modest bequest to me had eased that problem – until I spent most of it on helping stop a nuclear power plant at Hinkley Point. This, plus my sympathetic and flexible master thatcher, enabled me to take time off work at short notice to pursue my parallel investigation, and challenge the nuclear industry myself. Learning from Hilda's experience, I developed a network of supporters, including skilled researchers like Don Arnott and Kate, and took security precautions when harassment and intimidation ensued.

Initially, my genteel upbringing and conservative conditioning lulled me into trusting the police. However, I became increasingly alienated by their negligent initial response and subsequent failure to brief me as next of kin about major developments in the case. Their inexcusable blunder in allowing Hilda's body to decompose, requiring a sudden funeral, was followed by the inquest whitewash. Then came their outrageous interrogation of me in response to Dalyell's bombshell; refusal to connect dots over the arson attack on Fron Goch; pressure on whistleblowing telephone engineers; suppressing the Northumbria Report; disgraceful treatment of Con Purser, and sinister response to my slashed tyre outside Don Arnott's home. When police behave like this, the motive is either corruption or political pressure. Such uncharacteristically incompetent and/or vindictive behaviour gradually convinced me that, in Hilda's case, it was the latter. Ongoing surveillance and intimidation in New Zealand after I emigrated provided corroboration that this was a State crime.

Chronologically, the third and fourth wild cards were Gerard Morgan-Grenville and his long-standing friend Tam Dalyell. Both maverick establishment members, they were dangerous because they had good connections and information pointing to political conspiracies – in Dalyell's case the *Belgrano* connection, while Morgan-Grenville had sound reasons to support both that motive and mine about the nuclear industry. Worse for the State's gatekeepers, these two Old Etonians were financially independent and had too much integrity to be controlled. On the contrary, if they had been threatened they would have simply seized on it as corroboration. However, lack of corroboration from Hilda's diary about her last disturbing phone call to Morgan-Grenville, and Dalyell's refusal to name his most dangerous source because of political and social loyalties, let the police and MI5 off the hook.

Laurens Otter was wild card number five. Passionate about the need to get rid of nuclear weapons, he became Secretary of the Committee of 100, and worked for *Peace News*. Consequent awareness of the secret State, plus a streak of stubborn integrity, would have made him unusually difficult to intimidate. Thus, Hilda's last-ditch choice of Otter to try to pass sensitive material to for publication was shrewd.

The West Mercia Police came under public pressure from the moment farmer John Marsh made his first phone call about her crashed car at about 2.30 pm on the Wednesday. They could easily have visited Ravenscroft that afternoon – it takes only about five minutes to drive there from Monkmoor Police Station. Her calendar above the phone showed her lunch appointment with the Symondsons. Questioning them and neighbours would have quickly triggered a proper search around her car. DCS Cole admitted that, if she had been found that day, she would probably have still been alive. However, in these circumstances I suspect Hilda's body would never have been found.

To sustain a cover-up when whistleblowers are provoked by what they know is going on, the lying and denials become increasingly difficult and less believable. Friends of the victim are drawn in, and start connecting dots. When witnesses too frightened to go to the police see this, sometimes they feel strongly enough to come forward to those who will believe them, and can protect them with publicity.

The role of the media, as in Hilda's case, is therefore pivotal. It took Judith Cook's *New Statesman* article to persuade Dalyell to intervene. However, it can be a two-edged sword. From what he told me, MI5 probably exploited Cook's revelation of my role in the Falklands War. I must have been under suspicion as one of Dalyell's sources. After Ponting's arrest in August 1984, the State security authorities knew his most well-informed one was still active. They correctly judged Dalyell could not resist running with my Falklands link. He admitted that particular tip-off did not come from one of his usual sources. His spectacular Parliamentary intervention, two weeks after the inquest had finally been convened with minimal fuss, must have redoubled political pressure on the police. This explains their aggressive interrogation of me, probing whether I had leaked information to Dalyell – and even trying to intimidate me as a suspect in my aunt's murder – followed by their first attempt to frame a burglar.

Trying to make facts fit the panicking petty thief theory led to whistleblowing telephone engineers. No doubt from long experience there was an assumption that leaning on them would work. It did for the one who examined Hilda's faulty Fron Goch phone, but provoked the others to resist – and let the political cat out of the bag.

By then television had taken up the case. Harlech TV's John Osmond led the way with his tenacious and skilled succession of *Wales This Week* programmes, the last of which covered the tenth anniversary. Stuart Prebble did his best with *World in Action,* ensuring that the State version as depicted by *Crimewatch* backfired, provoking a far more dangerous whistleblower to break cover: a former MI5 agent. Wild card number six, Gary Murray became sufficiently motivated by the case to become involved.

Bringing in the Northumbria Police to review the case revealed the panic level on the eve of the first anniversary. Suppressing Peter Smith's report was probably wise in light of the terminal damage it could have done to several senior police officers' careers, especially if the telephone engineer had spoken out about his concerns. However, West Mercia Police faced fresh media ridicule and disbelief, generating huge publicity for Judith Cook's first book *Who Killed Hilda Murrell?* and providing a platform to break the Laurens Otter story. Of course Cook's harassment, and the dreadful attack on Dora Russell followed by the sinister postcard to her, strengthened my suspicions of State involvement.

Andrew Fox's courageous 1988 documentary clearly rattled the State cage. For a Central TV programme costing £40,000 to be pulled days before being broadcast, on a case where the police insisted it was just a petty burglary for cash gone tragically wrong, was unprecedented. Fox's experience of such crude censorship sustained his interest in the case. Twenty years on he agreed to help write early drafts of this book – thus qualifying as the seventh wild card.

The attempt to frame David McKenzie drove me to team up with Dalyell, a politician the Thatcher government had cause to fear. This decision to try to close the case must have been taken very soon after the Fox documentary was suppressed. Again, such heavy-handed abuse of the judicial system was risky – especially with two wild cards – myself and Dalyell – fired up and being fed new evidence from an outraged key witness, Rosalind Taylerson. Dalyell empowered me to challenge Thatcher's top legal adviser directly; and the result was not just failure for the government. Dalyell was provoked into picking up Hilda's case again; and he remained its Parliamentary champion until Andrew George's trial.

Trina Guthrie's dramatic affidavit in Gary Murray's book *Enemies of the State* made her wild card number eight and ensured media interest revived for the tenth anniversary. Murray corroborated revelations about surveillance of anti-nuclear activists and Sizewell objectors, and published Patsy Dale's affidavit.

John Stalker was a ninth wild card. When he attended the tenth anniversary public meeting with a Central TV film crew, I felt my pursuit of the truth had received a major boost. Here was a distinguished former senior police officer who had recently won his spurs challenging the State security system in Ulster. He had come through that and the fire of unfair dismissal with his reputation for no-nonsense integrity intact. Now he had a TV channel behind him and his own programme for a second 'independent' review of the case – but it was deeply disappointing. Nevertheless, it briefly shone a useful spotlight on the denial of Ian Scott's evidence by DCS Cole, and raised questions about the time of death.

A tenth wild card was the courageous dissident policeman who arranged for me to see two stolen files from Shrewsbury Police Station and receive a set of police photographs of Hilda's body and a copy of the Northumbria Report. This windfall revived my faltering quest. However, the files were relatively innocuous; and it took another ten years or so before I obtained enough evidence to expose the shortcomings of ACC Smith's review.

The news of multiple break-ins to my new home in Christchurch, New Zealand was a severe shock when I returned with Kate from overseas in 1999. After years living in Britain under surveillance, and having to keep sensitive documents in safe locations, I had hoped I was no longer enough of a threat to be followed to the other side of the planet; and the case had gone quiet for three years. Our harassment and intimidation warned us that the issues underlying Hilda's murder must have been extremely serious, and were ongoing. I found such corroboration encouraging: it meant I could trust my original gut feeling, and the sacrifices and stress entailed in my pursuit of the truth were worthwhile.

Involvement in the Cold Case Review had its healing, cathartic value. Also, it produced an eleventh wild card. When I wearily began briefing Kate and taking her through my archive, I discovered she should have been a detective. Her fresh mind on the case, energy, persistence, and aptitude for painstaking research and analysis were extraordinary, and sustained me. Allied to these skills, her significant role in the 1970s-80s campaign that convinced most New Zealanders to reject nuclear energy and deterrence for their security meant she understood those issues Hilda had grappled with as a woman campaigner.

Kate had other distinctive advantages and qualities. As a fourth-generation New Zealander, she was not deferential to those in authority. Her international experience representing citizen organizations had taught her how to speak truth to power without causing offence. On good terms with several leading politicians from a cross-section of parties, she included two prime ministers as friends. She had no career job to lose, but her academic skills and part-time lecturing at the local University of Canterbury kept her in touch with students, some of whom were inspired to work for us. Her role as mother of three girls kept her grounded; and having lived in her home for over twenty-five years, she had nurtured a strong family, neighbourhood community and network of friends, into which I was welcomed. This meant we had no shortage of support like house-sitters, a vital security need whenever we were away from home.

The two-week visit by DCI Tozer and DC Partridge in September 2002 was a one-off opportunity to help the police solve the case. However, the trial and George's subsequent failed appeal were travesties of justice. The West Mercia Police and State security system got what they desperately wanted: the case closed. For us, there was no closure, especially with a man imprisoned for 15 years for a crime he could not have committed. Police stonewalling at the two subsequent wash-up meetings was an ugly experience, renewing my sense of betrayal and alienation from them.

On the other hand, the flow of new, key information provoked by George's wrongful conviction infused us with fresh power and energy. I found it exhilarating to see the police thrown back on the defensive when we confronted them. Our belated discovery of so much suspicious activity around Hilda's house and Hunkington made me feel like a jigsaw puzzle player who, after struggling for too long, is visited by a friend who has nearly solved it. I need hardly mention that there are several people who have risked careers, if not their safety, for us to have reached this point.

⸙

Andrew George is the twelfth, and perhaps wildest, card in the case. While there is plenty of evidence to acquit him, he was undoubtedly in Hilda's house, and his aspermic seminal fluid was found on Hilda's slip.

George would have kept a sharp lookout as he loitered in the alleyway because, although he saw no car, a door left open suggested the owner had not gone far. Once inside, he probably quickly checked each room downstairs; but he would have had only a few minutes before hearing Hilda return. His escape route blocked, he might well have nipped upstairs to hide. All hell would have broken loose downstairs as Hilda confronted the team leader, was overpowered and removed in the Range Rover. The search for papers would have begun – whereupon he would have been discovered.

There would have been panic as a teenage truant threatened to blow the operation. The two men who he said held guns to his head could have killed him then and there, and had him disappear. As they did not suggests there was a contingency plan. Literally 'shitting himself', he would have done whatever they told him. Top of their list would have been that he must never tell anyone what had happened – or he was dead. Nevertheless, George warned his partner that "this is much bigger than the Shrewsbury police". He "said he thought the Government was involved". Also, she remarked that he "could only read comics". This meant he would not have been able to read details in the books or newspaper reports on the case. In addition, he told me Hilda "never was in the field – they took her somewhere else". Then there was the man in the Uckington pub after the inquest overheard saying: "That car was put there before she was dead".

One of the more intriguing twists was the police informant Mr A's attempt to talk to me. From what he told an experienced BBC TV journalist who had long followed the case, it seems even he had been disturbed by George's conviction. Mr A took quite a risk approaching me, especially if his intention was to tip me off that George had told him that at least three others, one of them a woman, were involved; and a white van followed the car. However, to stay alive George had claimed to him they were his brother, two friends nicknamed 'Cock-eye' and 'Laney', and his brother's girlfriend.

Mr A's role, and George's predicament, illustrate the power of the State security system to control evidence. Other pertinent examples in this case include the inmate who came forward to Trina Guthrie, and those he cited as members of the search and abduction team. All were struggling to survive after falling foul of the system where the State holds almost all the cards. It is too easy for witnesses to be intimidated, especially if they are in prison. This shows the huge difficulties of establishing that a State crime was committed – which means MI5 have an almost clear run to repeat such operations.

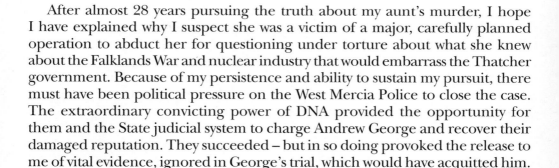

After almost 28 years pursuing the truth about my aunt's murder, I hope I have explained why I suspect she was a victim of a major, carefully planned operation to abduct her for questioning under torture about what she knew about the Falklands War and nuclear industry that would embarrass the Thatcher government. Because of my persistence and ability to sustain my pursuit, there must have been political pressure on the West Mercia Police to close the case. The extraordinary convicting power of DNA provided the opportunity for them and the State judicial system to charge Andrew George and recover their damaged reputation. They succeeded – but in so doing provoked the release to me of vital evidence, ignored in George's trial, which would have acquitted him.

I will now summarise my main outstanding concerns and unanswered questions about Hilda's case. There are nearly fifty of them:

- Gerard Morgan-Grenville's evidence that Hilda, uncharacteristically agitated, ended a half-hour phone call with him shortly before she was abducted and killed with the words: "If they don't get me first, I want the world to know that at least one old woman has seen through their lies."
- Tam Dalyell has never wavered in his allegation that "British intelligence were involved". He was corroborated by Judith Cook's separate source, and by a BBC TV journalist, Patrick Burns.

- From my experience as a Naval Intelligence officer with a top security clearance, MI5 would have discovered I knew there were things to hide over the Falklands War which were potentially more serious than the torpedoing of the *General Belgrano*.
- Dalyell's letter to Heseltine on 19 March 1984 triggered "a tremendous flap in Downing Street", two days before Hilda was abducted.
- Immediately after Dalyell detonated his 'bombshell' in Parliament early on 20 December 1984, there was a suspicious break-in at the flat of Lieutenant-Commander Peter Hurst, and subsequent problems with his phones.
- Hilda conferred with Don Arnott who, uniquely among anti-nuclear scientists, had discovered a serious flaw in the control rods of the US nuclear power plant design which had failed at Three Mile Island, but which Thatcher was determined to build. His concerns were later endorsed by Dr Edward Radford, chair of the TMI Scientific Advisory Board. At the time key leaders of the nuclear industry supporting Thatcher's plans took a close interest in what Don knew; he was tipped off that he was under surveillance, and some documents went missing. Before he could testify at the Sizewell Inquiry, he nearly died of a suspicious heart attack. In June 1985 he found his motorbike had been sabotaged. His death from natural causes in 2000 had nothing to do with his heart.
- Hilda was in correspondence with Ross Hesketh, a senior safety scientist in CEGB who had just been sacked for revealing that plutonium from British reactors was being secretly supplied to the Americans for nuclear weapons.
- At that time Hilda and I were closely conferring about her anti-nuclear paper for Sizewell, and I had suggested sending it to a scientist working at the secret reactor research centre at Winfrith whom I had met.
- Sizewell objectors were under surveillance; and at least four names on the list were in regular contact with Hilda.
- Laurens Otter's story, corroborated by Brian George. George Lowe's evidence suggests Hilda had time to drive to a callbox to phone Otter on her last drive home.
- Though no-one could prove any of Hilda's papers were taken, her document satchel and current handbag were not found.
- The suspicious deaths of Otter's friend Avraham Sasa, and Philip Griffith.
- Con Purser's experience after insisting on making a further statement that Hilda tried to leave documents with her three days before she was abducted.
- The strange, half-hearted arson attack on Fron Goch after Dalyell was challenged on TV that he might have been set up by MI5.
- The slashing of my car tyre outside Don's home, and the police and Forensic Science Service response.

- The advice from an ex-IRA man about use of a victim's car as a decoy in abductions in Ulster.
- Jill Finch's evidence of a Range Rover racing onto the by-pass to Atcham, and another report of a similar vehicle emerging rapidly from Ravenscroft, around the time Hilda was abducted.
- The last-minute withdrawal of Andrew Fox's 1989 CTV documentary.
- Why was the explosive evidence of male DNA under Hilda's fingernails and semen on her cardigan, both of which could not have been from Andrew George or his family, ignored by both prosecution and defence? The fingernail DNA established Hilda fought with another man.
- The likelihood that the semen was smeared onto Hilda's slip by someone other than Andrew George.
- Mr A's information that Andrew George had said other people were involved in the crime, and a white van followed Hilda's car.
- Andrew George could not have driven her car; so who was the well-built 25-40-year-old man who did?
- When police knew Hilda owned the crashed car in Hunkington by sunset on the Wednesday, why did they not immediately visit her house?
- Why did the police ignore the mass of evidence, provided within weeks of Hilda's murder, from reliable witnesses of changes in the appearance of Ravenscroft, and suspicious people and vehicles around it and her crashed car at Hunkington throughout the week Hilda was missing?
- The evidence from a reliable witness (who knew Hilda and had nearly collided with an unlit car reversing out of Ravenscroft late on the Wednesday night), about what she overheard from a group of men in an Uckington pub after the inquest.
- The lack of blood or fingerprints on and in Hilda's car, and its suspiciously clean bodywork; her car keys in her coat pocket; and the utter implausibility of her reaching the spot in Moat Copse where her body was found unaided without being seen, all point to the probability that she was stabbed later somewhere else, and was carried into the copse by more than one man.
- Circumstantial evidence that some cuts in her coat and skirt were made after she was stabbed, and she might not even have been wearing them.
- My suspicion that several items of Hilda's clothing plus boots, broken spectacles and kitchen knife, were planted to create a false trail from her crashed car to her body.
- The police confusion over footprints in Ravenscroft, whereby their initial search for a suspect with distinctive size 8-9 Romanian Gola trainers shifted to interest in Doc Martens, because Andrew George wore them – and the suspicious loss of casts of the trainer print.
- Police photographs of her body *in situ*, corroborating Ian Scott's certainty

she was not in his copse when he checked every tree over 24 hours after the police assumed she was left to die there, demolish their theory of a burglary gone wrong – so this was a much more complicated crime. Where was she until her body was found nearly two days later?

- Hilda's broken hyoid bone suggests she could have been strangled, not just placed in an arm-lock – by a teenage boy five inches shorter than her?
- Who were the mysterious police "swarming" on Marsh's farm on the Friday, "on a murder hunt"? Did they know there would be no farmworkers there that day?
- What were two detectives doing visiting a Shrewsbury sex counsellor at around that time asking if he knew of any man with sexual problems and a preference for violence to old ladies and interfering with their clothing?
- Who was the man seen conferring with PC Paul Davies before he became the first police officer to visit Ravenscroft on the Friday evening?
- Why did Acland not test for drugs, and the Forensic Science Service subsequently 'lose' the body sheet and crucial body parts associated with toxicology tests, including her brain, liver, stomach contents, bile and urine?
- Police pressure on telephone engineer Christopher Mileham to change his assessment of Hilda's phone that it had not been ripped out – and on Shropshire Councillor Derek Woodvine for leaking this information. Why did the relevant job card disappear?
- Why did police photographs show a redundant extension cable pulled away from its retaining staples? Mileham is adamant this was not the case when he examined the phone, and Brian George agreed it was like that when he saw it before the Scene of Crime unit arrived. So why were neither of them called as a defence witness in Andrew George's trial?
- The repeated intimidation of Ian and Thalia Campbell, and what they told us they knew about the case.
- Harassment of Judith Cook, the appalling attack on her supporter Lady Dora Russell and subsequent sinister postcard to her, and mysterious break-in at publishers Cecil Woolf of *Death of a Rose-Grower*.
- The highly unusual decision by West Mercia Police to get another police force to review their handling of the case, and the subsequent suppression of the Northumbria Report.
- Rosalind Taylerson's experience as a key witness of Hilda's car driver. Why were the police so determined to frame David McKenzie?
- Trina Guthrie's affidavit.
- Break-ins to my father's house and then our Christchurch home in which nothing was taken; endless interruptions to our phone and interference with mail; and the attempted break-in to our room in an English inn where we were the only occupants.

- The death threats to me via Patsy and Gordon Dale.
- The repeated slitting open of a letter to Kate from New Zealand after I and Dalyell declared George's conviction was unsafe.
- What George's ex-partner told us, and George told me.

Where to from here? First, there is the urgent need to release Andrew George – a petty thief who was known to be kind to old people, and unjustly incarcerated in a top security prison for hardened sex offenders for 13 years. DNA evidence in possession of the police and Forensic Science Service would probably acquit him, and establish beyond reasonable doubt that at least one other man, whom Hilda scratched, and possibly another man whose semen was on her cardigan, were involved in her murder.

Having re-opened the case, there has to be a proper Commission of Inquiry, led by a distinguished independent person with no links to the British State security apparatus. Only such an investigation can recommend how to prevent further corrupt, politicised abuse of the system of British justice and governance. Finally, I hope my pursuit of the truth about how and why Hilda died so violently will encourage others suspected of suffering injustice at the hands of the British security authorities to come forward.

One last comment. During the past quarter of a century and more, I have often felt like giving up on what has been a very personal Bunyanesque pilgrimage. At such moments, I found solace and encouragement in the following epigram, derived from an anti-World War One poem by the American workers' rights activist and conscientious objector Ralph Chaplin:

Mourn not the dead...
But rather mourn the apathetic throng
The cowed and meek
Who see the world's great anguish and its wrong
And dare not speak!

FURTHER READING

CHAPTER ONE:
Hilda Murrell website: www.hildamurrell.org
Jones, Lynne (ed.), *Keeping the Peace,* The Women's Press Ltd, London, 1983.
Roseneil, Sasha, *Disarming Patriarchy: Feminism and Political Action at Greenham,* Open University Press, Buckingham, 1995.
Radioactive Waste Management, Cmnd 8607, Her Majesty's Stationery Office, London, July 1982.
Royal Commission on Environmental Pollution (Chairman Sir Brian Flowers), Sixth Report, *Nuclear Power and the Environment,* Cmnd 6618, September 1976.
Smith, Graham, *Death of a Rose-Grower: Who Killed Hilda Murrell?,* Cecil Woolf Publishers, London, 1985.

CHAPTER TWO:
Sinker, Charles (ed.), *Hilda Murrell's Nature Diaries 1961-1983,* Collins, London, 1987.

CHAPTER THREE:
Bertell, Rosalie, *No Immediate Danger: Prognosis for a Radioactive Earth,* The Women's Press, London, 1985.
Foot, Paul with Smith, Ron, *The Helen Smith Story,* Fontana Paperbacks, 1983.
Gavshon, Arthur and Rice, Desmond, *The Sinking of the Belgrano: The act of war that finally killed off all hopes of peace,* New English Library Paper Back Edition, London, 1984.
The Ecologist, *A Blueprint for Survival,* Penguin Books Ltd, Harmondsworth, Middlesex, England, 1972.

CHAPTER FOUR:
Barker, Nick, *Beyond Endurance: An Epic of Whitehall and the South Atlantic Conflict,* Leo Cooper, London, 1997.
Chapman, Leslie, *Your Disobedient Servant,* Penguin Books Ltd, London, 1979.
Dalyell, Tam, 'A Way Forward for Nuclear Power', *New Scientist,* 16 October 1986.
Dalyell, Tam, *Misrule: How Mrs Thatcher has Misled Parliament from the Sinking of the "Belgrano" to the Wright Affair,* Hamish Hamilton Ltd, London, 1987.
Dalyell, Tam, *Thatcher: Patterns of Deceit,* Cecil Woolf, London, 1986.
Dalyell, Tam, MP, *Thatcher's Torpedo: The Sinking of the 'Belgrano',* Cecil Woolf, London, 1983.
Dalyell, Tam, *The Importance of Being Awkward: The Autobiography of Tam Dalyell,* Birlinn Ltd, Edinburgh, 2011.
Freedman, Sir Lawrence, *The Official History of the Falklands Campaign, Vol. II War and Diplomacy,* Routledge, Abingdon, Oxon, 2005.

Gould, Diana, *On the Spot: The Sinking of the 'Belgrano'*, Cecil Woolf, London, 1984.

Norton-Taylor, Richard, *The Ponting Affair*, Cecil Woolf, London, 1985.

Ponting, Clive, *The Right to Know: The inside story of the Belgrano Affair*, Sphere Books Ltd, London, 1985.

Ponting, Clive, *Whitehall: Tragedy and Farce: The inside story of how Whitehall really works*, Sphere Books Ltd, London, 1986.

CHAPTER FIVE:

Aubrey, Crispin, *Meltdown: The Collapse of the Nuclear Dream*, Collins and Brown Ltd, London, 1991.

Cook, Judith, *The Waste Remains: Intrigue and death on Suffolk coast*, Pluto Press, London, 1984.

Cook, Judith, *The Price of Freedom*, New English Library, Seven Oaks, Kent, 1985

Cook, Judith, *Who Killed Hilda Murrell?*, A New English Library Original Publication, London, 1985.

Cook, Judith, *Unlawful Killing: The Murder of Hilda Murrell*, Bloomsbury Publishing, London, 1994.

Gould, Jay M. and Goldman, Benjamin A., *Deadly Deceit: Low-Level Radiation, High-Level Cover-Up*, Four Walls Eight Windows, New York, 1991.

Hawkes, Nigel, Lean, Geoffrey, Leigh, David, McKie, Robin, Pringle, Peter and Wilson, Andrew *(The Observer)*, *The Worst Accident in the World, Chernobyl: The End of the Nuclear Dream*, William Heinemann Ltd and Pan Books Ltd, London, 1986.

Kemeny, John G., (Chairman), *Report of The President's Commission on The Accident at Three Mile Island, The Need for Change: The Legacy of TMI*, Washington, D.C., 1979.

McSorley, Jean, *Living in the Shadow: The story of the people of Sellafield*, Pan Books Ltd, London, 1990.

CHAPTER SIX:

Otter, Laurens, *The Arrogance of Uncontested Power*, Wrekin Libertarians, Wellington, Salop, 1988.

Ruane, Kevin, *To Kill a Priest: The Murder of Father Popliełuszko and the fall of communism*, Gibson Square Books Ltd, London, 2004.

CHAPTER SEVEN:

Cole, D.J., and Acland, P.R., *The Detective and the Doctor: A Murder Casebook*, Robert Hale Ltd, London, 1994.

Murray, Gary, *Enemies of the State: A sensational exposé of the security service by a former MI5 undercover agent*, Simon and Schuster Ltd, London, 1993.

Stalker, John, *Stalker: Did the Ulster Police Shoot to Kill? The True Story*, Penguin Books Ltd, London, 1988.

CHAPTER EIGHT:
Fagan Ginger, Ann, *Nuclear Weapons are Illegal: The historic opinion of the World Court and how it will be enforced*, The Apex Press, New York, 1998.
Lange, David, *Nuclear Free - The New Zealand Way*, Penguin Books, Auckland, 1990.
Templeton, Malcolm, *Standing Upright Here: New Zealand in the Nuclear Age, 1945-1990*, Victoria University Press in association with The New Zealand Institute of International Affairs, Wellington, 2006.

CHAPTER NINE:
Webb, Richard E., *The accident hazards of nuclear power plants*, Amherst, MA, University of Massachusetts, 1976.

CHAPTER TEN:
Gould, Russell, *Unsolved Murders: When Killers Escape Justice*, Virgin Books Ltd, London, 2002.

CHAPTER TWELVE:
Attorney-General's Office, http://www.attorneygeneral.gov.uk/Publications/Pages/DrKelly.aspx
Breach, Ian, *Windscale Fallout: A Primer for the Age of Nuclear Controversy*, Penguin Books Ltd, Harmondsworth, Middlesex, England, 1978.
Baker, Norman, MP, 'I believe David Kelly did not commit suicide – and I will prove it', *The Mail on Sunday*, 23 July 2006. http://dr-david-kelly.blogspot.com/
Baker, Norman, MP, *The Strange Death of David Kelly*, Methuen Publishing, London, 2007.
Bertell, Rosalie, *Planet Earth: The Latest Weapon of War, A critical study into the military and the environment*, The Women's Press, London, 2000.
Chowka, Peter Barry, 'A Tale of Nuclear Tyranny', *New Age*, August 1980, pp 26-69.
Cutler, James and Edwards, Rob, *Britain's Nuclear Nightmare*, Sphere Books Limited, London, 1988.
Hennessy, Peter, *The Secret State: Whitehall and the Cold War*, Allen Lane, London, 2002.
Rimington, Stella, *Open Secret: The Autobiography of the Former Director General of MI5*, Arrow Books Ltd, London, 2002.
Rashke, Richard, *The Killing of Karen Silkwood*, Sphere Books Ltd, London, 1981.

CHAPTER FOURTEEN:
Aaronovitch, David, *Voodoo Histories: The role of the conspiracy theory in shaping modern history*, Jonathon Cape, London, 2009.
Mansfield, Michael, *Memoirs of a Radical Lawyer*, Bloomsbury, London, 2009.

INDEX